SO-BPI-699

Parliaments and Legislatures Series

Samuel C. Patterson

General Advisory Editor

Parliaments and Legislatures Series

Samuel C. Patterson

General Advisory Editor

EDITORIAL BOARD

David W. Brady, Stanford University, USA
Gary W. Cox, University of California, San Diego, USA
Erik Damgaard, University of Aarhus, Denmark
C. E. S. Franks, Queen's University, Canada
John R. Hibbing, University of Nebraska, USA
Gerhard Loewenberg, University of Iowa, USA
Thomas F. Remington, Emory University, USA
Suzanne S. Schüttemeyer, Universität Lüneburg, Germany
Itler Turan, Koç University, Turkey

The aims of this series are to enhance knowledge about the well-established legislative assemblies of North America and western Europe and to publish studies of parliamentary assemblies worldwide—from Russia and the former Soviet bloc nations to Asia, Africa, and Latin America. The series is open to a wide variety of theoretical applications, historical dimensions, data collections, and methodologies.

OTHER BOOKS IN THE SERIES
Cheap Seats: The Democratic Party's Advantage in U.S. House Elections
James E. Campbell

Coalition Government, Subnational Style

Multiparty Politics in Europe's Regional Parliaments

WILLIAM M. DOWNS

JN
3971
.A988
D68
1998
West

Ohio State University Press
Columbus

Copyright © 1998 by The Ohio State University.
All rights reserved.

Library of Congress Cataloging-in-Publication Data
Downs, William M., 1966–
    Coalition government, subnational style : multiparty politics in
    Europe's regional parliaments / William M. Downs.
        p.   cm. — (Parliaments and legislatures series)
    Includes bibliographical references and index.
    ISBN 0-8142-0747-2 (cloth : alk. paper). — ISBN 0-8142-0748-0
(pbk. : alk. paper)
        1. Legislative bodies—Germany—States—Case studies.
    2. Legislative bodies—France—Regions—Case studies.
    3. Legislative bodies—Belgium—Regions—Case studies.   4. Coalition
    governments—Germany—States—Case studies.   5. Coalition
    governments—France—Regions—Case studies.   6. Coalition
    governments—Belgium—Regions—Case studies.   I. Title.
    II. Series.
    JN3971.A988D68   1998
    324'.094—dc21   98-26776
                                                                                  CIP

Text and jacket design by Nighthawk Design.
Type set in Baskerville by Brevis Press.
Printed by Braun-Brumfield, Inc.

The paper used in this publication meets the minimum requirements of the American
National Standard for Information Sciences—Permanence of Paper for Printed Library
Materials. ANSI Z39.48–1992.
9   8   7   6   5   4   3   2   1

CONTENTS

———————

ILLUSTRATIONS

Figures

Maps

TABLES

FOREWORD

The Parliaments and Legislatures Series provides for the publication of studies of parliamentary or legislative institutions in democratic societies. The names *parliament* and *legislature* are commonly used to label the representative assemblies of nations, states, provinces, or regions. Sometimes the term *parliament* is reserved for assemblies that mostly deliberate, ventilate, debate, or provide catharsis, while *legislature* is used to refer to assemblies that have strong lawmaking powers. In practice, this distinction can be misleading: some parliaments wield impressive legislative power, and some legislatures are "rubber stamps." The label *parliament* may be used to denote the representative assembly in a parliamentary system of government, where the working executive is chosen or confirmed by the assembly, while the name *legislature* may more readily be identified with nonparliamentary, separated systems. But this distinction is not universal. Accordingly, we consider both names for representative assemblies to be generic, using them interchangeably. And this series of books carries the title "Parliaments and Legislatures" to signify that all such assemblies, however named, may fall within the series' purview.

We are living in an age in which democratic constitutions and politics are being established, or are emerging, in parts of the world previously under authoritarian domination. Democracy is one of those rather uncertain political concepts susceptible to varying meanings. In contemporary writing about democratization, *democracy* often means the existence of a culture of civic participation in which free expression and free elections may thrive. Democratization, or democratic consolidation, is too frequently analyzed only in these terms, without giving attention to political institutions, and especially to legislative or parliamentary institutions. Yet it seems axiomatic that representative assem-

xiii

blies are essential institutions for democracy in large-scale societies. This series of books is founded on the assumption that parliaments and legislatures are at the heart of democracy. The study of democratic politics must entail anatomizing the selection, structure, performance, and impact of parliamentary or legislative institutions.

Heretofore, parliaments and legislatures have been studied mainly at the national level. Most of our knowledge about these institutions comes from research on assemblies like the United States Congress and the British and to some extent the Commonwealth parliaments, and there are a few scattered studies of parliaments elsewhere. The main exception to this national focus in legislative studies is provided by state legislatures in the United States, where 50 semisovereign subnational units have their own important lawmaking bodies.

Today, subnational legislative assemblies, apart from the American state legislatures, have emerged as vitally important entities for observation and analysis. Changes occurring across the democratic world stir demands for significant political participation in local communities, local control of crucial governing activities, political decision making by community institutions, and reduced centralization, devolving political power from national to regional, provincial, or local governments. William M. Downs's *Coalition Government, Subnational Style* grows out of his recognition of the new or enhanced importance of subnational, regional parliaments in major European countries.

As his inquiry evolved, Downs's curiosity about parliamentary institutions branched in two directions. First, he sought to investigate more fully the recurrent patterns of coalition politics in western European political systems. Second, he became curious about political party behavior in the French regional assemblies and thus decided to investigate subnational coalition politics in France and, comparatively, in Belgium and Germany. As he investigated coalitions within each of the subnational parliaments he analyzed, he sought to unravel the linkages between leaders, parties, and parliaments at the regional and national levels. He came to ask, "Is the politics of coalition formation observed at the national level similar to or different from coalition formation in subnational assemblies?"

The three country settings provide Downs with fruitful variations in the contexts for subnational assembly behavior. In France—a unitary political system often described as highly centralized—22 regional parliaments were operating by the 1980s, creating a fascinating new subnational environment for coalition politics. In Belgium, a formerly unitary system with 9 provincial councils was transformed in the mid-1990s into a federal state with directly elected regional assemblies in Flanders, Wallonia, and Brussels. Germany is a highly federalized system with 16 autonomous states, each with its own state legislature.

In these three countries, the composition of political party coalitions varies across regions and between regional and national levels; patterns of electoral competition differ in interesting ways; and the vertical linkages between the subnational and national governmental units are diverse. Downs's cogent analysis of these divergent subnational parliamentary institutions and parties makes an important contribution to knowledge about parliaments and legislatures. The journey is an informative and delightful one—from Luxembourg to Picardie, from Baden-Württemberg to Brabant, from Languedoc-Roussillon and Pays de la Loire to Lower Saxony and Liège. Their regional parliaments are lively and illuminating, with vigorous party leaders and party groups immersed in the politics of coalition building.

This is a theoretically and empirically rich analysis. It deftly draws upon historical and documentary evidence and upon survey data gathered from individual representatives in the subnational assemblies. Downs makes a particularly unusual contribution to comparative politics in the analysis across both regions and nations. There are also numerous fascinating nuggets of discovery in this book that can stimulate the imagination and lead to further inquiry. As regional parliaments become more common and more important, this study will come to serve as a landmark, a baseline for research on subnational representative assemblies. But for now, the reader will find in these pages the basis for a richer understanding of the role of parliamentary coalition politics in the process of democratization.

SAMUEL C. PATTERSON

PREFACE

Coalition government is a natural obsession for the American observer of European politics. At home in the United States, we sit comfortably election night after election night and watch as network news anchors tell us with ever-increasing rapidity who has won and who has lost. We retire to bed safe in the knowledge of who will govern and who will not. However, in much of western Europe, and in all multiparty systems characterized by even a modicum of proportional representation, election night usually marks the beginning—not the end—of the government formation process. When no single party secures an outright legislative majority, the postelection period is one of vast and varied possibilities marked by formal negotiations and backroom deals, by promises made and promises broken, and by optimistic public displays of unity from new partners all too aware of the fragility of any alliance among political competitors. The politics of coalition, especially for the American political scientist, is truly great theater.

The study of coalition politics in regional and local-level representative assemblies in continental European systems is, initially, rather a more difficult sell. I must admit that it did not immediately hold much allure for me after having long been captivated by the high drama of political machinations in national parliaments. After all, subnational politics was not supposed to get much more exciting than waste management, hospital administration, and land use planning—right? I came to the subject in the spring of 1989 rather by chance when, while on holiday in Normandy, France, I read in *Le Monde* about the fits Jean-Marie Le Pen's far-right Front National was giving the mainstream French conservative parties in many of the country's 22 regional assemblies. Three years earlier, while all party leaders had publicly refused to consider cooperating with the FN at the parliamentary level, newly elected center-right regional councilors from Aquitaine to Languedoc-Roussillon to Haute Normandie quietly collaborated with the FN to secure executive power. Now it seemed that the strategy had exacted high public relations costs, had pushed moderate and liberal voters to the left, and had superimposed national debate over immigration control, unemployment, AIDS, and crime onto the regional agenda. Even far from the National Assembly, coalition building—the politics of strange bedfellows—could be riveting stuff.

Three years and another French regional election later, my interest in coalition strategy in the periphery developed into a Ph.D. dissertation prospectus. Trained to think comparatively, like many in my generation of political scientists at Emory University, I recognized that embedded in subnational coalition government are some substantively interesting and theoretically challenging puzzles that could be tested in numerous countries: How and why do patterns of party alliances in the periphery differ in systematic ways from those witnessed in the capital? How closely do the outcomes of coalition negotiations conducted away from the glare of national politics appear to match electoral verdicts and patterns of electoral competition? Do coalitions produce consensual decision-making regimes within subnational assemblies or, alternatively, paralyze legislative processes with the ideological intransigence that often marks national parliamentary government? How much coalitional learning and diffusion of models is there between national and subnational assemblies?

Early forays into journalistic accounts of individual cases produced the kind of findings that beg for more sophisticated scrutiny. There were tales of internal party betrayal and of undisciplined secret votes, accounts of successful and enduring partnerships never attempted at the national level, and, most frequently, evidence that national figures (members of parliament and party leaders) were involved—by invitation or by imposition—in the process of negotiating the division of government spoils in the periphery. Armed with the political scientist's methodological tools, I set out to impose some order and understanding on a complex and fascinating reality.

My original fascination with the possibilities of coalition government and my subsequent but ultimately deep appreciation for subnational politics drove me to write a dissertation and now this book. During the course of these projects, I have accumulated a large number of acquaintances and debts, too numerous for me to mention all by name. It is indeed a pleasure, however, to acknowledge some of them here. I am especially grateful to Professor Thomas Lancaster, who inspired my approach to comparative political research and who gave me both the guidance and the intellectual space to produce an ambitious doctoral dissertation. My debt to Tom Lancaster goes beyond that first project: in helping me return to Europe so soon and to obtain a postdoctoral research/teaching position there, he pointed me toward the perfect opportunity to transform the dissertation into its present book form.

I have benefited from the advice, support, and time of numerous persons in different phases of researching and writing this book. For assistance in translating into French and German the survey questionnaire that provides much of the original data for this study, I thank Caroline Guichard, Bob King, Jeanne Fourneyron, Marianne Lancaster, Andreas Sobisch, and Geoffrey Roberts. I should also like to thank the Political Science Department at Emory University and the Graduate School of Arts and Sciences for their generous financial support of the survey questionnaire. Maggie Nicholson, Executive Director of the Fulbright Commission in Brussels, and Emile Boulpaep, President of the Belgian American Educational Foundation, deserve special recognition for supporting my first year (1992–93) of fieldwork in Europe. Equally deserving are the countless politicians, party executives, and bureaucrats whose willingness to meet and speak with me generated much of the original data for this study. Others assisted by providing valuable documents and source material. Several persons who contributed especially useful information do deserve recognition.

In Belgium, these were Paul Maertens at the Brussels Centrum Voor Politieke, Economische en Sociale Studies; Xavier Mabille at the Centre de Recherche et d'Information Socio-Politiques; Liewen de Winter at the Université Catholique de Louvain; Jan Peumans of the Limburg Volksunie; Freddy Clauwaerts of the Socialist Party Federation in Mons; Christiane Lemaire of the Namur Provincial administration; Charles Simon, Hainaut Provincial Council greffier; William Blondeel, communications officer of the East Flanders Provincial Council; Ghislaine Stevens-Maes at the Association des Provinces Belges; and Philippe Lamair of the Radio-Télévision Belge de la Communauté Française (RTBF).

In France, these individuals were Dominique Theo at the Picardie Conseil Régional in Amiens; Patrick Dos at the Auvergne Conseil Régional in Chamalières; Jean Callewaert, Director General of the Basse-Normandie Conseil Régional; and Monique Rousselin at the Ile de France Conseil Régional in Paris.

In Germany, these individuals were Heinrich Augustin at the Lower Saxony Landtag in Hannover; Michael Tolksdorf at the Berlin Abgeordnetenhaus; Reinhard Groß, Chief of Protocol at the Hesse Landtag in Wiesbaden; Ingeborg Ruopp at the Green Party secretariat in Stuttgart; Hendrik de Boer, press spokesman at the Mecklenburg-Vorpommern Landtag; Hinnerk Fock, press spokesman at the Hamburg Bürgerschaft; Gerald Wood, press spokesman at the Brandenburg Landtag; Dr. Gruß at the Sachsen-Anhalt Landtag; and Dr. Mittelsdorf at the Thüringer Landtag in Erfurt.

My thanks go also to Paul Pierson, Abby Collins, and their colleagues at the Minda de Gunzburg Center for European Studies at Harvard University. My visiting fellowship at Harvard provided a unique opportunity to produce the first version of this manuscript. The present book is a better one for my having had the experience. Invaluable, too, was the support of colleagues and friends during my final preparation of this book while I was at Odense University and Aarhus University in Denmark: Poul Erik Mouritzen, Mogens N. Pedersen, and Jørgen Grønnegård Christiansen. The chance to apply my ideas to the Scandinavian systems proved tremendously instructive—*mange tak!*

Of course, none of this would have been possible without the constant and overwhelming support of my family. This I have enjoyed from the very beginning. To my parents, thanks for your inspiration and pride. To "my girls"—Kimberly, wife and best friend, and Rachel, our beautiful daughter—this book is deservedly dedicated.

Part One

———

Introduction

Chapter One

Who Will Govern? Dilemmas of Coalition Government and Parliamentary Democracy

This book addresses a theme of central importance to the theory and practice of parliamentary democracy in western Europe: multiparty coalition government. Coalition government is the subject of a voluminous literature within the political science discipline; however, the present study is unique in its systematic and comparative focus on coalition government in the richly diverse yet underresearched institutional setting of *subnational* (i.e., regional, provincial, local) representative assemblies. Across western Europe in the increasingly powerful institutions of subcentral governance, the politics of coalition has become a high-stakes affair with consequences exceeding the limited confines of individual localities. In the state parliaments of federal Germany, for example, Green parties have since the mid-1980s upset the country's once predictable balance of power. In countries as varied as France, Belgium, Italy, and Austria, nationalist forces of the extreme far Right have gained toeholds in their respective political systems by venturing into power-sharing coalitions with mainstream parties at regional, provincial, and municipal levels. Even in Britain, where the Labour and Conservative parties monopolize power at Westminster and Downing Street, Liberal Democrats have taken advantage of majorityless "hung" county and city councils to gain a share of governing responsibility. With the politicization and nationalization of subnational government in recent decades, alignments on the geographical chessboard of political power in most European democracies have become increasingly volatile and complex.

"Winner-take-all" majoritarian electoral systems at both national and subnational levels, such as those in the United States, tend to take much of the mystery out of the question "Who will govern?" Conversely, the proportional representation systems common throughout the continental European democracies normally produce election results in which no single party holds a majority of council seats. Thus, as in national parliamentary institutions in these countries, elections to federal state legislatures, regional parliaments, provincial assemblies, county boards, and municipal councils tend to produce strong incentives for political parties to build alliances in order to form a governing majority. This book is premised on the observation that in the formation of coalition governments we find the crystallization of many of the political processes fundamental to representative and parliamentary democracy: interpretation of electoral verdicts, postelection compromising of campaign pledges, trade-offs between policy and power, indirect selection of executive authority, temporary cooperation between long-term adversaries, collective decision making, and, with collective responsibility, a blurring of lines of accountability.

The prima facie importance of coalition formation is widely accepted in the context of national parliamentary institutions, but the subject is much less analyzed, much less compared, and therefore much less understood in the context of subnational assemblies. Seeking to remedy this deficiency, this book has three guiding objectives:

1. To depict the building of power-sharing coalitions in subnational parliaments as outward and well-defined manifestations of political motivation, governing intent, and democratic responsiveness

2. To assemble and analyze observations and statements of motivations and beliefs made by middle-level legislators—elected representatives whose obligations, experiences, and ambitions are for the most part overlooked by students of parliamentary government

3. To build upon existing theories of coalition politics to identify cross-national behavioral similarities and to highlight within-nation differences as they are revealed in actual high-stakes political situations

Elections, Coalitions, and Representation

Two centuries ago, Jean-Jacques Rousseau, in *The Social Contract,* insisted that "the instant a people gives itself to representatives, it is no longer free" (103). For some, Rousseau's radical critique of democratic representation may be a bit overstated. In today's world, few would contend that perfect direct democracy is really possible on any useful scale; still, Rousseau effectively reminds us that the relationship between representatives and the represented is at best imperfect. One particular concern voiced by some observers of political systems characterized by coalition government is whether the quality of democratic representation and of the electoral mechanism itself is diminished when legislative parties—not voters—ultimately answer the question "Who will govern?"

Two decades ago, Abram De Swaan (1973) also wrote of representative democracy's imperfections: "If different governments, varying in party membership and policy, may result from a given election outcome, either there is no 'verdict of the electorate' or . . . the verdict is not necessarily, or even usually realized in multi-party systems" (1–2). De Swaan at that moment put his finger on one of the supposed weaknesses of coalition systems, namely that they remove any direct linkage between votes and the formation of a government. According to basic tenets of liberal democratic theory, voters—not party leaders locked in secretive backroom negotiations—should determine the political complexion of a governing executive body. In political systems that encourage government by coalition, however, popular will is instrumental only in that it decides which political parties will sit in parliament. Once this initial matter is determined, deputies and party leaders are ultimately free to choose from among a potentially huge number of cross-party combinations and permutations in search of a winning majority. This process may produce "strange bedfellows," governments that fail to resemble the messages sent by voters some days, weeks, or even months earlier. "Coalitions of minorities," groups of small parties whose policy preferences may be starkly incompatible, can unite for the sole purpose of evicting a larger party from its hegemonic place in government. Similarly, "coalitions of losers," parties and adversaries whose electoral scores have just dropped precipitously, can join forces to cling to power and forestall their mutual demise. The failure to come to any cross-party agreement may also produce "coalition avoidance" and thus minority governments, often weak and beholden throughout their terms to transient legislative voting majorities or to the threat of blackmail from some external party. Indeed, it would seem that almost anything is possible in postelection coalition formation.

A growing number of rigorous studies of government formation now suggest that, in reality, the realm of possible cross-party coalitions is systematically and significantly constricted by the rules, structures, and norms of the parliamentary institutions to which parties gain access (Bergman 1995; Laver and Schofield 1990; Strom 1994; Strom, Budge, and Laver 1994). These attempts at reconciling a neoinstitutionalist approach with that of formal rational choice theory have clearly enhanced the already rich literature on cabinet coalitions in European national governments (see Bogdanor 1983; Browne and Dreijmanis 1982; Dodd 1976; Luebbert 1986; Pridham 1986). Still, efforts to understand coalition behavior in a "constrained real world" (Laver and Schofield 1990, 195) remain deficient in at least two respects, the first of which is their general failure to consider broader issues of democratic representation. Indeed, inseparable from our desire to better explain and anticipate the political composition of coalition governments should be the goal of evaluating the dynamics of coalition formation within the larger democratic process. Political science can, for example, evaluate popular claims that political parties purposefully manipulate the coalition process in order to circumvent electoral verdicts. We can look further to determine if, as is often charged, the secretive postelection bargaining and deal making characteristic of government formation undercut the electoral process, thus weakening a supposedly fundamental link between citizens and their representatives. These concerns help stimulate thought on coalition formation not only as a curious behavioral puzzle but also as an ambiguous mechanism in the machinery of parliamentary democracy.

Existing efforts also remain deficient by failing to exploit alternative data sources outside the national parliamentary arena. Scrutiny of coalition politics in subnational institutions of representative governance is especially overdue; the topic has been described as "an almost entirely unworked field in political science" (Mellors 1989, 8) and a "largely forgotten area" (Pridham 1987, 374). At subnational levels, processes of institutional and political decentralization during the past two decades have created new political expectations and new political opportunities. In some countries (e.g., France, Belgium, Italy, Spain), decentralization has created entirely new institutions of representative government, directly elected councils and parliaments located at an intermediate, or "meso," position between national and local governments. In other countries (e.g., Germany, Denmark, Sweden, Norway), decentralization has empowered existing institutions with new fiscal and deliberative responsibilities. In all countries, a common justification for breathing new life into subnational institutions has been that they bring government closer to the people, increase the opportunities for citizen participation, decentralize economic decision making, and, in short, increase the state's "democraticness" (Putnam 1993; Schmidt 1990; Sharpe 1993). Thus we have one of our first puzzles to solve: How does the "decentralization as democratization" ideal square with observations indicating that in many instances local electoral competition, local public opinion, and local policy issues are not the driving forces behind party strategy and key decisions, such as government formation, at subnational levels? As an artificial act, and as the immediate act following an election, the process of manufacturing a governing majority is one area in which parties' choices can be evaluated in light of their professed intentions to enhance transparency, accountability, and responsiveness in decision making.

Designed to contribute to serious thinking along these lines, this book raises three essential sets of questions:

1. If different local and regional governments, varying in party membership and policy, may result from a given election outcome, then is the process that yields such "strange bedfellows" genuinely responsive to the preferences of the electorate? In other words, *do electoral competition and electoral verdicts really matter in coalition systems?*

2. Do politicians elected to subnational parliaments follow the strategic instructions of central party leaders, or do regional and local parties have a free hand in their coalition decisions? In short, when national/subnational divisions over strategy arise, *are local and regional politicians loyal to their national leaders or their local constituents?*

3. In demonstrating the (in)compatibility of parties, their (in)efficacy in governing, and the electoral (un)popularity of a partnership, do coalitions in regional and local parliaments supply part of the "perfect information" that national party leaders need when they sit down at the bargaining table to negotiate a new national government? In what sense *are subnational parliaments "proving grounds" for future national coalition governments?*

Answers to these questions can help explain one of the most important recurrent events in parliamentary democracy. Moreover, they allow deeper understandings of the meanings of *representation, power,* and *cooperation* outside the more familiar institutional arena of national parliamentary politics.

Coalition Politics in the Real World of Subnational Assemblies

To get a flavor for the politics of coalition as it plays out in subnational institutions, we can point to a mix of examples. When, for instance, a party holding just 8 seats in a parliament of 113 members in France's third-largest region emerges from postelection coalition bargaining in sole possession of the regional presidency, in control of the regional cabinet, and in command of a Fr 3.9-million regional budget, the process by which relative electoral weakness transforms itself into substantial governmental power becomes central to the concerns of political science.[1] When a party gains the plurality of votes and seats in five consecutive elections in Belgium's largest province and is on five consecutive occasions excluded and denied any share of provincial power, then the process by which relative electoral strength transforms itself into complete governmental weakness is again clearly important.[2] And when a radical right-wing party led by an unrepentant veteran of the Waffen SS for the first time enters the parliament of one of Germany's wealthiest Länder with 11% of the vote, forces the election's two big losers—the Christian Democrats (CDU) and the Social Democrats (SPD)—into a rare "Grand Coalition," and thus leaves the Landtag with virtually no democratic opposition, then the ability of representative government to function effectively under such circumstances must certainly be examined.[3] In short, many substantively important political outcomes stand to influence large numbers of people but are generally overlooked in the literatures on coalition government and parliamentary democracy.

Journalistic treatment of these outcomes is extensive. There is, moreover, a small but growing body of literature that addresses individual cases and single countries. Good work has been done, for example, on the Dutch municipal councils (Denters 1985, 1993; Kuiper and Tops 1989; Steunenberg 1992), on the Danish municipal councils (Pedersen and Elklit 1995; Thomas 1989), on the Belgian municipal and provincial councils (Mabille 1982, 1986; Pijnenburg 1987, 1988, 1989), on the Italian municipal and regional councils (Pridham 1984, 1986; Zariski 1984), on Germany's Land legislatures (Gunlicks 1977; Roberts 1989), on the so-called hung county and regional councils in Britain (Laver, Rallings, and Thrasher 1987; Mellors 1983, 1984, 1989; Temple 1991), on the regional assemblies in post-Franco Spain (Botella 1989; Robinson 1989), and on France's new regional councils (Hainsworth and Loughlin 1989; Mazey 1986; Perrineau 1987; Schmidt 1990). What these works lack, unfortunately, is genuine comparison. Little effort has been made to understand varying political responses to power-sharing opportunities at subnational levels across these various countries. Comparison, then, is one area to which the present study seeks to contribute.

What existing works do tell us very clearly is that coalition outcomes are valued by political parties and by voters. This, they conclude, is axiomatic. Government status is critical in subnational assemblies, and competition for government status is a struggle for resources—both political and economic. Provincial and regional governments oversee budgets that in past decades have generally grown at rates faster than those in local or national government. The overloaded, overburdened modern welfare state has "off-loaded" many of its traditional tasks to the subcentral units (Batley and Stoker 1991; Jones and Keating 1995; Sharpe 1993). Provincial and regional executives not only are charged with managing grants and fiscal transfers from the state and from the European Union but also have authority and responsibility in such areas as investment, regional development, transportation, infrastructure, education, professional training, social services, environmental management, supervision over local governments, and, of course, taxation.

Beyond service delivery, part of "responsible" democratic governance is responsive and representative institutions of subnational governance. Subnational institutions can fulfill purposeful obligations. If subnational governance "matters," as a survey of its functional importance would indicate, then the partisan composition of the governing executives themselves should also matter in a practical sense. Research indicates that subnational assemblies are increasingly the domain of disciplined political party groups and not simply of individuals only titularly attached to national party organizations (Dunleavy 1980; Mellors and Pijnenburg 1989; Selle and Svåsand 1983). Despite morose academic predictions of the "end of ideology" and the "decline of party," we may still assume that the policies of a single-party Socialist regional government will differ predictably from those of a single-party Christian Democratic or Liberal regional government. Indeed, there is evidence to support the general proposition that, all else being equal, Left-controlled regions have tended to tax, spend, and borrow more heavily than Right-controlled regional authorities (Denters 1993; Mazey 1993; Page and Goldsmith 1987). To cite just one example, in the so-called red Hainaut province in Belgium—"red" because it is the bastion of the Socialist Party—taxes and spending per capita are three times those of neighboring East Flanders, which has had a conservative provincial majority for two uninterrupted decades (Bernard 1992; Hugé 1989, 1991).

We must wonder, however, how well a multiparty coalition government will perform, especially if it is the product of untried alliances, such as those between Socialists and Liberals, traditional parties and ecologists, or centrist parties and extremists. What are the effects of coalition on subnational budgets, taxes, services, or the distribution of central government outlays? Does coalition encourage perpetual legislative "gridlock," or can multiparty power sharing in subnational assemblies cultivate pragmatism and cooperation? Clearly, each coalition outcome in a local or provincial parliament is a story in itself. Each coalition has policy implications, both in terms of substance and in terms of intergovernmental coherence. Each coalition says something about the degree to which competitors and even avowed adversaries can cooperate in democratic systems. Each coalition provides important indications as to the locus of power and influence in political parties and in representative assemblies. These are nontrivial concerns; a nonsuperficial understanding of modern parliamentary governance, therefore, requires that they be addressed.

Theoretical Justification

The study of subnational coalition formation provides the opportunity to collect empirical observations concerning behavioral outcomes and to test alternative causal hypotheses against them. For example, one set of outcomes that raises a host of theoretical questions concerns those multiparty governing arrangements that deviate from the more familiar patterns established in national parliamentary politics. In fact, our study could begin by making a single observation: in most multiparty systems with directly elected territorial assemblies, power-sharing alliances at national and subnational levels of government rarely match. Despite the numerical possibility of faithfully mirroring the national government-versus-opposition pattern, regional and provincial coalitions are frequently "incongruent," with party allies at one level of government facing off as opponents at the next.

The phenomenon prevails throughout the European democracies. The Free Democrats in Germany, for example, participate in regional-level governments with Social Democrats while playing partner to the Christian Union parties in Bonn. The conservative parties in France collude with the extremist Front National in the regions while boasting a clear and safe distance from the "lepénistes" in Paris. Socialists and Liberals in Belgium defy traditional ideological divisions to form joint regional, provincial, and municipal governments while refusing cooperation at the national level. Italian Socialists and Social Democrats have shared power with the Communists in regional administrations without any similar arrangements evolving in Rome. Even county branches of the Conservative and Labour parties in Britain have established de facto governing coalitions, although this has been unthinkable in national government.

The puzzle of two levels of the same political party belonging to different coalition camps raises an array of questions: Are the incentives and constraints that compel political parties to ally with one another in territorial parliaments the same as those that guide parliamentary parties at the national level? For any given party, where are the fundamental decisions about participation in subnational coalitions made—at the subnational or the national level? On what bases are these decisions made? How much influence is brought to bear on subnational party groups by the national party leadership, and vice versa? Are governing coalitions at subnational levels more or less responsive to the will of the electorate than those at the national level? Finally, to what extent do political parties use subnational assemblies either as experimental laboratories for future national coalitions or as outlets for diffusing internal party dissent?

Turning to what is a rich theoretical literature on coalitions and government formation for answers to these questions proves somewhat less than satisfactory. Many extant theories are "policy blind." Most insist that researchers consider political parties to be a priori "unitary actors" or "single-minded bargaining entities." All but a few view government formation as anything but a single-shot "game"—a static, discrete contest that neither is influenced by nor is itself influencing coalitions being formed at a different time or at different locations in the political system. No theories address the linkages between party alliances in national government and those developing in subnational government. None address the direction of coalition change within the system. There is little theoretical provision, moreover, for the provincial or regional party group whose coalition preference comes into conflict with that of its national leadership, for the pressures of maintaining national-subnational congruence, or for the possibility of local experimentation in alternative alliances for possible future use in national government. Previous efforts have all generally focused on motivation or ideological compatibility as *the* causal agents. Few, if any, have suggested that situation or context may systematically condition what rational actors may be expected to do in coalition situations. In short, the existing literature is rather ill equipped to deal with the questions that emerge once the analysis of coalition government expands to include regional and local representative institutions.

Any theoretical approach that intends to have broad, comparative applicability must start, if not from scratch, then at least at the level of eclectically borrowing the least objectionable tenets from the existing literature on coalitions, parties, and democratic representation. The fundamental task, taken up in subsequent chapters, is not to concoct a model purporting an exact "fit" but to construct some meaningful alternative hypotheses and to test for linkages among significant variables. We need, in short, to develop a lens through which to view and compare coalition behavior across subnational assemblies. Such a lens should allow us to arrive at useful comparative generalizations and at the same time allow us to be sensitive to some of the peculiar qualities of individual regions, provinces, and parties.

Structure of the Book

This introduction has argued the merits of investigating dilemmas of coalition politics in subnational parliamentary assemblies, in particular the well-defined and regularly repeated political act of government formation. The analysis endeavors to compare the process, its outcomes, and its broader implications for democratic representation.

Our comparison focuses on western Europe and specifically on three countries: France, Belgium, and Germany. There are compelling reasons for considering these three countries as worthy arenas for intrasystem and cross-national comparison. The countries are different as are the electoral cleavages that separate their parties. Yet in each country, recent and major alterations in basic territorial and institutional structures have called new attention to fundamental political processes and performance at regional and local levels. Subnational governance in each of the three countries runs the full range of possibilities: single-party majorities, single-party minorities, multiparty coalition majorities, multiparty coalition minorities. Power-sharing coalitions also demonstrate a variety of characteristics: oversized coalitions, ideologically "unconnected" coalitions, coalitions of "losers," and coalitions excluding the party with the plurality of seats. In each country, moreover, parties frequently appear to reject the national coalition of the day in favor of some alternative regional or provincial arrangement, even when election results would allow for a duplication. Similarly positioned parties in different regions, when faced with similar coalition opportunities, are known to choose different strategies. Variation, of both the within-nation and the cross-national kind, begs for explanation.

In search of explanation, ensuing chapters explore evidence from a mix of sources. Evidence comes first from historical events data: more than 260 government formations in the Belgian conseils provinciaux and conseils régionaux/gewestraad, the French conseils régionaux, and the German Länderparlamenten since the early 1960s. To these historical data are added cross-sectional survey data, collected from 608 elected representatives in the three countries in 1992. These sources are then supplemented by material from 107 interviews conducted with deputies, councilors, and party officials during the September 1992–September 1993 period. Such evidence should not only add depth to our existing knowledge of coalition politics in Belgium, France, and Germany but also demonstrate how coalition arrangements in subnational assemblies can sustain or complicate the coalition environment within any multiparty democratic system.

The book has four parts with nine chapters. In part 1, following this introduction, chapter 2 provides a formal discussion of the relevant literature and its application to our particular research questions. In doing so, it summarizes the conventional wisdom on coalitions, outlines the many and varied criticisms of formal theory, and surveys recent attempts to use subnational coalitions as alternative data sources. In this way, we can assess the utility of importing concepts and assumptions from the existing literature for purposes of describing and explaining the payoffs of government status in Europe's subnational assemblies. Identifying the stakes for politicians also allows us to identify the key issues for comparative analysis and to evaluate the status of our current theoretical understanding of those issues.

Part 2 presents theory and methods. Chapter 3 takes a fresh and ambitious look at coalition theory from the perspective of subnational institutions. In developing a general theory of coalition formation for the subnational governmental arena, the chapter constructs testable hypotheses regarding system-level, group-level, and individual-level influences on strategic choice. Chapter 4 provides an explanation of the techniques used to collect and analyze the various kinds of data assembled for the book. This chapter delineates a three-pronged research methodology and defends the logic of the selection of cases for analysis. The tools of investigation, including events data analysis, attitudinal survey administration, and elite interviewing, are elaborated and justified.

Part 3 commences the empirical analysis in earnest, with chapter 5 narrowing the discussion by focusing on coalition politics in three particular (and in some ways peculiar) European nation-states. The German (federal), French (unitary/regionalizing), and Belgian (regionalized/federalizing) systems are detailed, including comparisons of key parties, institutional "rules of the game," and historical patterns of coalition behavior. Comparisons reveal that, unlike the behavior posited by existing theory and anticipated by our understanding of national-level politics, coalition behavior in peripheral legislatures does not necessarily reflect electoral verdicts, obligatory duplications of national arrangements, or strict adherence to zero-sum competition.

Chapter 6 asks, "Do electoral competition and electoral verdicts matter in strategic approaches to power sharing at subnational levels?" Ideally, the act of majority formation in territorial parliaments should serve to determine and legitimize the direction of public policy in the province, region, or state. But when election results are not the most important influence in the choice of government, the veracity of this legitimizing function becomes suspect. In such cases, a fundamental principle of representative democracy—that the government, at whatever level of the polity, should enjoy the support of the electorate—seems lost. Combining aggregate-level and individual-level data, the analysis compares the relative influences of electoral competition, electoral accountability, and electoral change on coalition outcomes.

Chapter 7 suggests that in a perfect democratic world where party competition and cooperation in regional institutions reflected and reacted to the opinions and wishes of regional electorates, we would expect regional party groups to enjoy decision-making autonomy in their own parliamentary affairs. In the imperfect democratic systems of the real world, however, political decisions that hold weighty consequences for local voters may become "nested" in the larger, national coalition game and thus subject to the direction of central party leaders and other organizational actors external to the region or province. The effort to identify the personal motivations and internal party pressures that influence coalition behavior in the subnational arena is taken up in this chapter. Attitudinal data are tested for disparities between subnational councilors and national party leadership. These data suggest the conditions under which councilors at subnational levels submit to national party leadership and those under which there is more likely to be attitude-related conflict over strategic choices.

Part 4 provides applications of the theoretical points made in preceding chapters and presents the principal conclusions drawn from the study. Chapter 8 broaches the important and timely subject of bottom-up coalition influence and change. Here the task is to demonstrate linkage between coalition systems at the national and subnational levels of government. Can coalitions formed in territorial assemblies restrict or enlarge the universe of coalitions available to the same set of parties in a national parliament? Which subnational coalitions are consciously deemed "proving grounds" for future national governments? Comparison of individual cases from Belgium, Germany, and France, reporting firsthand accounts of postelection coalition formations, allows some substantively interesting political stories to be told that otherwise would be left out of accounts of multiparty government in the three countries.

In chapter 9 the discussion returns to the purposes, practices, and potential of the subnational parliamentary institutions introduced in chapter 1. In turning away from the particular German, French, and Belgian cases, this final chapter synthesizes the results garnered from the empirical investigation and suggests the primary conclusions and contributions of the analysis. Thus, the book concludes with an agenda for future research in the fields of subnational parliamentary institutions, political parties, and coalition government.

Chapter Two

Negotiating Power in Europe's Subnational Parliaments: Issues for Analysis

There is no more important event in the life of our council than the act of forming a working majority. It means almost nothing to be in the opposition. And so in the hours, days, and sometimes weeks after an election we must carefully negotiate until we achieve a workable solution. We ask ourselves: What have the voters just told us? What does our party want? How well can individuals work together? What policies are most important? And we normally arrive at a successful arrangement that benefits us all.

—Provincial Assembly Member,
West Flanders, Belgium

Distributing the important posts between the parties is usually a joke. There is no consultation with the voters or with the party. There is little discussion of policies or programs. It is a simple exercise in political self-preservation. I usually end up angry and depressed.

—Provincial Assembly Member,
Namur, Belgium

Negotiating the formation of a new government is a fundamental and regularly repeated political act in subnational assemblies. Politicians elected to representative bodies at municipal, county, cantonal, provincial, regional, and state levels frequently face dilemmas analogous to those of national parliamentarians who must bargain across party lines to form a governing majority. Presented above are the starkly contrasting observations of 2 of Belgium's 726 provincial council deputies, projecting entirely different images of postelection coalition bargaining.[1] On the one hand, there is a suggestion that the government formation process is a serious occasion for deliberation and cooperation to the mutual benefit of politicians, parties, and the public. In this vision, coalition building is a process that legitimizes political leadership and establishes a clear direction for future public policy. On the other hand, there is a suggestion that the government formation process is simply politics at its worst—cynical, self-serving, and unaccountable. While it is up to subsequent chapters to demonstrate how reality varies systematically along a continuum between these polar extremes, the two descriptions at the very least call upon us to look closely at the government formation process, to identify the key players and their motivations, to recognize the stakes and payoffs of coalition bargaining, and to search out and interpret the internal party battles that occur over local strategy.

The politics of forming governments in assemblies where no party has an overall majority thrives in a large institutional universe. As table 2.1 shows, across western, southern, and northern Europe there are approximately 92,000 directly elected local authority councils, more than 800 county and provincial councils, and over 100 regional assemblies. While some of these will either occasionally or consistently enjoy single-party majorities, such is in fact rarely the case. Indeed, in countries with directly elected regional parliaments, an overwhelming proportion of the legislative bodies at the beginning of 1996 contained no party with 50% + 1 of the available seats. Clearly, coalitions are part of political life in subnational parliaments.

The absence of a natural majority increases alternatives and thus choices. There are always $2^n - 1$ possible coalition alternatives in any n-party parliament (Hinckley 1981; Laver, Rallings, and Thrasher 1995; Shubik 1967). For example, the entry of 10 parties into the 42-seat legislature of the Italian regional assembly in Calabria following its April 1995 election produced a universe of 1,023 possible coalition outcomes (table 2.2). A portion of these alternatives would fail to secure a legislative majority and thus yield only minority administration; an institutional rule requiring passage of a 50% + 1 threshold is therefore important and is present in varying forms cross-nationally (Budge and Laver 1986; Laver 1986; Laver and Schofield 1990; Strom 1990b). The outcome that Calabria's politicians chose from the 1,023 possible was a four-party center-right coalition supporting regional president Giuseppe Domenico Nisticò (Forza Italia) with the barest of majorities

Table 2.1
Directly Elected Local, Provincial, and Regional Assemblies in Europe

	Local Authority Councils	N	County, Provincial Assemblies	N	Regional Assemblies	N	%Single-Party Majority, 1996
Austria	Gemeindenrat, Stadtrat	2,475	Bezirksvertretung	23	Landtag	9	33.3
Belgium	Conseil Communal	589	Conseil Provincial/ Provincieraad	10	Conseil Régional/ Gewestraad	3	
					Gemeinschaftrat	1	0.00
Denmark	Byråd	275	Amtsråd	14	—	—	—
Finland	Kunnanvaltuusto	461	Landsting	1	—	—	—
France	Conseil Municipal	36,551	Conseil Général	100	Conseil Régional	22	0.00
Germany	Gemeindenrat, Stadtrat	16,160	Kreistag	426	Landtag	16	37.5
Greece	Demotico Symvoulio	6,036	—	—	—	—	—
Iceland	Bæjar/Sveitarstjórn	196	—	—	—	—	—
Ireland	Urban, Town Council	75	County Council	34	—	—	—
Italy	Consiglio Communale	8,085	Consiglio Provinciale	94	Consiglio Regionale	20	0.00
Luxembourg	Conseil Communal	126	—	—	—	—	—
Netherlands	Gemeenteraad	636	Provinciale Staten	12	—	—	—
Norway	Bystyre	435	Fylkestinget	19	—	—	—
Portugal	Assembleia Municipal	305	—	—	Assembleia Regional	2	100.0
Spain	Ayuntamiento	8,077	—	—	Asamblea Regional	17	35.3
Sweden	Kommunfullmäktige	288	Landsting	23	—	—	—
Switzerland	Gemeinderat	3,000	—	—	Kantonsparlement	21	19.0
United Kingdom	Local Council	8,500	County Council	76	—	—	—

Table 2.2
Distribution of Seats in Calabria Consiglio Regionale,
April 1995

Party	Seats
National Alliance	9
Party of Democratic Socialism	7
Democratic Union	6
Forza Italia	6
Christian Democratic Center	4
Popular Party	3
Refounded Communists	3
Democracy Yes	2
Independents	1
Social Democratic Federation	1
Total	42
Coalition possibilities $(2^n - 1)$	1,023
Winning coalition	Forza Italia + Christian Democratic Center + National Alliance + Popular Party

(22 of 42 seats). How scholars have attempted to conceptualize, describe, and explain the process of choosing and successfully negotiating one option out of an often vast pool of alternatives is the subject of this chapter.

Defining Coalitions

The term *coalition* may encompass a wide range of activities. There are "electoral coalitions," in which cooperating political parties agree to systematically transfer votes among themselves to their mutual advantage, as in the French double-ballot system. There are "legislative" or "voting coalitions," in which members of political parties agree to join forces in support of specific policy or legislation, as in the United States Congress. More familiar and more relevant to the present study is the notion of "power-sharing" or "governing coalitions," in which political parties agree to share executive offices—that is, ministerial portfolios.[2] Outside the Anglo-American democracies, from Italy to Israel and Belgium to Germany, such governing coalitions are the norm. For purposes of clarity, the definitions articulated by Kelley (1968) serve as the standard references: coalitions exist when two or more groups or parties "agree to pursue a common goal or a common set of goals, pool their resources in pursuit of this goal, and communicate and form binding commitments concerning the goal." Specifically, a governing coalition entails "the agreement of two or more parties to serve in the same government" (62–63).

Understanding coalitions helps to answer one of the immutable questions of politics: Why do avowed adversaries cooperate? If politics is largely about bargaining and compromise, then the transformation of political competitors into allies is of the utmost importance, whatever the situation, setting, or scope. Scholars have asked three classes of questions about governing coalitions: those concerning *coalition formation,* those concerning *coalition maintenance,* and those concerning *coalition termination.* Observers of coalition formation attempt to explain, and purport to "predict," the outcomes and payoffs to political parties engaged in bargaining over the composition of a cabinet government (see Budge and Herman 1978; De Swaan 1973; Franklin and Mackie 1983; Laver 1974; Lijphart 1981; Strom, Budge, and Laver 1994; Taylor 1972). Much less studied but no less important is coalition maintenance. The concerns of coalition maintenance shift analysis from outcomes to processes, asking questions about communication among partners, joint decision making, policy output, and the efficacy of an alliance (see Blondel and Müller-Rommel 1993; Robertson 1983; Rudd 1986; Schmidt 1983). A more recent concern with coalition termination seeks to identify the sources of coalition breakup, such as a constitutional crisis, a no-confidence vote, elections, a policy disagreement, or the replacement or death of a government minister (see Budge and Keman 1990; Frendreis, Gleiber, and Browne 1986; Gunlicks 1977; King, Alt, Laver, and Burns 1990; Lupia and Strøm 1995). Our concern here is ultimately with all three of these aspects of coalition behavior, although with much greater and more immediate emphasis on coalition formation. Maintenance and termination are secondary concerns, but both are logically connected to the prospect that the mix of coalitions existing in subnational parliaments can influence the rise and fall of those at the national level.

Explaining Coalition Formation

Much of the theoretical literature on coalition governments embraces the assumptions of rational political behavior. Faced with decisions, rational political actors possess sets of alternative strategies, ordered preferentially, from which options connected with more preferred outcomes are consistently chosen over those associated with less preferred outcomes (Strom 1990a, 30). The game-theoretic tradition, which has dominated coalition research, emerged from this general presumption of rational decision making (Axelrod 1970; Gamson 1961; Tsebelis 1990). Game theorists view the process of government formation as "a particular type of social interaction, one forcing the actors to bargain with each other before they can 'win' and one that can, therefore, be modelled by constructing *deductive* theories on the basis of sets of *a priori* assumptions about the bargaining objectives of the actors" (Laver 1989, 16). In particular, four a priori assumptions have guided the game-theoretic approach, or what is generally labeled "formal coalition theory" (Laver 1986; Riker 1962; Strom 1990a):

1. Relevant players in the coalition game are unified parties, each of which can be considered a single bargaining entity with indivisible motives.
2. The coalition game is zero sum; what is gained by one party in pursuit of government office (i.e., cabinet portfolios) is lost by another party.
3. The universe of possible coalition governments is formed by all "winning" combinations of parties.
4. Each game of government formation is an isolated event, independent of any previous or future bargaining between the parties.

From these basic assumptions, formal theory has generated two types of research: size-criterion studies (the "office-seeking" tradition) and ideological/policy distance studies (the "policy-seeking" tradition).

"Office-Seeking" Tradition

Pioneering the office-seeking tradition, William Riker in his seminal contribution, *The Theory of Political Coalitions* (1962), deduced a "size principle" by which in *n*-person, constant-sum "games" coalitions of minimum size could be expected to form. Seeking to create a "minimum winning coalition" large enough to win but no larger, rational players in Riker's model would, for example, systematically decide to form coalitions of no more than 101 members in a 200-seat parliament. The clear assumption is that the exclusive motivation of rational party actors is the zero-sum maximization of seats in government so as to best exploit a fixed prize, namely the spoils of office. Subsequent modifications to the minimum-size rationality maintained that a minimum winning coalition not only should have no unnecessary individual members but should include as few parties as possible (Leiserson 1968). In the hypothetical 200-member parliament, a coalition of two equally powerful parties combining for 60% of the seats would be preferred to a coalition of four equally powerful parties with 60% of the seats.

The frequency of nonminimal-size coalitions in European national parliaments casts doubt on the size criterion as a fundamental determinant of multiparty government formation. "Oversized" and "undersized" coalitions are the most common deviations from the minimal winning solution. The oversized coalition "develops when a cabinet has obtained majority status, but at the expense of bringing more political parties into the government than are necessary to ensure a majority of votes in parliament" (Robertson 1983, 935). Conversely, an undersized coalition "may simply be a single minority party holding all the ministerial portfolios, yet entirely dependent upon a voting alliance within parliament to sustain votes of confidence" (Robertson 1983, 936). Formal office-seeking theory would have difficulty, then, in explaining coalition avoidance[3] and minority governments in Norway, Denmark, and Finland or oversized, "surplus majority" governments in Italy, Belgium, and the Netherlands. Undersized and oversized coalitions are more than "outliers" among European coalition cabinets: 37% of European governments in nonmajority legislatures from 1945 to 1987 were minority administrations, while 25% of all European governments during the same period contained surplus majorities (Laver and Schofield 1990, 70).

"Policy-Seeking" Tradition

Countering the generally disappointing results of empirical tests using the size principle, students in the policy-seeking tradition of government formation contend that parties seek to build coalitions with those parties closest to them ideologically (Axelrod 1970; De Swaan 1973; Leiserson 1970). According to this vision, the rational collective choice of political actors is to minimize the range of policy disagreement and ideological heterogeneity among members of a potential coalition. Members of winning coalitions, it follows, would all be adjacent or "connected" if placed on an ordinal, single-dimension, Left-Right ideological scale. "This implies that considerations of policy are foremost in the minds of the actors and that the parliamentary game is, in fact, about the determination of major government policy. . . . From the interaction of the actors on the basis of these preferences, certain coalitions are more likely to emerge than others. Such coalitions are not necessarily minimal in the sense of any of the theories presented before: they may well include unnecessary members" (De Swaan 1973, 88). Still, tests of the pioneering policy-distance models revealed more than a few cabinet coalitions to be ideologically unconnected (Browne and Franklin, 1986). Of 31 postwar Italian national government coalitions, for example, only 18 are predictable given the assumptions of policy distance (von Beyme 1983). Such predictions thus score only slightly better than chance.

New Directions

Recent theoretical and empirical works on national government formation have sought to reach beyond the traditional office-seeking versus policy-seeking dichotomy. Responding to the "poor fit between one-dimensional predictions and the empirical consequences of coalition behavior" (Schofield 1993, 3), some scholars now borrow from spatial theories of party competition to model coalition bargaining in legislatures on the basis of two or more policy dimensions. Schofield's (1993) model of "core parties" that can "typically guarantee themselves membership of every government coalition" (5) purports to explain "the occurrence of minority (non-majority) governments in countries such as Sweden as contrasted with the frequent occurrence of surplus (supra-majority) governments in Italy" (5). Austen-Smith and Banks (1990) and Laver and Shepsle (1990) contribute a "portfolio allocation model," suggesting that the credibility of alternative allocations of cabinet portfolios proposed during coalition bargaining is crucial: the "equilibrium solution" to coalition bargaining comes from identifying a discrete alternative in which the coalition awards each key portfolio to the party controlling the median legislator on the policy dimension associated with the portfolio in question (Laver, Rallings, and Thrasher 1995). Others, such as Baron (1991, 1993), add to the debate by contending that the very definition of "winning" has to be relaxed so as not to be strictly confined to those parties who become formal members of the cabinet; minority coalitions can, accordingly, be "winning" if they systematically secure support from outside the coalition.

These new directions in coalition research constitute fertile ground for future thought and study in the field of coalition government. They do not, however, resolve some of the standing indictments leveled against previous research. Models of unconstrained minimalist rationality operating within the context of laboratory-pure "games" fail to adequately explain the two aforementioned types of coalitions that commonly deviate from the minimum winning solution: oversized coalitions and undersized coalitions. More important, the "pure" rational choice approach is "inadequate because it does not allow one to account empirically for the *environmental phenomena,* or *context,* within which coalitions take shape and later collapse" (Robertson 1983, 935, emphasis added). ˙ ˙e are learning that behavior and choices are systematically structured. Politicians and parliamentary parties in minority legislatures should accordingly be seen as constrained actors within particular, and variable, political and social environments. In studying environments, we should, for example, assess the impact of *electoral competition* (e.g., interelection volatility and stability) on coalition negotiations. Likewise, *party goals* and *party systems* deserve greater attention. Lessons from the "new institutionalism" further suggest that it is "possible to develop intriguing and powerful models that are driven by assumptions about the *structural features* constraining coalition bargaining" (Laver and Schofield 1990, 198, emphasis added). If a "reality gap" exists in our understanding of the theory and practice of coalition government, then the way forward may be through systematic investigation of the roles played by contextual influences such as electoral competition, party goals, and institutional rules.

More damning than any reality gap is the stinging methodological critique that in coalition studies "the relationship between theory and data has become extremely incestuous" (Laver 1989, 16). New theories, innovations built upon the early works of Riker, De Swaan, and others, continue to be tested with the same set of data—namely, the universe of national governments in postwar Europe—from which the early theories themselves were originally derived. This poses a predictable problem: "It is simply no longer possible, for example, to construct a general theory from *a priori* assumptions and then to run off to 'test' it against the data, since the general properties of this data set are by now very well known. . . . In short, there are not enough national government coalitions to be very useful as a test bed for new theories" (Laver 1989, 16–17). There is, then, a "data gap" in coalition studies that hinders efforts to increase our understanding of this most basic political process.

To summarize the most basic and contentious shortcomings of conventional approaches to the study of coalitions, it is possible to make the following initial claims:

1. Theories that predict coalition behavior solely on the basis of universal, game-theoretic assumptions of minimal size or minimal policy range are insufficient for an accurate account of actual patterns of government formation.
2. Extant theory largely underdevelops party goals and electoral systems. The methodological choice between laboratory-pure theory (based upon deductive assumptions about rational behavior) and simple description (detailing case and systemic characteristics) is a false one. Contextual constraints—when they can be measured in meaningful fashion—cannot be ignored and should be included in deductive models.
3. Further development in our theoretical understanding of government formation and coalition bargaining is restricted by a paucity of fresh data.

Recognizing these shortcomings, we need to rectify the "accumulated dissatisfactions" (Browne and Franklin 1986, 469) and the "apparent gulf between theory and practice" (Mellors 1989, 5) in coalition studies.

Importing Coalition Theory to Explain Multiparty Subnational Government

Do the shortcomings of previous efforts designed to explain national government formation preclude the possibility of importing coalition theory to understand government formation in subnational institutions? The difficulties of doing so are certainly exposed when we try to make sense of individual instances of coalition bargaining. Consider, for example, the case of Belgium's Limburg Province in 1991. The

Belgian general election of 24 November marked the beginning of a
108-day odyssey that ultimately gave the country a new national government. Voters sacked a five-party coalition that had ruled since
1988. The Flemish Christian People's Party (CVP), whose uninterrupted presence in Belgian government dated from 1958, lost 4 of its
43 previous seats in the 212-member Chamber of Representatives.
The CVP's partner in the Christian Democracy family, the francophone Christian Social Party (PSC), relinquished 1 of its 19 seats. The
Flemish (SP) and Walloon (PS) Socialist parties lost 4 and 5 seats, respectively. The Flemish People's Union (Volksunie), a regional nationalist party, could salvage but 10 of its original 16 seats. In the wake, a
total of 13 parties with parliamentary representation stood ready to
either build or block the formation of a new cabinet.

The protracted crisis in Brussels coincided with smaller crises
throughout the country. No single party secured a majority in any of
Belgium's oldest institutions, the nine provincial assemblies. Nor could
a single party claim outright victory in any of Belgium's newest institutions, the regional councils. Indeed, the game being played in the
capital was duplicated in microcosm across all institutional levels of
representative government.

In Limburg province, where linguistic conflict has twice felled national governments,[4] the game was quick, decisive, and seemingly full
of broader implications. There the Catholic CVP had literally always
been in the majority, often with an outright monopoly of provincial
power but at times in coalition with the Flemish Socialists and on one
occasion with the Flemish Liberals (PVV). This time, voters had reduced the CVP's representation in the provincial council (Provincieraad) by 1 seat, leaving it with 24 on a council of 70, as shown in table
2.3. Needing just 12 more seats to secure a majority, the Christian
Democrats could choose immediately from the Socialists or the Liberals or even from some combination of the regionalist Volksunie, the
ecologist Agalev, or perhaps the right-wing extremist Vlaams Blok.
Most theoretical expectations would have led us to predict the winning
coalition to be one that minimized the number of parties, council seats,
and ideological distance: for example, a center-right CVP-PVV provincial government.

In reality, the outcome bore little resemblance to theoretical expectations. Unbeknownst to the CVP leadership, however, an anti-CVP
coalition had already taken shape months before the election when SP,
PVV, and Volksunie militants drew up a secret pact promising a tri-

Table 2.3

Distribution of Seats in Limburg Provincieraad,
21 November 1991

Party	Seats
Christian People's Party	24
Socialists	18
Liberals	12
Flemish People's Union	10
Ecologists (Agalev)	3
Vlaams Blok	3
Total	70

partite division of provincial power if voting results allowed.[5] The die had long before been cast. Following public announcement of the "palace revolution,"[6] the CVP found itself evicted from power in a Flemish province for the first time in 161 years! The Limburg government thus contained an excess number of parties and an excess number of council seats and was ideologically "unconnected" with left-wing and right-wing parties governing together without the centrist CVP.

Not only would coalition-theoretic expectations have led us to a faulty prediction, but they would also have masked the most interesting dimensions as well as the wider importance of coalition bargaining. Specifically, conventional theoretical approaches would have missed the significance of subnational-national linkages in coalition bargaining. In local terms, the Limburg coalition was rather astounding, a small but impressive victory for those campaigning on an anti–status quo theme. Origins and implications of the provincial coup, however, exceeded Limburg's own boundaries. The written coalition agreement, signed in the provincial capital, Hasselt, the night after the election, itself suggests a much wider importance attached to the outcome. Nine persons signed the 21-point document, pledging accord for eight years. Among the signatories, not one was an elected member of the provincial parliament itself; all were from each party's national leadership. For the Socialists, Willy Claes, the vice prime minister, signed. For the Volksunie, the party president, Jaak Gabriëls, signed. For the Liberals, the party's highest-ranking member in the Flemish executive, Patrick Dewael, signed.[7] The provincial coalition appeared to have gained the attention of each party's top leaders.

The coalition thrusting the CVP into opposition in Limburg would be attempted again by party leaders at the national level. Fifteen days after the announcement of the SP-PVV-VU Limburg alliance, King Baudouin designated Guy Verhofstadt, president of the PVV, as *formateur* of the next Belgian government. For eight furious days, Verhofstadt attempted what no *formateur* had attempted since 1958—to put together a government coalition *without* the Catholic parties. The effort ultimately stalled on 18 December amid bitter disagreements over the inclusion of the ecologist parties, Ecolo and Agalev, and the old center-Left government—a "losers coalition"[8]—was revived. Verhofstadt's mission proved historic but short-lived. Socialists and Liberals could not duplicate their Limburg coup; nor could they build upon their long-standing alliances in the provinces of Liège, Luxembourg, or Namur. Although the venture had failed, "It was psychologically important, a premonition of what could happen in the future in the whole country."[9]

The kind of deal making that transpired in Limburg province illustrates many aspects of the process in which we are interested. In the Flemish Christian Democrats we see a party whose long-standing hegemony in provincial coalition politics suddenly disappears despite an apparent advantage in bargaining power, only to be followed quickly by a direct challenge to the party's parallel status as hegemon in national coalition politics. We see, in the Flemish Socialists, a party choosing to "betray" its long-time coalition partner and determined to trade in its status as junior member in one coalition for a stronger position in another, albeit ideologically "unconnected," coalition arrangement. In Guy Vehofstadt we see the political entrepreneur attempting to translate provincial coalition innovation into national coalition change. We have linkages between coalitions at the provincial and national levels that cause us to question: When do national party leaders become directly involved in questions of government participation at subnational levels? Do members of subnational assemblies, those persons who must live with the consequences of coalition decisions, share the same preferences for coalition partners as their colleagues in national parliament? How, moreover, do coalitions at subnational levels influence the making and breaking of coalitions at the national level? Answers to these questions can inform our understanding of strategic political behavior not only in Belgium but in all multiparty coalition systems.

The Limburg case does not stand alone. Examining 45 coalitions formed in Italy's regional parliaments between 1970 and 1980, Zariski

(1984) finds that only 6 cases (13.3%) conform to Riker's prediction of minimal winning coalitions and that in only 10 cases (22.2%) do the winning coalitions contain no numerically redundant parties. Testing the expectations of formal coalition theory against 44 Flemish municipal council coalitions in Belgium, Pijnenburg (1987) finds that "the majority coalition that has actually been formed does not conform at all to the minimalist rationality put forward by the formal theories [compared to the alternative possibilities, it is actually the worst off]" (61–62). In a more ambitious test of the predictive power of size-oriented, policy-oriented, and actor-oriented models using data from 483 cases of Dutch municipal council coalitions formed between 1978 and 1986, Steunenberg (1992) concludes with the less-than-promising finding that "although the predictions of most coalition models proved to be statistically significant, their performance is still rather poor" (245–71). Steunenberg's efforts, together with those of Pijnenburg and Zariski, raise doubts about the possibility of making precise predictions about the formation of "minimal" coalitions. The questions most relevant to subnational coalitional behavior cannot be adequately addressed by drawing inferences exclusively from data on votes, seats, and office payoffs. These outward signs of coalition bargaining do provide a necessary and useful basis for analysis, but more creative measures are also required.

In particular, two nontraditional dimensions of coalition behavior deserve closer consideration: the vertical dimension and the internal party dimension. Recognition of these two arenas addresses the central theme of new thinking concerning coalitions: namely, that "context matters." Strom, Budge, and Laver (1994) perhaps put it best in their admission that "the real world of coalition politics is one of constraints, in which it is quite definitely *not* the case that everything is possible" (307). By looking "inward" and "downward" at government coalitions, for example, it may be possible to relax the conventional axioms of parties as unitary actors and government formations as isolated events.

The Vertical Dimension

The vertical dimension reveals a two-way problem: "How do national leaders or party strategists control through the state structure sub-national coalitional behaviour (vertical-downwards), and what effect have developments at the sub-national levels on the pursuit of party strategies (vertical-upwards)?" (Pridham 1988, 6). Do we assume that national parties allied in coalition will want to impose the same coalition at all levels where election results allow? Or do we explore the possibility that national politicians use certain subnational institutions as test markets for future national coalitions? Are subnational coalition agreements "nationalized," or are they based purely on local concerns? Granted, coalitions in provincial, regional, and state governments have less visibility than those at the national level; nevertheless, it must be investigated whether they tend to "enter the strategic considerations of national party leaders," to what degree they "complicate the coalition environment across the country," and in what fashion they may also "act as some determinant of actual coalition behavior" in the capital (Pridham 1984, 240). In pursuing answers to these questions, the vertical dimension allows us to see linkages and perhaps even interdependence between national and subnational coalition systems.

The Internal Party Dimension

The internal party dimension likewise forces us to address the consequences of internal party struggles for the bargaining process. Party leaders, whether at the national level or in regional parliaments, are not free from real or potential internal constraints. These constraints may condition a party leader's behavior toward other parties in coalition situations, and they may be seized upon and exploited by competitors at the bargaining table. Peering inside the internal party "black box" leads us to ask: Do national elites communicate demands to subnational actors that compel the latter to alter their preferred course of action or to tolerate actions of their national colleagues that the local or regional politicians would not have accepted in the absence of intervention from above? Does the national party have the capacity to remove courses of action from the subnational party's set of feasible choices without engaging in an explicit controversy and without imposing national preferences? Inversely, do authoritative decisions about coalition strategy flow upward as well as downward? Along the internal party dimension, then, party structures, levels of party centralization, elite control over followers, and party factions are all relevant variables indicating the interaction between interparty and intraparty relationships (Heidar 1984; Panebianco 1982; Sjoblom 1968). By shifting attention to coalitions at multiple levels of government and by recognizing the interdependence of parties and coalitions at different levels of the polity, a successful departure can be made from the usual assumptions, units of analysis, and arenas that limit conventional analyses.

Issues for Analysis: Actors, Motivations, Outcomes, Time, and Data

Variation in party coalition behavior across national and subnational levels of representative government forces us to rethink the extent to which political parties really can be considered "unitary actors," each with a "single set of preferences concerning the range of potential coalitions" (Laver and Schofield 1990, 21). The possibility that coalition outcomes in regional government may influence future coalition outcomes in national government suggests as well that government formation need no longer be considered the "discrete event" assumed by many theoretical models. A further assumption that the universe of possible coalition governments is determined by all "winning" combinations of parties, although partially redeemed by the greater propensity of parties to "experiment" at the subnational level, may also deserve some refinement. We look more closely at each of these possibilities in succession.

Parties as Unitary Actors

Coalition theory depends in large part on the supposition that parties ultimately behave as unitary actors. Theoretical parsimony has seemingly obliged this oversimplification of the reality of "party" in macrocomparative studies of government formation at the national level. The unitary actor assumption envisions an organizational oligarchy that permits party leaders, backed by their respective national executive bureaus and obliging party congresses, to speak to potential coalition partners at the bargaining table with one voice.

Existing knowledge of political parties does, however, indicate that all parties have regional factions or strongholds that may or may not approve of strategic decisions made by national party leaders. If regional party groups distinguish themselves from the national parliamentary party and the extraparliamentary party leadership in either basic goals or policy positions, the predictable result may be conflicting coalition preferences. When coalitions so induce conflict between party layers, dissenting members can exercise their options either to voice discontent or to exit the organization. This raises the possibility that the dichotomy offered by national/subnational party layers is a useful way to relax the dubious unitary actor assumption. If we extend the analysis of coalition behavior to the subnational legislative arena, the axiom of parties as single bargaining entities becomes by necessity an empirical question, not an a priori assumption. Examined at multiple levels, coalitions may be as much products of vertical *intra*party politics as they are of horizontal *inter*party bargaining.

To accept the unitary actor assumption is to view regional party organizations as little more than compliant local organs of national political parties, with national party elites consistently determining the strategic choices and coalition formulas involved in government formation in regional assemblies. All that remains for their lower-level counterparts is to play the part of faithful implementors. Viewing the party as unitary across levels of government further assumes that subnational coalitions are negotiated in the context of a particular coalition government at the national level (Laver, Rallings, and Thrasher 1987, 502). It assumes no significant variation in policy positions or ideological proclivities across levels of the party. It assumes, in short, a fixed process of top-down unilateral control. By this logic, if we can explain and predict the coalition behavior of parties at the national level, then we can do so by the same means and with equal success at the subnational level.

It may be similarly problematic to consider, a priori, subnational party groups as unitary, independent bargaining actors in and of themselves. To do so would be to consider the formation of governing majorities in subnational assemblies as discrete localized events, entirely removed from the government formation process at the national level. Further, to do so would be to once again ignore intraparty influences, the possibility of mixed motives within parties toward government participation, and the interest and influence of central party leaders. Even in the case of federalized Germany, it would be imprudent to assume in advance that Länd parties operate wholly independent of influence from their colleagues in Bonn.

The vertical dimension thus provides an opportunity to legitimately operationalize a concern that has long haunted models of coalition behavior. In particular, deviant subnational coalitions, those in which parties pass up the opportunity to reproduce the alliances of their national party, appear to violate the unitary actor assumption. Even if we accept that "parties are run by autocratic leaders who determine strategy in accord with their own ideal points" (Laver and Shepsle 1990, 496), by introducing a levels-of-analysis dynamic to the study of coalition behavior we must acknowledge at least two sets of leaders with two sets of putatively incompatible bargaining strategies, ideological proclivities, and policy goals within the same party. Moreover, "It may be misleading to assume a priori that officials associated with national political institutions are automatically more powerful than officials associated with local political institutions: that is a key question for empirical research" (Kesselman and Rosenthal 1974, 22).

The unity of parties is questioned further if we envision that "stratarchy" is a possible alternative to oligarchy. Parties are, in this alternative conception, stratified by different territorial levels and party organs, each of which has autonomy over its internal policies and affairs (Kitschelt and Hellemans 1990): "The desperate need in all parties for votes, which are scarcely mobilized at the apex of the hierarchy, results in at least some, if not pronounced, deference to the local structural strata where votes are won or lost. Thus a kind of 'balkanization' of power relations occurs, with variations in the extent of autonomy in middle and lower hierarchical strata from one habitat to the next" (Eldersveld 1964, 9). Locating the patterns of such variation is, of course, an empirical matter.

In sum, coalition politics in subnational assemblies provides convenient laboratories for challenging the unitary actor assumption and for testing the depth of partisanship, ideology, and organizational discipline across vertical party layers. To the extent that there are discernible and systematic differences, these factors must be considered as influencing the process of government formation.

If Not Single-Headed, Then Singularly Motivated?

By adding both vertical and internal party perspectives to the analysis of coalitions, it is possible to give fresh consideration to the traditional assumption that coalition players all pursue identical goals. If parties are indeed not making uniform coalition choices across institutional levels of power, as suggested above, then the question must be whether the basic goals of parties in regional, provincial, and local assemblies differ in some real way from those of parties in the national bargaining arena.

The basic division in the theoretical literatures on coalitions and competitive parties pits pure "office seekers" against pure "policy seekers." Ideal-typical office seekers are motivated by office as an end in itself, while ideal-typical policy seekers are motivated by office as a means to influence policy. Office-seeking party politicians who are motivated, ceteris paribus, by the fixed-sum pursuit of seats and by the overwhelming desire to capture the spoils of national cabinet portfolios (e.g., status, salary, staff) tend to see the virtues of policy compromises if these increase the party's chances of getting into government. Conversely, policy-seeking party politicians who are concerned, ceteris paribus, with ideology pursue office with equal vigor but tend to avoid the policy compromises necessary to enter certain coalitions. Neither classification is new, and most experts find it realistic to consider real-life politicians and parties as being somewhere in between the two ideal types. Still, most research assumes that political parties are motivated by either one or both of two ambitions: to get into government and to realize their policy goals.

Evaluating the motivations of political actors involved in coalition bargaining at subnational levels cannot by itself resolve the office-seeking versus policy-seeking controversy. Almost all politicians and political parties offering themselves for election are seeking office with an eye towards its benefits, and most politicians and political parties must pay some deference to policy concerns both before and after an election. Problems arise, first, when the stakes of coalition bargaining are presumed to be zero sum and, second, when these stakes are presumed to be identical for all actors and parties involved.

Formal theory is severely constrained by assuming that coalition actors pursue identical goals. The pursuit of goals may be identical only to the extent that all actors wish to maximize their expected utility. All parties and politicians must be considered rational decision makers, with their motivations for cross-party alliances based upon rational calculations. But are not the motivations of coalition actors influenced systematically by *situation*? It is possible that the "characteristics of the setting within which the coalition forms crucially influence what a rational actor should do. . . . A model created to explain coalitions in one type of setting may be inappropriate for another" (Reisinger 1986, 552). If the assumed payoffs of coalition membership are systematically and independently influenced by some measurable aspect of the context of the bargaining arena, then the basic motivations for entering into alliances may indeed vary.

What are the implications, for example, of one set of national party elites crafting coalition strategy to suit its basic appetite for the zero-sum capture of seats and power, while regional militants in the same party find themselves constrained by electoral or organizational pressures and thus are less willing to trade fundamental policy objectives for a share of the rewards of office? Will the regional group submit to the national strategy or perhaps choose the option of remaining outside government to maintain the purity of its message or to keep certain campaign promises? Motivations and rewards are important because they largely determine the nature of patronage, the nature of bargaining compromise, and the ability to ally with supposed enemies—all elements critical to coalitions at any level. The national/subnational divide affords the opportunity to examine the balance between motivations within parties, and it also allows for some test of the constraints that may alter the basic motivations of coalition actors. If individuals at various levels of polity and party are subject to the effects of multiple roles and cross-pressures, then coalition setting may indeed influence what a rational actor can be expected to do. Such influence is neglected by a theoretical axiom that stipulates that the coalition game is zero sum, with parties motivated solely by the desire to gain executive office at virtually any cost.

Allgemeine Koalitionsfähigkeit?

One additional theoretical supposition is that all coalition actors rationally calculate the benefits of any and all potential coalitions, and thus that the universe of all mathematically possible combinations of political parties constitutes the universe of coalition possibilities. In addition, the probability of all coalitions forming is often presumed to be equal. This, like most other such a priori assumptions, is debatable. One outspoken critic of this "American assumption" is von Beyme (1983): "The polarization of the major components of some party systems in Western Europe makes most of the theoretically possible coalitions—which according to coalition theory increase with the number of parties—politically impossible. Even coalitions that are considered as politically possible by the elites are resisted from the grass roots" (342). By expanding the analysis of government coalitions to subnational parliaments, it should be possible to test with new data the openness of parties to the entire range of coalition possibilities. If parties appear to experiment with alternative coalitions to a greater extent in subnational institutions than in national government, it may very well prove that this supposition of "allgemeine Koalitionsfähigkeit" actually makes more sense in the subnational arena than in the national arena. We would then have to question whether ideological compatibility is less important at regional and local levels; alternatively, it might mean that electoral exigencies or the desire to experiment with new coalition arrangements can loosen the usual constraints that confine parties in national parliament. If the universe of coalitions is wider or narrower depending upon level of the polity, then it should open up the possibility that coalitions at one level effectively eliminate or enlarge the set of feasible coalitions at another level.

Discrete Event or Continuous Process?

Should acts of government formation be modeled as one-shot contests, discrete events determined by the legislative weights of the respective parties and not by any past experiences or anticipation of future consequences? The possibility that subnational coalitions offer both experience and information to parties in the national bargaining arena, and thus serve as critical links in a dynamic process, has rarely been considered or systematically examined.

Is it really useful, we must ask, to assume a priori that parties and their leaders are both amnesiac and myopic? More likely, "Their strategies in elections and coalitional bargaining are typically conditioned by past events, as well as by the anticipation of future benefits" (Strom 1990b, 569). Clearly, one of the sources of this conditioning may be the success or failure of party relations in regional coalitions. The compatibility of parties as partners, their loyalty to one another, their efficacy in governing, and the electoral popularity of a coalition are all crucial criteria that provide part of the presumed "perfect information" that allows parties to make rational coalition choices during government formation at the national level.

Given that one of the principal criticisms of formal theory is that its laboratory-pure assumptions—like that of coalitions as discrete events —mask significant influences on coalition decisions, it would seem desirable that some attention be given to coalition behavior as a continuous process. "Government formation is typically a recurrent event. And the behavior of actors in a sequence of games (a so-called supergame) can differ radically from that of players in a single game. In a sequence of games, rational actors will adopt strategies maximizing their pay-offs in the supergame, rather than in each consecutive game separately" (Denters 1985, 297). Granted, there is no real scientific benefit in documenting every development in party relations or every threat to an alliance that occurs between the formation and termination of a national coalition. However, the periodic formation of coalitions in subnational institutions is the most outward manifestation of coalition behavior outside the national bargaining game. These are events that may be "pregnant with national connotations" (Hainsworth and Loughlin 1989, 169). They should be included in a more dynamic explanation of governing coalitions, one that improves upon existing static models by focusing on political learning processes and memory effects.

Both Gold Mine and Minefield: Methodology

Put simply, the evidence provided by coalition behavior in subnational assemblies can serve to ameliorate the so-called data gap in coalition studies. An enormous supply of untapped data exists at the subnational level of analysis. This is tantamount to a "gold mine" for observers of coalition behavior who have exhausted the same set of post-1945 national cabinet formations in Europe. At the same time, the very fact that this huge reservoir of data is both unrefined and largely uncollected scares away all but the most determined would-be pioneers in the field. This is to say nothing, of course, of the perceived minefield of problems in comparing coalition data from territorial units across different systems. The argument here, however, is that the benefits of gaining a fresh perspective on multiparty coalition government through the use of subnational data far outstrip the difficulties of collecting and organizing the data itself.

If the accretion of coalition governments in Europe cannot keep pace (despite the best efforts of the Italians!) with the development of theory and the demands of hypothesis testing, then we can and should turn to subnational coalitions. Doing so produces a new universe of coalition cases, the total number of which is "virtually incalculable" (Pridham 1987, 374). The study of subnational coalitions makes it possible to analyze a large number of coalitions simultaneously within a single country, allowing variables such as political culture and party system to be controlled, as well as to analyze an even larger number of coalitions longitudinally across countries.

Investigating coalition behavior in subnational assemblies, especially with regard to the conditions under which such behavior varies systematically from coalition behavior in national parliaments, can therefore help refine our understanding of parties as unitary actors. It can, simultaneously, help determine the goals and constraints that motivate party politicians to choose certain coalitions from a universe of alternatives. Further, it is possible through the study of subnational coalition behavior to gain a clearer understanding of coalition building as a continuous process instead of accepting the more traditional assumption of government formations as discrete events. Table 2.4 summarizes many of the principal issues at stake, the varied criticisms of existing theoretical approaches, some of the solutions offered by analysis of subnational parliaments, and some of the pressing questions that should be pursued in comparative fashion.

Summary

Although government formation provides one of the most heavily theorized and empirically tested fields in political science, there exists too much dissatisfaction over the current state of research to ignore the benefits of incorporating subnational legislatures and vertical intraparty politics. Critics will no doubt suggest that the explanatory and predictive powers of the field's most fashionable models would be sacrificed by including subnational institutions. The easiest retort to this charge is that any such assumed "powers" are themselves dubious. A more meaningful rejoinder, however, is that expanding the study of coalitions to a new level of analysis does more to advance our insight into an important political process than do the logical but often cryptic models whose coalition "solutions" depend on laboratory conditions. Charting new territory, with all its risks, seems preferable.

Progress on a new research frontier has to this point been slow, often imprecise, and at times simplistic. Moreover, previous research into regional and local coalition politics has not ventured beyond single case studies and within-nation comparisons. Now is the time to push research to a new level, moving beyond descriptive case studies to theory-driven, cross-national comparative analysis. Chapter 3 tackles this task by formulating a theoretical framework that will allow for rigorous thinking and systematic cross-national analysis of coalition formation in subnational parliaments. While challenging many of the common assumptions in the study of coalitions, the explanation detailed in this next chapter maintains the general presumption of rationality. A new

Table 2.4
Analytical Issues in Study of Coalition Government

Importance of studying coalition government formation	• Illustrates capacity of competitors to cooperate • Indicates relative openness of political system to rule by diversity of parties • Demonstrates relative responsiveness of parties to electoral verdicts • Provides first evidence of future direction of public policy • Reveals basic motivations of politicians and parties • Exposes process of collective decision making in mixed-motive situations
Approaches to the study of coalition government formation	• Deductive/game-theoretic • Inductive/empirical • Size principle models • Policy distance, ideological range models • Actor-oriented models (core party)
Criticisms of approaches to the study of coalition government formation	• Neglect power-sharing coalitions outside national parliamentary arena • Neglect internal party influences on strategic choice • Fail to account for "oversized" and "undersized" governments • Fail to account for contextual constraints (electoral and organizational) • Consider government formation static and discrete; ahistorical • Data poor
Solutions offered by studying coalition formation in subnational government	• Supplies new and fast growing set of outcomes for within-nation and cross-national comparison • Focuses attention on parties' internal politics of strategic choice and forces a reassessment of the "unitary actor" assumption • Raises possibility that government formation is a continuous process, interdependent on developments across government tiers
Key questions	• Does coalition behavior in subnational arena mimic that in national arena? • What are the determinants of coalition choice at subnational levels: motivations, compatibility, situation? • How responsive are parties to electoral competition and electoral change? • How influential are national politicians in forming subnational governments? • Do coalitions in subnational parliaments serve as "experiments" for future national use?

set of testable propositions is deduced from this unifying criterion of rationality, permitting the collection and analysis of cross-national data and thus the pursuit of solutions to the puzzles offered by subnational coalition politics.

Part Two

————

Theory and Methods

Chapter Three

Theory: Constraints on Rationality in Government Formation

What determines coalition choice in subnational legislatures? Reviewing the "state of the art" in chapter 2 demonstrated that theoretical approaches to the study of government formation commonly identify actor motivations and policy distance as the exclusive agents of causality. Power aggrandizement and ideological proximity clearly do play important roles in government formation in subnational institutions, as they do in national parliaments, and for this reason they deserve classification and analysis. However, blankly crediting politicians and parties with zero-sum mentalities and with uniform power- or policy-seeking motivations does little to explain the immense variety of political responses to coalition opportunities found in regional and provincial assemblies. Assuming constant and consistent motivations fails to explain, for example, why separate subnational branches of the same political party choose different coalition strategies when confronted with similar alternatives. This raises the logical question: Does *context* matter?

Context, situation, and environment are normally "red flag" variables in comparative political analysis—how can we generalize about structures, processes, or outcomes if all are dependent upon the unique setting in which they occur? The purpose of this chapter is not to seek explanation in the peculiar qualities of regions such as Catalonia, Flanders, Lombardy, or Schleswig-Holstein. Instead, the argument put forth below is that important and measurable characteristics of political environment systematically condition the courses of action that rational actors will pursue in the high-stakes affair of government formation. The argument will be advanced, not that "contextual variables" are themselves the only causal agents in coalition formation, but that they can add considerably to our understanding of the power game in subnational institutions.

Figure 3.1 locates the question of contextual influence within a general model of coalition formation. Suggested originally by Groennings (1970), the model includes "situational" variables among the factors influencing coalition bargaining. Situational variables include stability of situation, numerical strength of parties, positions of parties, constitutional variables (e.g., election laws), conventions or informal rules, external pressures (e.g., public opinion, threat), and the values and norms of the political culture (449). Of these, we will focus on *stability* (e.g., the impact of electoral change) and *external pressures* (e.g., national party intervention). These factors address key linkages between voters and their representatives as well as those between representatives and their parties—two sets of relationships whose qualities are at the heart of contemporary concerns over subnational governance.

A related problematic involves *national-subnational coalition linkages*. Are power-sharing arrangements across levels of government interdependent? In figure 3.1's depiction of the coalition formation process, "compatibility perceptions" play an important role in developing a party's strategic orientation. Included among compatibility variables are "prior party relationships: precedent, tradition, mutual reliability." Focusing on top-down and bottom-up directions of coalition change and experimentation tests whether the strategies and interactions leading to government participation at one institutional level are significantly influenced by the coalition "game" as it is played out at other levels or in other settings (figure 3.2). If parties are interested in precedent, tradition, and mutual reliability, then it should follow that "vertical political learning" occurs. Empirical support for this assumption would contribute temporal and spatial dimensions to the theoretical understanding of coalitions and government formation.

We now have the seeds of our own theoretical approach. Our dependent variable has five dimensions. At root, we are interested in strategic choices and coalition outcomes, namely, the characteristics of actual multiparty governments formed as a result of postelection bargaining. But we recognize that these outcomes have individual-level, party-level, and system-level components. At the individual level, we want to know, first, if and to what extent politicians perceive constraints

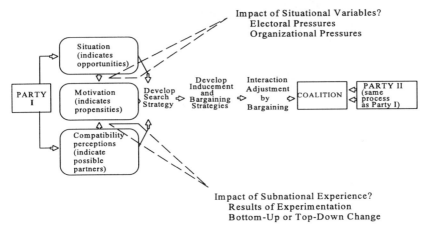

Figure 3.1 General Model of Coalition Formation. *Source:* Adapted from Groennings (1970).

on their behavior emanating from electoral and organizational environments, and second, how politicians react to these pressures (i.e., the extent to which they are responsive to, or conditioned by, their environments). At the party level, we want to measure and explain the strategic importance assigned to the congruence of party alliances in territorial parliaments with those in the national parliament. Finally, at the system level, our concern is with assessing the diffusion (both vertically and horizontally) of alternative coalition arrangements experimented with in the periphery.

Accepting the basic premise of rational political behavior, this study recognizes that underlying motives and preferences are key factors contributing to strategic choice and coalition outcomes. Our postulate, however, is that this relationship is conditional. Electoral context and organizational context condition the translation of political preferences into decisions and behavior. Electoral context and organizational context alter politicians' perceptions of bargaining environments, assign variable weight to such factors as electoral verdicts and party discipline, and ultimately define the stakes and broader implications of any experimental governing alliance. Motives, electoral environment, and organizational environment are thus the key explanatory variables in this study. The remainder of this chapter details the causal logic linking these explanatory variables with the politics of coalition in subnational parliaments.

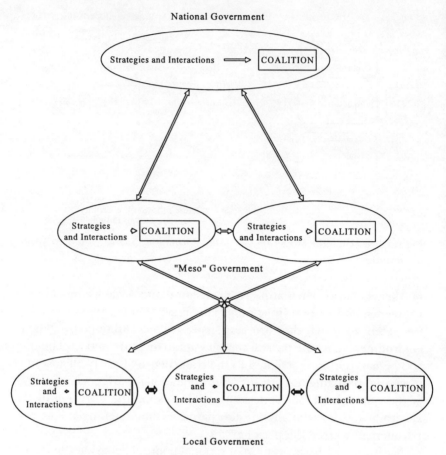

Figure 3.2   Coalition Linkages across Governmental Tiers

Propositions

The choice of coalition strategy by parties forming governments in subnational assemblies depends in part on the presence or absence of two key sets of constraints, one electoral and one organizational. Each constraint is a function of the competitiveness and uncertainty of electoral environments. When politicians in the subnational arena believe that their own behavior has a direct impact on electoral outcomes, their strategic choices are duly constrained by the necessity of appearing credible to the local electorate. Likewise, when politicians under conditions of electoral uncertainty perceive that their coalition behavior has a direct impact on internal party relations, then their strategic choices are constrained by the necessity of reconciling local imperatives with national party preferences. Strategies of deferring to national wishes or deviating from them are in turn influenced by the balance of "organizational radicalism" within the subnational party group. Thus, both a logic of electoral competition and a logic of party organization will guide the theoretical explanation and subsequent empirical investigation.

The initial basis for this theoretical understanding derives from previous work by Denters (1985), Strom (1990b), and Kitschelt (1989a). The "conditional model of coalition behavior" developed by Denters suggests that coalition behavior varies with the competitiveness and instability of the subnational political "market" or arena. Competitiveness and instability, in turn, determine the degree to which national party leaders—"entrepreneurs" in Strom's conceptualization—attempt to influence coalition outcomes in the periphery. In conjunction, the notion of "organizational radicalism" refined by Kitschelt proposes that coalition decisions, and the influence of national leaders on them, ultimately vary by the relative weights of internal party factions and the efficiency of the strategies to which each subscribes.

Electoral Constraints on Coalition Bargaining: The "Conditional" Model

According to Denters (1985) and following Downs (1957), politicians in competitive electoral markets are constrained by the need to "compete for the electorate's favours in order to attain or retain office" (Denters 1985, 296). Conversely, politicians in uncompetitive electoral markets "can, without seriously damaging their election result, behave in a way that is directly conducive to their ultimate goals" (Denters 1985, 296). Competitiveness, in short, restricts coalition choice.

Given these possibilities, two factors may lead regional and local politicians to consider whether they are operating under the pressure of an electoral constraint. First, the *political volatility* of the subnational electoral system itself can determine the presence of such a constraint on behavior. The more vote and seat shares for parties fluctuate across consecutive elections, the more politicians are likely to believe—both individually and collectively—that their electoral fortunes are directly tied to their own behavior. Thus, an electoral constraint can be said to be operative. However, the less results for parties vary across successive elections, the more politicians are likely to detach election outcomes from behavior, including coalition behavior. In this latter case, politicians would be less constrained by electoral imperatives in their strategic choices, given the marginal utility of votes.

Second, the *extent of nationalization* in subnational markets may also influence the role an electoral constraint plays in coalition behavior. When fluctuations in election results in the subnational arena are tied to those in the national arena, choices of coalition strategy by subnational party groups are again likely to be unrestricted. The opposite may be true in more "localized" systems in which changes in party vote and seat shares are not related to those at the national level. In such situations politicians and party groups have incentives to appear "consistent and reliable" to the local electorate and are more inclined to pursue a restricted set of coalition possibilities.

By dichotomizing the electoral volatility and nationalization variables, we may envision a classification scheme of subnational electoral environments (figure 3.3). Electoral markets have either low or high rates of political volatility and are deemed either "nationalized" or "localized." Cross-classifying territorial units by these criteria yields four distinct categories of subnational electoral markets: low-volatility/nationalized, low-volatility/localized, high-volatility/nationalized, and high-volatility/localized.

The principal hypothesis emerging from this scheme is that volatility tends to "increase the inclination of parties to pursue short-term strategies" (Denters 1985, 298). Especially in localized, high-volatility systems, parties have the greatest electoral constraint and thus should have the strongest incentives to pursue conservative coalitions that minimize ideological distance, even if such coalitions are larger than the normally optimal minimum winning combination. In nationalized, high-volatility systems, parties do have a partial electoral constraint, but volatility is largely a function of national political considerations and trends. In this latter context, parties are more likely to concentrate on the maximization of seats in government: in other words, they will prefer a minimum winning coalition that maximizes their share of the rewards of political office. The conditions and constraints posited by the model are summarized in table 3.1.

The theoretical model constructed thus far suffers from the sins of omission rather than those of commission. The approach as formulated does not fully explore the nationalized/localized distinction, nor does it introduce the possibility that national party leaders enter the subnational coalition game when the game itself is nationalized or

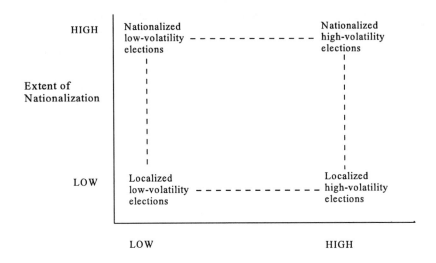

Figure 3.3 Typology of Subnational Electoral Environments. *Source:* Denters (1985, p. 297).

Table 3.1

Constraints on Coalition Actors in Different Electoral Environments

Electoral Condition	Electoral Constraint	Level of Risk	Scope of Strategy	Range of Alternatives	Strategic Orientation
High-volatility, localized	Full	High	Short-term	Narrow	Competitive
High-volatility, nationalized	Partial	↑	↑	↑	↑
Low-volatility, localized	Partial	↓	↓	↓	↓
Low-volatility, nationalized	None	Low	Long-term	Broad	Cooperative

when the stakes are high. Nor do we yet have evidence to support the proposition that "in electoral systems lacking competition, political parties are more likely to opt for co-operative strategies, than in systems where politicians are forced to compete" (Denters 1985, 305). Also unexplored is the question of whether individual parties respond differently to electoral constraints when volatility manifests as success (i.e., electoral gains) as opposed to failure (i.e., electoral losses). These are crucial gaps that must be addressed and are addressed below.

It suffices to note at this point that the model of conditional coalition behavior does provide a useful foundation for the study of subnational assemblies. The model's appeal lies in its apparent success at "conciliating elements of the formal theories and the alternative real-life analysis of coalition dynamics" (Pijnenburg 1987, 73). The approach "standardizes the dimension of party competition and electoral volatility in such a way that (a) it can easily be operationalized, (b) will lend itself perfectly to the formulation of both precise and readily verifiable hypotheses, and (c) could prove a relevant and interesting concept for cross-national comparisons" (Pijnenburg 1987, 73). This is no small feat, given the widely presumed impossibility of conducting rigorous cross-national comparisons of subnational coalition politics (see Laver 1989; Mellors and Pijnenburg 1989). Still, the model is neither complete nor without its problems.

Specifically, the model must address the role of national-subnational linkages in the coalition game. When discussing government formation in regional or provincial parliaments, it is rather unrealistic not to provide for the possibility that the process of subnational coalition choice is "nested" within a larger process of coalition formation at the national level.[1] Allowing for this potentiality brings into focus some important questions: In which cases are national party interest and involvement in subnational coalitions likely to be greatest? In which scenarios is national control over subnational coalition decisions likely to be most effective? And when, finally, does a party's electoral constraint come into conflict with its internal organizational constraints? Clearly, a theoretical explanation that looks "downward" at subnational coalitions must also look "inward" at party relations and organizational constraints on bargaining.

Organizational Constraints on Coalition Bargaining: Entrepreneurs, Radicals, and Loyalists

A model of government formation, especially one that purports to explain behavior across different levels of the polity, cannot avoid the presence of an organizational dynamic. To do so would be to accept the purity of the unitary actor assumption dispelled in the preceding chapter. The games of coalition bargaining and formation in regions or provinces may not occur in complete isolation from the "supergame" between parties at the national level. These games, whether at the national or the subnational level, are in part constrained by the organizational properties of the players. The trouble is how to work this particular concern, or what may be called "parties' internal micro-politics of strategic choice" (Kitschelt 1989a, 401), into the relatively parsimonious framework of the conditional model of coalition behavior.

One logic of this combination can be summarized as follows: Rational party leaders value certain political goods, namely, party power and status. They seek to maximize these goods in the various institutions to which the party gains access. Further, pursuit of these goods is most important to party leaders when their attainment is most in doubt. In other words, the interest of party leaders is likely to be greatest when the goods they intrinsically desire are either in jeopardy or newly within their grasp. Under conditions of uncertainty, as in coalition formation, and under conditions of political volatility, as in highly competitive electoral environments, party leaders are forced to focus attention on the protection and aggrandizement of these valued goods.

Just as volatility increases the inclination of subnational party groups to react with short-term strategies, so too should high volatility increase the inclination of national party leaders to react with their own short-term strategies. Herein lies the potential for conflict. Indeed, if we accept that "parties, regardless of their organizational characteristics, face different incentives in different institutional settings" (Strom 1990b, 579), then we must also accept that national parties and their constituent subnational groups may approach the same highly volatile situation with dissimilar, though individually rational, short-term motivations and strategies.

Since Downs (1957), the rational motivations of party politicians have been the subject of protracted debate. Borrowing from recent contributions to the debate by Strom (1990b) and Kitschelt (1989a), it is possible to construct a set of assumptions concerning the utility calculations of national party leaders and subnational-level party politicians as they approach coalition strategy. This is best accomplished by conceptualizing party leaders, on the one hand, as *entrepreneurs* and elected councilors, and on the other, as a mix of organizational *loyalists* and *radicals*.

NATIONAL PARTY LEADERS. National party leaders may be thought of as entrepreneurs, primarily motivated by the anticipated benefits of converting government status into private goods. "Office benefits must figure prominently in the utility calculations of the individuals who become party leaders. Left to their own devices, then, party leaders should pursue office benefits rather than votes or policy" (Strom 1990b, 574). The rational short-term priority of entrepreneurial party leaders, all other things being equal, is to maximize the prize of government office. The behavioral manifestation of this priority is an attempt to get the party into government office wherever election results allow and to do so in a manner that maximizes the rewards of office, such as portfolios, power, and prestige. As entrepreneurs, however, party leaders must, when able, also be concerned with longer-term strategies that can help them compete electorally in the future. When given the luxury, entrepreneurial party leaders may, for example, experiment with alternative coalition formulas in subnational assemblies and thus boost their leverage with national coalition partners by increasing the threat of coalition breakup. To meet the concerns of short- and long-term strategies as well as the requirements of a rational, self-interested leadership intent on protecting its status and power, national party leaders accordingly create a hierarchical, top-down party decision-making apparatus (Kitschelt 1988; Michels 1962; Schlesinger 1984).

These twists on the Downsian notion of parties and party leaders relate directly to coalition behavior as classified in the conditional model. Under conditions of uncertainty and competitiveness, the short-term strategy of rational, unconstrained national party leaders is a zero-sum survivalist strategy: that of maximizing the power of the party vis-à-vis that of its opponents. In practical terms this means minimum winning coalitions and/or the imposition of the national coalition arrangement in all cases permitted by election results. Alternatively, under more stable conditions, rational, unconstrained party leaders can pursue ideologically "unconnected" alliances or even experiment with anti-incumbent coalitions of minorities. In all cases, the entrepreneurial party leader assumes the deference and adherence of party groups at lower echelons. The alternatives for national leaders determining party strategy in both low- and high-volatility subnational electoral markets are summarized in figure 3.4.

The deference of regional deputies and provincial parliamentarians to the strategic preferences of superior party levels is a rational expectation under certain conditions. National party leaders should have the greatest concern for coalition outcomes in highly volatile subnational electoral markets. The stakes will, it follows, be highest in high-

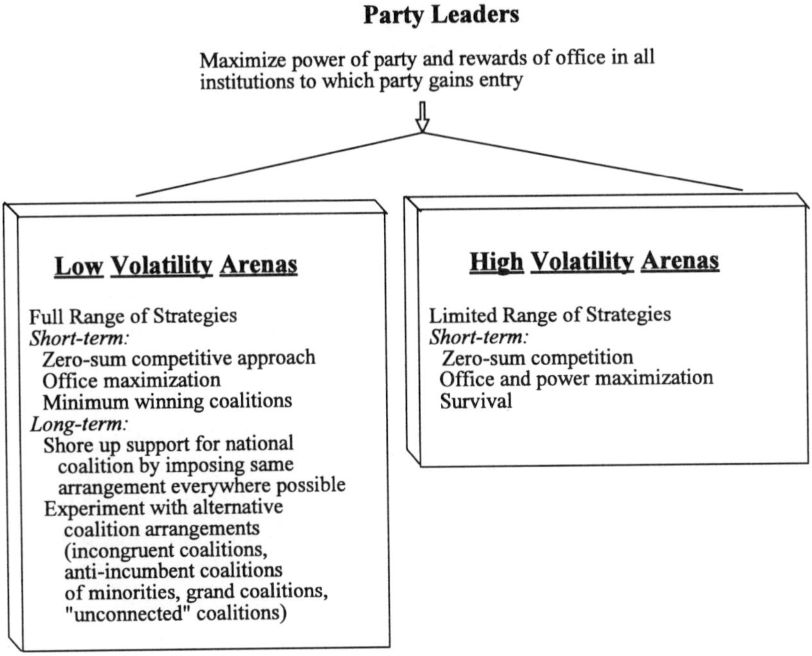

Party Leaders

Maximize power of party and rewards of office in all
institutions to which party gains entry

Low Volatility Arenas

Full Range of Strategies
Short-term:
  Zero-sum competitive approach
  Office maximization
  Minimum winning coalitions
Long-term:
  Shore up support for national
    coalition by imposing same
    arrangement everywhere possible
  Experiment with alternative
    coalition arrangements
    (incongruent coalitions,
    anti-incumbent coalitions
    of minorities, grand coalitions,
    "unconnected" coalitions)

High Volatility Arenas

Limited Range of Strategies
Short-term:
  Zero-sum competition
  Office and power maximization
  Survival

Figure 3.4 Conditional Strategies of National Party Leaders

volatility, nationalized arenas. With the outcome being of greatest importance to the national party and at the same time appearing to be minimally tied to the behavior of the subnational party group itself, deference to national strategy is to be expected. Conversely, the stakes and interest will be lowest for the national party leadership in low-volatility, localized electoral arenas. While deference to national preferences is still an expectation—in this case prudent—entrepreneurial party leaders have both the luxury and the incentive to grant a degree of strategic autonomy, a "carrot" of sorts, to the subnational group. In uncompetitive, localized electoral arenas, party leaders have little to lose but perhaps something to gain by granting partial or total control over coalition decisions to subnational groups.

In between such poles are those electoral markets that can be classified as "low volatility/nationalized" or "high-volatility/localized." Where electoral competition is nationalized and stable, the motivation for politicians at either the subnational or the national level to pursue short-term strategies is not fulfilled. Provincial or regional politicians are not restricted by a pressing need to appear reliable and consistent to the local electorate, and national party leaders are themselves free to direct their immediate attention to more contentious arenas. Thus, with neither an electoral constraint nor an organizational constraint operative, parties in low-volatility nationalized cases are free either to pursue coalitions that maximize primary goals (e.g., office benefits) or to experiment with alternative coalition formulas. Each option is equally rational for both national party leaders and subnational party groups.

It is the final case, that of the high-volatility localized electoral markets, in which the strategies of entrepreneurial party leaders may meet resistance. Here both the power and standing of the party are clearly at stake, thus making the party's participation in government a matter of some concern for the national leadership. If, under conditions of competition and uncertainty, party leaders pursue short-term strategies, they are likely to view the subnational coalition game as a struggle in which only the fittest survive. The consequence is that competition easily becomes zero sum and coalitions take on the character of power-maximizing, minimum winning arrangements. This logic, while efficient and optimal from the vantage point of national party leaders, may stand in contrast to the preferences of subnational party groups.

For a regional party calculating the consequences of its ultimate coalition decision, the rational choice under conditions of a full electoral constraint is to pursue a conservative coalition of minimal policy range in order to "minimize the damage post-election compromising is bound to inflict upon the credibility of coalition parties" (Denters 1985, 298). Here powerful incentives exist for parties to adjust their strategies to local electoral preferences and vote maximization. Such, however, may not be in keeping with the national leadership's own preferences. Thus, there is the potential for internal party disagreement, even conflict, and hence the presence of organizational risks and constraints.

National party leaders may indeed condone and concur with such a cooperative, policy-sensitive local strategy, but only after calculating it in terms of costs and benefits to the national coalition strategy. They may, however, choose instead to impose alternative coalition formulas on their colleagues in the periphery. This could require party groups in subnational assemblies to share power with nontraditional partners, to break preelection promises, or to concede large portions of their electoral platforms simply to increase acceptability as a coalition partner. Subnational party leaders and assembly members must then calculate the costs and benefits of alternative coalitions not only with respect to the local electorate but also with respect to the national party leadership.

Coalition choice under electoral and organizational constraints is largely a choice between deference and dissention, between toeing the party line and exercising the options of "voice" and "exit" (Hirschman 1970). Under these conditions, the game is no longer a discrete event between unified parties but is instead a kind of "two-table" bargaining process in which subnational parties negotiate simultaneously with their local rivals *and* with their own central party leaders. It may be rational in the short term, for example, for the regional party group to conform to national policy and exclude one or more major parties from a coalition. This avoids intraparty conflicts, ensures policy consistency, and engenders harmony between the national coalition partners. The strategy, however, may be counterproductive and suboptimal if it dilutes public support—perhaps by excluding the party with the plurality of votes—and if the other regional party or parties retaliate by excluding the first party from all future coalitions.

For their part, national party leaders must themselves assess the trade-offs between dictating their will and diffusing internal dissention. So-called strong leaders can neutralize internal conflicts by imposing their preferences on subordinate colleagues. As conventional wisdom suggests, such centralized, oligarchic leadership produces the strongest and most credible actors in coalition bargaining (Groennings 1970; Maor 1992; Panebianco 1988). We might expect this in, for example, the German Free Democrats (FDP). Other, "weaker" leaders may see in subnational coalitions the opportunity to retain the support and membership of party factions or groups by granting them a free hand in their own coalition decisions. Leaders of parties racked by faction, such as the Belgian Social Christian Party (PSC), may be expected to adopt such a posture.

The key here is simply that the opportunities offered by government formation and coalition bargaining can, under certain conditions, appeal to the disparate motives of subnational and national party leaders. When this occurs, the interparty coalition game itself can become an intraparty contest as well. The possible conditional dynamics of organizational constraints are summarized in table 3.2.

ELECTED COUNCILORS. Outcomes of internal struggles over coalition strategy depend as much on the goal-related tendencies of internal party groups as on static organizational rules and structures. By

Table 3.2

Organizational Constraints on Coalition Actors in
Different Electoral Environments

Electoral Condition	Electoral Risks	Organizational Constraint	Potential for Intraparty Conflict
High-volatility, localized	High	Full	High
High-volatility, nationalized	↑	Partial	Low, favors deference
Low-volatility, localized		None	Low, favors autonomy
Low-volatility, nationalized	Low	Partial	Low, favors either deference or autonomy

invoking the concept of "organizational radicalism," it is possible to anticipate in which parties or in which regions subnational leaders and elected party representatives will give in to external prodding and where instead they will choose to dissent. By allowing for multiple goals across party layers, we should be better able to explain some apparently nonrational actions taken by party groups in bargaining situations.

The central assumption of rationality employed so far holds that all party politicians, regardless of their position in the polity, have a primary goal, whether office maximization or policy maximization, ideology advocacy or constituency representation. Politicians, whether in subnational parliaments or in positions of national party leadership, make deliberate and conscious choices to pursue their respective primary goals within the constraints offered by the electoral and organizational environments in which they operate.

If the Weberian notion of parties as bureaucratic organizations were always true, there would be little need in the study of strategic choice to proceed past an investigation of national party leaders' primary goals. When primary goals within voluntary associations (e.g., political parties) are mutually conflicting, party representatives at lower tiers of the organizational and governmental pyramids should consistently accede to the primary goals of the top leadership under the threat of discipline. In reality, however, national party leaders are themselves rarely unconstrained or omnipotent. Their leverage is constrained by the balance of power within the party.

All political parties, regardless of their organizational properties, have antagonisms between leaders and followers, between pragmatists and ideologues, even between conservatives and progressives. Subgroups of parties, such as those brought together in territorial parliaments, contain similar mixes of antagonisms. Borrowing from the notion of organizational radicalism, it is possible to identify one such antagonism that may influence parties to commit to a particular coalition strategy under both electoral and organizational constraints.

All political parties contain a mixture of persons either satisfied or discontented with the distribution of power within their respective organizations (Pierre 1986). Following Harmel and Janda (1992), it may be assumed that along with vote-, office-, and policy-maximization goals, some party politicians may also include *intraparty democracy maximization* among their aims. The antagonism between organizational "loyalists," those satisfied or unwilling to challenge decision-making norms, and organizational "radicals," those discontented and critical of power relations within the party, should help explain outcomes in parties' micropolitics of strategic choice.

Ideal-typical loyalists subscribe to strategic moderation in matters of internal party politics and are inclined to pursue strategies that maximize party unity as well as their personal careers within the party. For organizational loyalists, the objects are efficiency and discipline, even if a particular party group has to sacrifice its autonomy and immediate interests. They are, in a slight twist on Edmund Burke, "trustees" of party policy. Organizational radicals, conversely, call for strategies that maximize local identity, local priorities, and decentralized decision making rather than the imperatives of party unity. For radicals, the object is party democracy, even if the party's ability to speak with one voice at the bargaining table has to be compromised. Completing the Burkean analogy, organizational radicals are the "delegates" making decisions based on their own best judgment. This characterization of dichotomies and antagonisms within subnational party groups is summarized in figure 3.5.

The theoretical connection with the conditional model of coalition behavior and its associated electoral and organizational constraints is apparent. When the choice of coalition strategy in a competitive

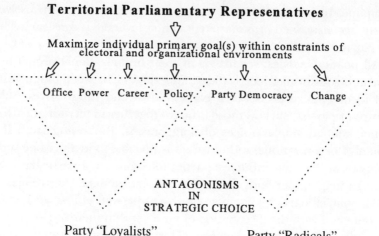

Figure 3.5 Micropolitics of Subnational Coalition Choice

environment—that is, high-volatility, localized electoral markets—induces national-subnational disagreement, politicians may respond (both individually and collectively) to organizational demands in different ways depending in part upon their organizational radicalism. In the absence of both electoral constraints and pressure from national elites, debate over the power of party layers is moot. Politicians can pursue unrestricted the coalitions that maximize their primary goals. Under the weight of both electoral constraints and organizational constraints, however, radicals are more likely than loyalists to pursue their own strategy and risk sanction rather than to defer to that of their putative superiors.

Actors within the same voluntary association can disagree over strategic choice, and the manner in which one level of party members responds to the organizational demands made by another level is a function of the value placed on intraparty democracy as opposed to party unity and deference. Higher degrees of organizational discontent and greater concentrations of organizational radicalism can therefore condition the behavior of competitive parties in coalition situations.

While clashes over internal party democracy are well documented within the so-called new politics parties (e.g., Greens), it is unrealistic to ignore those that occur within traditional parties, such as the German Christian Democratic Union (CDU) after its 1973 restructuring, the French Socialist Party (PS) ever since the Epinay Congress of 1971, and the Belgian PSC following its decision to abolish organized tendencies in the early 1980s. Though outside the context of coalition systems, the U.S. Democratic Party in the late 1960s and early 1970s is an additional example of the effect that debates over party democracy can have on strategic orientations.

Bottom-Up "Feedback"?

The theoretical exposition has thus far concentrated on the electoral, organizational, and individual constraints that restrain political motivations and condition the behavior of actors in subnational coalition situations. A matter of final theoretical importance is the relationship between coalition building in peripheral parliaments and that which occurs in national government.

In his benchmark contribution, *Coalitions in Parliamentary Government,* Dodd (1976) proposes that "provincial or state parliaments could provide an experimental setting in which party coalitions could be attempted between long-term adversaries, with the intermediate provincial experience making national-level coalitions more possible than they would be without the provincial experience" (217). Related is Hinckley's (1981) more formal contention that "coalition behavior in one situation both affects and is affected by behavior in other situations" (81). Little theoretical effort has, however, been devoted to exploring the possibility of bottom-up coalition influence, experimentation, or "feedback." We know little of whether subnational coalitions borne of certain electoral conditions produce better experimental gauges for future national-level cooperation. Little is known, either, about the extent to which decision makers at the regional or provincial level are motivated by the expectation that their strategic choices can influence those taken at the national level.

Extrapolating from the logic posited in preceding sections, it follows that those coalitions formed in "low-volatility, nationalized" subnational electoral markets should hold the greatest value as test beds for future coalition arrangements. Here purposive coalition experimentation is most feasible, given the absence of immediate electoral constraints. Moreover, since election results consistently follow national patterns, subnational politics can more easily be seen as national politics on a reduced scale. Coalitions obliged by electoral mathematics or by unique local concerns would not be true "proving grounds" for national collaboration. For example, it might be expected that a "red-green" (i.e., red = Social Democrats, green = Greens) experiment in Germany's Lower Saxony, where voting in Landtag elections has been comparatively stable and where existing voting shifts tend to follow national patterns, could better serve as a proving ground for future national-level collaboration than one of the so-called traffic light coalitions (i.e., red = Social Democrats, yellow = Liberals, green = Greens) in Bremen, where voting shares fluctuate wildly and where elections are usually won or lost on "local" issues.

We should anticipate that the value of a subnational coalition in terms of its "vertical-upward" ability to influence national coalitions is directly related to the nationalization of the electoral environment but inversely related to the volatility of the electoral environment. Establishing causality between subnational coalitions and national coalition change is a demanding task. To a certain extent, the definitive establishment of such causality is beyond the immediate scope of this investigation. The real goal is to establish that both association and influence exist and that under certain measurable conditions the linkages between subnational and national coalition systems are stronger.

Summary

The preceding discursive exposition has placed this study's theoretical basis within the context of current thinking on coalitions and competitive party behavior. The overarching premise has been that coalition behavior is conditional; it is not necessarily a one-shot contest among unified parties. The strategic behavior of parties in the subnational bargaining arena can be conditioned by the local electoral environment as well as by the internal organizational environment. Further, the context in which an alternative regional power-sharing arrangement emerges determines its worth as an agent of national change. Together, these propositions revise our existing understanding of the motivations, outcomes, and consequences of government formation.

The following sections transform the expository discussion into a more limited, formal set of statements that enable subsequent empirical analysis. Underlying assumptions and testable hypotheses are presented and are followed by a formal depiction of the process of subnational government formation.

Explaining Coalition Bargaining and Government Formation in Subnational Assemblies

Assumptions

Our theoretical approach to understanding coalition politics in subnational parliaments rests upon the following assumptions:

A1. Politicians are goal oriented; each is motivated by and pursues some intrinsically desirable political good or goods.

A2. Politicians have incentives to pursue utility-maximizing courses of action. Politicians are rational agents.

A3. Outcomes of government formation are valued by politicians, parties, and voters.

A4. In government formation, rational politicians make conscious and deliberate decisions concerning participation in government.

A5. In political parties, conscious and deliberate decisions concerning government participation are collective decisions, influenced by the balance of goals and power within the party.

A6. For a constraint on individual or collective behavior to be operative, critical actors must perceive its presence. "'Perception' is the intermediate variable that has to be placed between objective facts and the reactions of the parties" (Deschouwer 1992, 17).

These six assumptions allow us to "break free" from the "shackles of conventional coalition theory" (Laver and Shepsle 1990, 495). Together, they lay the foundation for an informed, reasonably parsimonious interpretation of a complex process. They simply allow us to recognize coalition formation as a rational endeavor with a collective outcome, produced from individual preferences aggregated within an electoral and organizational framework. They make no predetermination that parties are unitary actors or that coalitions are discrete outcomes. These matters are left open for testing.

Hypotheses

Hypotheses are arranged in three sections, addressing system-level, party-level, and individual-level influences on subnational strategic choice. Premised on acceptance of the assumptions set forth above, a group of hypotheses concerning electoral constraints on strategic choice and coalition behavior in subnational assemblies is presented first. The dependent phenomena to be explained include strategic preferences (i.e., attitudes and perceptions) and the actual outcomes of government formation in subnational assemblies (i.e., behavior). The basic question is whether different political responses to coalition opportunities emerge from different electoral contexts. The essential view of the world anticipated by these hypotheses is that, all else being equal, electoral volatility and localization should increase the risks of coalition decisions, restrict coalition choices, and reinforce adversarial strategies.

H1. Volatility increases the perception among politicians that coalition choices affect election outcomes.

Volatility heightens risk and accountability

H2. Localization increases the perception among politicians that coalition choices affect election outcomes.

Localization heightens risk and accountability

H3. Electoral traditions of high volatility and localized voting patterns increase incentives to restrict coalition choices on the basis of local electoral concerns and thus increase the likelihood that parties will adopt vote-maximizing strategies vis-à-vis government participation.

Corollary. Electoral stability and nationalized voting traditions eliminate incentives to restrict coalition choices on the basis of local electoral concerns.

H4. Electoral success reinforces noncooperative strategies.

Corollary. Electoral failure reinforces cooperative strategies.

Testing these hypotheses should allow us to dispel the null hypothesis that context does not influence what rational actors may be expected to do in coalition situations. It should, therefore, demonstrate that level and change of electoral support do affect perceptions of strategic situations. It should, moreover, shed important light on the strength of linkages between electoral verdicts and government formations at regional and provincial levels of governance. Alternatively, if testing these hypotheses produces little or no real evidence of a relationship between electoral context and strategic choice, then the influence of the electoral mechanism on government composition— presumed to be robust by the democratic ideal—will be proven weak. If, finally, no connection can be found between electoral context and perceptions of strategic situations, then the indifference of elected representatives to popular opinion will be exposed.

Next, a set of hypotheses regarding organizational influences and constraints on coalition choice is presented. These hypotheses suggest those conditions under which the involvement and influence of national party leaders in the coalition affairs of their subnational colleagues is likely to be greatest. In conjunction, a hypothesis suggesting the conditions under which national involvement in subnational coalition choice is likely to provoke internal disputes is advanced. Here again, the competitiveness of subnational electoral environments influences the degree to which organizational constraints (i.e., national-subnational intraparty relations) condition coalition outcomes:

H5. Volatility and nationalization increase the incentives for national party leaders to participate in decisions of subnational government formation.

H6. Stability and localization increase the incentives for party leaders to grant subnational colleagues strategic autonomy.

H7. Volatility and localization increase the potential for national-subnational conflict over coalition strategy.

If strategic orientations and questions over government participation at the provincial or regional level are indeed sources of organizational conflict, then it is important that some effort be made to understand the likelihood that subnational politicians will behave independently of pressure from their national leadership.

H8. Organizational radicalism reinforces vertical strategic factionalism.

H9. Informal party organization reinforces local autonomy in coalition decision making.

H10. Participation in the organs of party decision making outside the region or province is inversely related to vertical strategic factionalism.

A final set of hypotheses concerns the extent to which coalitions in subnational parliaments serve as precursors for future coalitions in national government. There may, of course, be numerous factors and circumstances that connect the choice of strategy in one arena with that in another. For the purpose of testing a "conditional" understanding of strategic choice, however, it is useful to focus again on the key variables of volatility and localization:

H11. The risks of coalition experimentation decrease with electoral stability and nationalized voting patterns.

H12. Traditions of electoral stability and nationalized voting results increase the utility of subnational coalition "experiments" for future use in national government.

H13. Strategic "openness" facilitates coalitional learning.

These possibilities hold weighty theoretical and practical implications for party system change. With empirical evidence to support these propositions, it will be possible to contend that coalition outcomes are interdependent, not discrete.

Synthesis

The theoretical explanation outlined above does not endorse an understanding of subnational governance as the exclusive domain of unconstrained, self-interested office seekers. Instead, it contends that in the government formation process, political self-interest is conditioned in systematic ways by the characteristics of the electoral environment in which parties compete. Subnational branches of national political parties entering coalition bargaining situations are conditioned in their behavior by the competitiveness of the electoral environment, which in turn conditions the involvement and influence of national party leaders. Context and situation can condition collective outcomes. Moreover, when the best rational strategy of a subnational party group conflicts with the preferences of its national party leadership, the decision to conform or to deviate is influenced by organi-

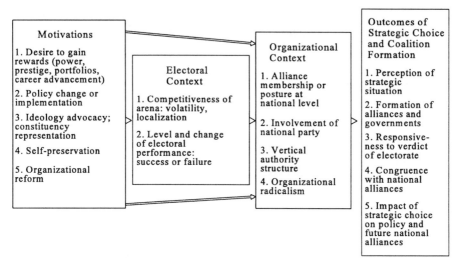

Figure 3.6 Determinants of Strategic Choice in Subnational Government

zational structures and levels of discontent and radicalism within the party group. This vision by necessity simplifies a complex reality. It does, however, possess a greater sensitivity to the determinants of party behavior in coalition situations than do existing explanations that use size and ideological orientation as exclusive independent variables and that consider parties as homogenous groups of decision makers.

The essential tenets of this vision of strategic choice are depicted in figure 3.6.[2] Here coalition choices are driven by the rational pursuit of certain preferred goods (primary goals such as office benefits) but are constrained by pressures external to a pure utility calculation. These constraints include the necessity of adapting to the immediacy of the electoral environment and to the preferences of party superiors.

What needs to be reinforced in this representation is the dynamism inherent in the process leading to new coalition governments. It is therefore appropriate to depict the same variables within a broader systemic context, as in figure 3.7. Visualizing the determinants of coalition choice in this manner adds both vertical and temporal aspects to the explanation. The vertical dimension shows that coalition bargaining in subnational assemblies may take place within the larger context of national coalitions. Hence, the subnational process is not a priori a discrete event but is instead "nested" within national coalition systems. Moreover, the possibility that coalitions at one level of government can influence coalitions at another level is denoted by the two-

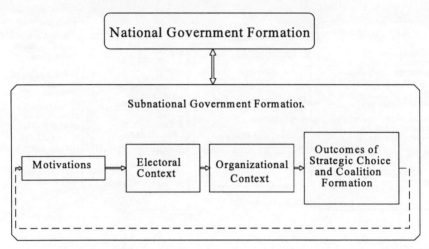

Figure 3.7 Dynamic Process of Coalition Government Formation

way arrows connecting subnational and national coalition processes. Adding a temporal dimension also discounts the extent to which coalitions may be considered unique events, suggesting instead that a "feedback loop" connects past, current, and future iterations of the government formation process.

Of course, figures such as these are but attempts to capture patterns in behavior across a variety of cases. Given some basic assumptions of rationality and of microeconomic behavior, the explanation posited above permits the systematic collection and analysis of comparative data and facilitates pursuit of a solution to the puzzle of subnational coalitions. The proposed explanation should give us a clearer picture of how politicians and parties adapt to their institutional, organizational, and representational duties. With this explanation, we should be better able to determine if pressures from voters make party politicians more accountable in their strategic choices. Similarly, we should be better able to gauge whether the nationalization of subnational politics allows politicians to place party discipline in strategic decision making above personal popularity in their home districts. The exact methods employed in this pursuit are detailed in chapter 4.

Chapter Four

Methods of Investigation

We have established the need to know more about what goes on in that murky period between election day and the actual formation of a government. We have recognized that this period is one during which party leaders and elected councilors consider the consequences of alternative alliances—consequences based in part on the legislative weights of potential partners, the prospect of policy concessions, and the ideological as well as individual compatibility of possible allies. We have more narrowly defined as our particular concerns the electoral and organizational constraints that may influence strategic choice. Finally, we have identified the universe of cases and the evidence available from subnational parliaments as both a gold mine and a minefield. Because some of the central advantages offered by the study of coalition politics in regional and local assemblies are methodological, it is essential that the techniques and data sources used in this study be discussed before presentation of the empirical evidence. This is all the more true if, as is hoped, this book is to spawn future research into a broader array of comparative cases.

To investigate the influence of electoral and organizational constraints on government formation, the ideal research design would rely on nonparticipant observation of postelection negotiations among party leaders in the proverbial "smoke-filled backrooms" of council chambers and among newly elected councilors gathered at regional, provincial, or local party headquarters. While perhaps feasible in single-locality or single-party studies, the "fly-on-the-wall" approach is difficult, if not impossible, to achieve in comparative multilocality, multiparty contexts. The best alternative is to document actual decisions and to pose questions directly and systematically to those individuals most

67

involved in—and most affected by—the process of forming coalition governments. In this spirit a three-pronged research strategy was designed and applied to the intermediate-level subnational assemblies of three West European countries: Germany, France, and Belgium.

The Countries

Why study and compare coalition politics in the subnational parliaments of Germany, France, and Belgium? Although chapter 5 will detail the historical and institutional factors that make comparison of these particular countries appealing, it is useful here to lay out briefly the principal reasons for their selection. Political relevance, variation along a range of key variables, and subnational-national linkages are among the most important criteria.

Political Relevance

The three countries are of considerable interest, first, because in each case territorial assemblies occupy prominent roles in contemporary political affairs. Belgium, a country that in recent decades has been obsessed with state reform and territorial restructuring, contains nine provinces (ten since a 1993 constitutional revision) dating from the country's 1831 founding that continue to be minibattlegrounds for political parties seeking to expand their respective power bases throughout the country (see map 4.1). Through coalition building at the provincial level, federalist parties first gained a share of governmental power in the 1970s, the country's three party "families" first experimented in bilingual tripartite governance, and mainstream parties now try to fight off challenges from upstart ecologists and far-right extremists. Since 1995, direct election of the new federal state's three regional parliaments in Flanders, Wallonia, and Brussels-Capital (see map 4.2) has created an even more prominent institutional arena for coalition politics and has greatly increased the stakes of subnational government formation (Downs 1995, 1996).

In Germany 16 autonomous states (see map 4.3) enjoy wide executive, legislative, and budgetary competences. Politically, the chessboard of Germany party competition finds the Christian Democrat (CDU/CSU)–Free Democrat (FDP) governing coalition in the Bundestag coexisting with an increasingly varied set of arrangements in

Map 4.1 Belgian Provinces

the Länder: CDU-SPD, SPD-FDP, SPD-Grüne, SPD-FDP-Grüne, even SPD–Statt Partei ("Instead Party," a breakaway faction of the Hamburg CDU). State-level coalitions are repeatedly held up as models for future federal governments. For example, CDU-SPD *Große Koalitionen* formed in Berlin and Baden-Württemberg in the early 1990s were pointed to during the 1994 national parliamentary election campaign as models for a possible Christian Democratic–Social Democratic coalition in Bonn. Similarly, Rolf Scharping, one-time leader of Germany's opposition Social Democrats, predicted that a "red-green" SPD-Grüne coalition government established in May 1995 in the country's most populous state of North Rhine–Westphalia would prove to be a model for changing federal government after the 1998 election. For parties in opposition nationally, hope springs eternal from the periphery. Bleaker are the unpopular economic consequences of East-West unification, which continue to fuel the fortunes of far-right parties (e.g., Deutsche Volksunion and Die Republikaner) in state politics and so introduce elements of uncertainty into coalition formation. The addition of five Länder from the former German Democratic Republic also adds a new wrinkle to coalition politics in Germany, with former Communists, reconstituted as the Party of Democratic Socialism (PDS),

Map 4.2 Belgian Regions

now seeking legitimacy as worthy players in the power game. In terms of political relevance, regional politics and coalition government in Germany clearly score high marks.

In France the construction of 22 regional parliaments following François Mitterrand's assumption of the presidency in 1981 has created new arenas for party competition and new necessities for coalition building (map 4.4). Since the first direct elections of these parliaments in 1986, French politicians have been faced with realigning themselves to conform to new regional strategies, strategies that may link them with parties they have opposed for years at the local, departmental, or national levels. Conservative parties find themselves sharing regional power with the far Right, and embattled socialists struggle to build alliances with communists and ecologists. The extent to which the French Greens and the far-right Front National will be able to transform their regional power-sharing experiments into greater payoffs (e.g., legitimacy, acceptability as coalition partners, stepping-stones to national power) is a timely and real concern. Part of the allure of including France in our analysis is, therefore, that regional-level coalition politics is now in its formative stage and as such is the subject of considerable academic and popular curiosity.

Map 4.3 German Länder

Variation

Provincial and regional-level parliamentary government in all three countries exhibits the phenomena identified by previous chapters as meriting explanation. Subcentral governments in Belgium, France, and Germany run the full range of possibilities: single-party majorities, single-party minorities, multiparty coalition majorities, and multi-

Map 4.4 French Regions

party coalition minorities. Power-sharing coalitions also demonstrate a variety of characteristics: oversized coalitions, ideologically "unconnected" coalitions, coalitions of "losers," and coalitions excluding the party with the plurality of seats. In each country, moreover, parties frequently appear to reject the national coalition of the day in favor of some alternative regional or provincial arrangement, even when election results would allow for a duplication. Indeed, similarly positioned parties in different regions, when faced with similar coalition opportunities, are known to choose different strategies. There are, in short, numerous instances of the kinds of coalition politics that we have previously deemed worthy of study.

There is, moreover, variation along a number of potential explanatory variables. If we are to ask, "Does context matter?" then it is clearly important that context itself vary. As will be demonstrated thoroughly in chapter 6, patterns of electoral competition in the territorial subunits of Belgium, France, and Germany vary substantially and systematically. Certain regions, provinces, and states are demonstrably more competitive (i.e., electorally volatile) than others. Size, history, and timing of elections make certain regions or provinces more or less important in national terms, thus making electoral competition more "nationalized" or more "localized" across regions. This variance makes it possible to examine whether different political solutions to coalition problems emerge out of different electoral contexts. The party systems of each country also present useful variation in organizational style, from the supposed "basis democracy" of the German, Belgian, and French green parties to the outwardly more authoritarian regimes of the German FDP, the French Communists (PCF), and Belgium's francophone Liberals (PRL). Along the organizational axis, then, there is also relevant variation.

Subnational-National Linkages

A final reason for focusing on these three particular countries is the important consequences of subnational coalition outcomes for national politics in each. In Belgium, Germany, and France, direct as well as indirect linkages connect subnational and national politics and policy. The clearest example of this is Germany, where the majority in the federal council, or Bundesrat, is always a direct reflection of the governments in the 16 constituent Länder. Any change in the partisan composition of government at the state level can alter the balance of power in the Bundesrat and thus influence the fate of most federal legislation. Similarly, in Belgium, a portion of the national senate has traditionally been determined not by the voters but by the majorities in the provinces. More recently, the massive devolution of legislative and executive powers to regional authorities and the federal senate's transformation into an arbiter of regional disputes has led to a highly complex network of linkages between the executives of the three regions and the national government. In France national-regional linkages are also strong, since the ability to accumulate multiple elected offices has meant that national deputies, senators, government ministers, and even party presidents are often simultaneously regional councilors and executives. Of the 577 deputies elected to France's National Assembly in 1993, 523 held at least one other mandate at the local or regional levels. Vertical linkages such as these make evident the broader system-level importance of government formation and coalition politics at subnational levels.

The Behavior

Having selected these three country cases, the task of constructing an accurate image of coalition behavior begins with accumulation of relevant historical data. For Belgium the analysis includes a 33-year span, namely, the period 1961–94, covering 12 national/provincial elections and 109 provincial government formations. Additional data derive from regional-level coalition building in Flanders (1995), Wallonia (1995), and the Brussels-Capital Region (1989, 1995). For Germany, the historical reference frame commences with 1961, the year in which the liberal Free Democrats began playing their role as indispensable federal coalition partners, and it ends with 1992, a year that saw crucial state elections in Baden-Württemberg and Schleswig-Holstein. In the interest of comparability, the formal analysis is limited to governments formed in the 11 states of West Germany, and only briefly do we examine the data from recent coalition governments in the five new eastern Länder. During this period the Germans have held more than 90 elections to the 11 western Landtage. Since direct elections to regional councils in France date only from 1986, the historical context of coalition politics at the institutional level of representative government is by necessity much narrower than in the Belgian and German cases. The 1986 and 1992 elections yield 44 cases of regional government formation.

The historical data derive from two main sources: election results and primary documents. Electoral statistics for Belgium, France, and Germany provide a vivid historical picture of context and coalition behavior at the subnational and national levels in each country. The Belgian Ministry of the Interior provided the data on vote and seat distribution for national parliamentary and provincial elections for the three-decade period. Additional electoral information for Belgium, including the outcomes of government formations, comes from a series of postelection analyses published in *Res Publica* since 1972 (Brans 1992; Costard 1972, 1974; Mabille 1982; Toelen 1986, 1987) and from the weekly publications of the Centre de Recherche et d'Information

Socio-Politiques (CRISP) in Brussels. German electoral data have been collected from the annual editions of *Statistisches Jahrbuch für die Bundesrepublik Deutschland* (Wiesbaden: Statisches Bundesamt, 1961–1995), from *Wahlen in der Bundesrepublik Deutschland* (Ritter and Niehuss 1987), and from the *Handbuch der deutschen Bundesländer* (Esche and Hartmann, 1990). Detailed statistics published in select editions of *Le Monde* provide the electoral database for the French case. These data, including percentage of votes won by party, seats obtained, and coalitions formed, help construct a statistical compendium of coalition cases at both the subnational and national levels.

Primary documents provide the second source of information regarding the historical evolution of subnational coalition politics in Belgium, Germany, and France. Documentary sources include published material such as newspapers and journals, official government publications, accounts of party conferences, records of parliamentary debates, party statutes and election manifestos, and texts of actual coalition agreements. Press accounts proved especially useful in highlighting those government formations that were especially racked with conflict of both the interparty and the intraparty variety. Employed in this regard were the principal Belgian dailies (*Le Soir, La Libre Belgique, Het Volk, De Standaard*), two key German papers (*Frankfurter Allgemeine Zeitung, Süddeutsche Zeitung*), and the leading French journals (*Le Monde, Le Figaro, L'Express, Le Point*). Without saturating the analysis with specifics, which rigorous cross-national analysis must avoid, these source materials do allow for a fuller, historically sensitive interpretation of the patterns observed in subsequent cross-sectional survey analysis.

The Survey

The second principal source of evidence comes from a cross-national survey questionnaire. Survey research, if properly designed, can produce generous quantities of comparable data that can then be used to test and refine research hypotheses. The survey instrument used in this analysis, a mail questionnaire, provides a "snapshot" or cross-sectional image of perceptions, attitudes, and behavior across a selected range of parties, regions, and countries. The use of surveys in single-country subnational coalition studies is not in itself new. Noteworthy attempts include Bueno de Mesquita's (1975) analysis of "stra-

tegic predispositions" in Indian state parliaments; investigations into
Britain's "hung" local and county councils by Rallings and Thrasher
(1986) and Temple (1991); and Brearey's (1989) survey of German
municipal councilors and local government coalitions in North Rhine–
Westphalia. Absent, however, are any true cross-national surveys of
regional assembly members of the type attempted here.

To uncover relevant attitudinal patterns, motivational discrepancies, and behavioral observations, an extensive closed-ended mail questionnaire was deployed. Containing more than 80 items, the questionnaire covers a variety of topics relating to government formation,
coalition building, electoral competition, legislative affairs, and internal party relations. Respondents were asked, for example, to characterize their personal involvement in coalition negotiations, to rank the
concerns that motivated them and their parties in pursuit of government office, and to describe the influence of national party leaders in
local coalition bargaining. Especially critical to our theory are a set of
questions dealing with the local electoral environment: Had elections
grown or diminished in intensity during the respondent's tenure? Had
the determining themes and personalities of the most recent election
been local or national in nature? To what extent had electoral accountability motivated the respondent to support or to oppose certain coalition options? In addition, other questions attempted to locate a
respondent's discontent with internal party relations, as well as his or
her ideological proclivities and future political ambitions. Still other
questions sought to tap respondents' awareness of concessions won and
lost during coalition bargaining, as well as the occurrence of less overt
forms of coalition building. A list of the questions included in the questionnaire is provided in Appendix 1.[1]

In the recognized technique of area sampling, each element of a
survey population is associated with a particular geographical area. In
this way, "a sample of elements is drawn, and either all elements in the
selected areas are included in the survey or a sample of these elements
is included" (Kalton 1983, 8). Following this basic methodological
premise, territorial parliaments were selected in each of the three
countries on the basis of multiple theoretical and substantive criteria.
Once selected, all elected members of the respective provincial councils, regional councils, or Landtage were then included in the survey
population. Lists of the members, their party affiliations, their positions within the subnational legislatures and governments, and their
political as well as professional backgrounds were in most cases ob-

tained directly from the information bureaus of the provincial, regional, and state authorities. Each Belgian *greffier provincial/provinciegriffier* supplied detailed information regarding the membership of its respective council.[2] Each German Landtag publishes some form of a *Volkshandbuch,* which generally includes relevant political and biographical data. Comparable information was obtained through the *Direction Général* of each French regional council and was supplemented by *Le Guide: L'annuaire du monde de la politique et des pouvoirs* (Profession Politique, 1992), a compendium of local, regional, and national political figures.

Occurrence of substantively interesting and politically meaningful coalition outcomes topped the list of selection criteria. Effort was made to include within the sample those provinces, regions, or Länder in which the formation of the sitting government had been unusual—those in which there had been an unprecedented party alliance or a major coalition shift. This is because it is important to be able to tap into the observations, perceptions, and attitudes of representatives who take part in or who observe such major events. And for theoretical purposes it is important to include within the sample cases representing subnational-national coalition "incongruence" as well as those representing subnational-national coalition "congruence."[3] If national-subnational coalition incongruence is an indicator of differential motives or of internal party disagreement, then it is instructive to compare responses across such coalition types. Moreover, since electoral volatility and localization are crucial variables, it is also necessary to have cases whose traditions of electoral behavior clearly represent different levels of each. These selection criteria were easily met in each of the three country cases. Coalition types and national-subnational congruence are summarized below, and chapter 6 addresses more directly the dominant characteristics of the electoral environments of each.

Belgian Provinces and the Brussels Regional Council

For Belgium, five of the country's nine provinces elected in November 1991 produced a manageable and representative set of cases. In the Liège, Luxembourg, and Namur provinces, Socialist (PS)–Liberal (PRL) coalitions stood in apparent contradiction to the Socialist (PS/SP)–Christian Social (PSC/CVP) alliance in national government, as did the "grand" Socialist (PS/SP)–Christian Social (PSC/CVP)–Liberal (PRL/PVV) coalition in Brabant province. In contrast, the Socialist–

Christian Social coalition in Hainaut's provincial council mirrored the national formula of the day. At the time of the survey, Belgium's only directly elected regional parliament was in the Brussels-Capital Region. Elected in 1989, the Brussels regional assembly chose a governing coalition that included the center parties (CVP/PSC), the Left (SP/PS), and two linguistic community parties, the Francophone Democratic Front (FDF) and the Flemish People's Union (Volksunie). These governing alignments are summarized in table 4.1.

In the provincial assemblies of Liège, Luxembourg, and Namur, possibilities existed following the 1991 elections to duplicate the national center-Left coalition, but these were in each case rejected in favor of ideologically "unconnected" (i.e., skipping the center party) socialist-liberal power-sharing arrangements. Given its relevance to our research questions, this deliberate rejection of the national formula warranted inclusion of these provinces in the sample. Alternatively, Hainaut's provincial assembly members chose to mimic national party alignments. This "congruence" is important and warrants Hainaut's inclusion in the sample, as does the fact that for the Hainaut Socialists the 1991 coalition was their first with any partner since 1978. Marked by its electoral stability and clear "national" character due to its location in the province containing the capital city of Brussels, the Brabant provincial legislature during the period 1991–94 was of substantive interest because it represented the first time in any of Belgium's legislative assemblies that one linguistic party wing entered a governing coalition without its companion party wing. This occurred when the Flemish CVP joined the Brabant provincial government without its "sister" party in the Christian Social family, the francophone PSC.[4]

German Land Parliaments

The Land parliaments of Baden-Württemberg, Bremen, Hesse, and Lower Saxony provide the area samples for the German case. The Christian Democrat–Social Democrat "grand" coalition in the southwestern Landtag of Baden-Württemberg, reminiscent of the same rare alliance in the Bundestag from 1966 to 1969, was pointed to at the time of the survey as a precursor of some form of "solidarity government" to be constructed after the 1994 federal elections. Baden-Württemberg's importance derives also from the fact that it was the scene in 1992 of the first state-level attempt at uniting Christian Democrats

Table 4.1

Belgium: Provincial and Regional Assemblies Included in
Survey Population, 1992

Provincial Councils	Partisan Composition of Government		Congruence with National Parliamentary Alliances
Brabant	Socialists + Christian Socials + Liberals	PS/SP + CVP + PRL/PVV	×
Hainaut	Socialists + Christian Socials	PS + PSC	√
Liège	Socialists + Liberals	PS + PRL	×
Luxembourg	Socialists + Liberals	PS + PRL	×
Namur	Socialists + Liberals	PS + PRL	×
Regional Parliament			
Brussels-Capital Region	Socialists + Christian Socials + Regionalists	PS/SP + PSC/CVP + FDF + VU	×

Note: National government: Socialists + Christian Socials (PS/SP + PSC/CVP).

and Greens in a so-called black-green or eco-libertarian coalition. In the city-state of Bremen, the Free Democrats left their federal allies, the CDU, for an SPD-FDP-Grüne "traffic light" coalition in the 1990–94 senate. The Länder of Hesse and Lower Saxony were included in the sample because their respective "red-green" SPD-Grüne governments could be considered "congruent" coalitions. The Hesse and Lower Saxony governments represented unions of parties in opposition nationally and as such matched the national majority-versus-opposition alignment. They are worthy of study also because most observers regarded them as "experiments." Table 4.2 summarizes the German Länder selected for inclusion in the survey.

The context in which new governments are negotiated in these four German states clearly varies, as will be shown in chapter 6. Bremen—the historically rooted, small, urban Land—is characterized by an electoral history replete with wide interelection vote swings and significant discrepancies between party vote shares at federal and Land elections. Lower Saxony—the artificially constructed, large, rural Land—is generally one of the more electorally stable German states and one in which election results for federal and Land legislatures appear remarkably similar over time. Between these two extremes in the Protestant north are Baden-Württemberg and Hesse in the Catholic south. Both states are characterized by high levels of interelection volatility. However, elections in Baden-Württemberg are more often "not fought on matters of national policy" (Braunthal 1982, 193), retaining an ele-

Table 4.2
Germany: State Parliaments Included in Survey Population, 1992

State Parliaments	Partisan Composition of Government		Congruence with National Parliamentary Alliances
Baden-Württemberg	Social Democrats + Christian Democrats	SPD + CDU	×
Bremen	Social Democrats + Free Democrats + Greens	SPD + FDP + Grünen	×
Hesse	Social Democrats + Greens	SPD + Grünen	√
Lower Saxony	Social Democrats + Greens	SPD + Grünen	√

Note: National government: Christian Democrats + Free Democrats (CDU/CSU + FDP).

ment of localism despite the state's size and importance in the Bundesrat. Voting patterns for federal and Land elections in Hesse, conversely, more closely mimic one another, which may indicate a national rather than a "local" electoral dynamic.

French Regional Councils

The same process of area selection guided the choice of French regions for inclusion in the survey population. Only months before the survey questionnaires were distributed, France held direct elections to its 22 metropolitan regional councils. At the time of the regional elections, which were for the first time uncoupled from national legislative elections, the 29-member cabinet of Socialist Prime Minister Edith Cresson contained figures not only from the Parti Socialiste (PS) but also from the smaller Mouvement des Radicaux de Gauche (MRG) and France Unie (FU).[5] This group of parties is considered the national majority of the day, while the "Union pour la France" (UPF) electoral alliance, incorporating the Rassemblement pour la République (RPR) and the Union pour la Démocratie Française (UDF), is but one of several national oppositions. Other separate parties, including the Parti Communiste (PC), the Greens (Les Verts), Génération Ecologie (GE), the Front National (FN), and Chasse, Pêche, Nature et Traditions (CPNT), are classified as unallied national oppositions. Any regional coalition that mirrored the PS-MRG-FU national majority or the RPR-UDF oppositional alliance could be included as "congruent." Any other alliances would be deviations from the national pattern and could be included as "incongruent" coalition cases.

Nine particular regions stood out as representative of the patterns of alliance building following the 22 March 1992 elections and the formation of regional governments. In two regional councils (Pays de la Loire, Provence-Alpes-Côte d'Azur), the national RPR-UDF alliance duplicated itself in electing the regional president and in forming the regional cabinet. In Aquitaine, Midi-Pyrénées, and Picardie, the same RPR-UDF alliance found itself making postelection deals with the radical antiecologist CPNT, rewarding the small party with executive posts in both Aquitaine and Midi-Pyrénées. Campaign promises to the contrary, the center-right RPR-UDF forces in Alsace accepted the support of right-wing extremists and Front National dissidents, and in Languedoc-Roussillon, the parties of Jacques Chirac and Giscard d'Estaing rallied a strange mixture of Communists, Greens, and "Chasseurs" (CPNT) to elect a UDF regional president. In Bourgogne and Lorraine the Socialists joined with the France Unie movement, both ecologist parties (Verts, Génération Ecologie), and, in the case of Lorraine, the Communists. Charges of collusion with the Front National divided the coalition majority in Lorraine, leading to its quick collapse and the subsequent formation of an RPR-UDF regional government. The necessity for the Socialists and the conservative parties to cope with new, smaller partners holding the balance of power in the regions makes these cases particularly valuable.

Given these substantively interesting outcomes, and given that they display variation in an important theoretical phenomenon (national-subnational congruence), these nine regions were chosen for inclusion in the survey. Table 4.3 summarizes the regional councils selected for the French sample and their coalition majorities.

Responses

A total of 608 completed questionnaires were returned, giving the survey a relatively high overall response rate of 38.7%. This rate is especially satisfying for U.S.-based cross-national surveys of elected representatives in European subnational assemblies. The response rate is generally consistent across countries and area units, and the respondent pool generally reflects the territorial parliaments' overall characteristics in terms of both party affiliation and legislative expe-

Table 4.3

France: Regional Assemblies Included in Survey Population, 1992

Regional Councils	Partisan Composition of Government		Congruence with National Parliamentary Alliances
Alsace	Gaullists + Democratic Union + National Front	RPR+UDF+FN	×
Aquitaine	Gaullists + Democratic Union + Other Rightists	RPR+UDF+CNI+CPNT	×
Bourgogne	Socialists + Other Left + Greens + France United	PS+MRG+Verts+GE+FU	×
Languedoc-Roussillon	Gaullists + Democratic Union + Green Dissidents	RPR+UDF+Diss. Verts	×
Lorraine	Socialists + Communists + France United + Greens	PS+PCF+FU+Verts+GE	×
Midi-Pyrénées	Gaullists + Democratic Union	RPR+UDF	✓
Pays de la Loire	Gaullists + Democratic Union	RPR+UDF	✓
Picardie	Gaullists + Democratic Union + Other Rightists	RPR+UDF+CPNT	×
Provence-Alpes-Côte d'Azur	Gaullists + Democratic Union	RPR+UDF	✓

Note: National government: Socialists + Left Radicals + France United (PS+MRG+FU).

rience (i.e., number of terms served). A complete tally of the survey returns, broken down by region and party, is provided in Appendix 2.

It is instructive to note here some characteristics of the respondent pool in each country. Contained within the Belgian sample are 10 of 27 (35.7%) *députés permanents*, the provincial executives analogous to national cabinet ministers. In addition, 2 of 5 (40%) provincial council presidents responded to the survey questionnaire, as did 4 vice presidents and 15 ordinary members of the executive bureaus. Six provincial party groups leaders (*chefs des groupes*) returned their surveys, as did 2 party federation presidents. The national vice president of one Belgian political party, also a provincial councilor, provided answers to the questionnaire as well. Among the German respondents are 2 minister-presidents, 1 Landtag president, and 3 Landtag vice presidents. In addition, 5 Land government ministers and 5 former Land government ministers answered the questionnaire. German parliamentary party leaders are also well represented, with 6 Landtag *fraktionsvorsitzenden* and 9 deputy *fraktionsvorsitzenden* responding.

More impressive is the list of high-ranking politicians in the group of French respondents, this being due in large part to the French tradition of *cumul des mandats*, or the accumulation of elective offices across multiple levels of government. On the level of regional government itself, all 9 council presidents, 30 vice presidents, and 11 *commission permanente* members replied. Regional councilors with positions in national government answering the questionnaire include 5 cabinet ministers and 1 junior minister (*secrétaire d'etat*), 6 senators, 9 Assemblée Nationale deputies, and 2 former deputies. In addition, 4 of the French respondents are European deputies. Regional councilors holding elective office below the regional level are also generously represented, including 30 departmental councilors (*conseillers généraux*), 36 municipal councilors, and 48 mayors. There is, then, more of an opportunity with the French data to gauge the responses of persons in multiple positions of party power and with experience and stature in national government.

Reliability and Validity

The prevention of any systematic error ranked high among the goals during the design of the survey.[6] To estimate the reliability of indicators, parallel measures were constructed for key items and placed at different points in the questionnaire. Strong correlations between items and generally equal mean values signal that the measures are to a large extent reliable. Limitations on the length of the questionnaire itself, however, prevented the use of parallel measures tests for all indicators. Beyond reliability, the validity of the measures is of crucial importance. Several steps were taken to ensure that indicators for such tricky concepts as "influence," "pragmatism," and "deference" would be sufficiently valid. First, pretesting the questionnaire with a small sample of respondents helped eliminate certain problematic indicators. Second, soliciting the critical assessments of academic observers with expertise in the field also improved the validity of the measures before administering the survey. One final, and perhaps most important, method of determining the validity of selected indicators as guidelines to what "really" happens was to check them against the responses of both party actors and nonparty political observers in open-ended discussions. This technique, facilitated by 12 months "in the field," more than any other technique contributed to reliable and valid measures and analysis.

The Interviews

To complement and validate the data derived from survey responses, a final empirical base is supplied in the form of interviews conducted with elected representatives and party leaders at both subnational and national levels in Germany, Belgium, and France. Such interviews were necessary to produce the qualitative and contextual material essential for full interpretation. Moreover, open-ended discussions helped ameliorate some of the inherent restrictiveness of closed-ended questionnaires.

The interviews, conducted during the September 1992 to September 1993 period, included discussions with regional and provincial councilors and deputies, subnational party leaders, national parliamentarians, central party executives, and extraparliamentary party staff officials in each of the three countries. In all, representatives from 17 political parties, 14 subnational assemblies, and 3 national governments were interviewed. Interview subjects were selected on the basis of several criteria. Participation in coalition negotiations, government membership, legislative and party tenure, position in party hierarchy, and dual office holding (national and subnational) were among the principal concerns. Of primary importance were party group leaders (*chefs des groupes, fraktionsvorsitzenden*) in selected territorial assemblies. These persons occupy key decision-making positions and are involved more than others—at least outwardly—in the formulation and nego- tiation of coalition agreements. They are likely also to be the persons who feel the most pressure from national party officials and who, at the same time, can exert the most pressure on the national party.

Using what is generally deemed the "nonschedule-structured inter- view method" (Nachmias and Nachmias 1987), the strategy of the in- terviews was to raise specific questions concerning previous decisions of coalition participation, the intraparty causes and consequences of these decisions, and the prospects for future collaboration with other parties. Asking the same question of a simple councilor, a regional party group leader, a regional government executive, a national par- liamentarian, an extraparliamentary national party official, and a party president best served the comparative purposes of this analysis. Was the interviewee aware of the party's coalition strategy? How did the interviewee believe the party's coalition strategy in Region A or Region B fit into the party's national coalition strategy? What factors did the interviewee believe were most influential in the party's sub- national coalition decision, and how likely was it that this decision would influence future coalition choices in national government? Fre- quently, the answers from persons in the same party in the same re- gional parliament were not the same. Together, however, they supplied important clues and different pieces of the puzzle that ultimately re- vealed meaningful empirical patterns.[7]

Summary

This chapter has delineated a three-part research methodology de- signed to describe, explain, and to some extent "predict" coalition be- havior and government formation in subnational assemblies. The tools of investigation include the analysis of historical events data, attitudi- nal survey administration, and interviewing of elites. Simple reliance on one of these three methods would probably not supply an informed account of the coalition game as it plays out in territorial parliaments; it has been argued, however, that combining historical, quantitative, and qualitative approaches—what Putnam (1993) calls "marinating yourself in the data" (190)—allows for useful insights into patterns of behavior in Belgium, France, and Germany.

Part Three

Empirical Analysis

Chapter Five

The Province, the Region, and the State: Rules of the Game in Three European Systems

R ules, structures, and history matter. Any treatment of power politics and coalition behavior in parliamentary assemblies must recognize substantial elements of each to be plausible. To explain important phenomena across countries, we tend to look first for similarities and differences in procedural rules, institutional design, and underlying processes of change. Only then can we move on to search for explanations of behavioral patterns within countries by focusing on environmental conditions—for instance, those to be found in electoral competition and organizational pressures. To establish the institutional and historical background for our analysis, this chapter is intended to fill some of the gaps in our knowledge about structures, functions, actors, government formation processes, and the historical evolution of coalition politics in the intermediate-level territorial parliaments of Belgium, Germany, and France.

Our first goal is to find answers to the following questions: Where and how do the provinces, regions, and states fit into their respective political and administrative systems? Who are the key players in the power game? How are new governments formed—in other words, what are the "rules of the game"? Are there aspects of the government formation process that generate criticism, either for their lack of transparency or for their lack of democratic accountability? In what ways have the dynamics of coalition building at subnational levels mimicked or departed from national alliance patterns? The methodology is to ask these questions of each country separately and, once this is done, to draw together some of the most important comparative characteristics. It is this drawing together of history and institutional development that leads to the chapter's second goal, namely, the close examination of the outcomes of coalition bargaining. Our methodology here represents a preliminary exploration of evidence from more than 300 acts of government formation, illustrating the types of governments formed, their size in seats and party members, their congruence with national coalitions, and their apparent responsiveness to electoral verdicts.

Belgium

"L'accord institutionnel de Saint-Michel," an eleventh-hour agreement patched together in October 1992 and ratified in April 1993, pushed forward Belgium's transformation into a federal state and at least temporarily forestalled the country's anticipated descent into domestic ungovernability. As a federation, Belgium now has greatly strengthened regional parliaments, whose deputies were directly elected for the first time in the May 1995 general election. In these regional parliaments, coalition decisions assume the level of "high politics" as parties in Flanders, Wallonia, and Brussels must choose between subnational governments that either complement or complicate the usually shaky alliance arrangement in national government. Coexisting with the new regions are the provinces, Belgium's traditional meso-level institutions of representative government, which "have pursued 'provincial interests' in a creative way during the past 150 years" (Delmartino 1993, 52). So urgent is the task of contemporary Belgium to find common ground between disparate cultures, parties, and ideologies that any lessons concerning cooperation culled from the grass roots should be of great practical value. This is the justification for exploring coalition behavior in the elected assemblies of both the provinces and the regions.

In Belgium's oldest political and administrative institutions, the provincial councils (*conseils provinciaux, provincieraad*), political parties often coalesce in manners strikingly different from their national counterparts. With the centrist Christian Socials and left-of-center Socialists allied in national coalition following the 1995 election, for example, parties in only 2 of the 10 provincial councils adopted the national center-left formula. The same had been true following the previous election in 1991, and in 1987 *none* of the provincial council majorities matched the parliamentary majority constructed in Brussels. "Unnatural" alliances between left-wing Socialists and right-wing Liberals, "grand" or all-party coalitions, and the possibility of power sharing with regionalist or ecologist parties are all provincial phenomena with indirect and direct system-level implications. While observers of Belgian politics frequently refer to such phenomena as "interferences" in the process of national government formation, little or no attempt has been made to determine their magnitude.[1]

In Belgium's newest institutions, the regional parliaments (Conseil Régional Wallon, Vlaamse Gewest, Conseil Régional Bruxellois/Brusselse Hoofdstedelijk Gewest), legislative parties have much less government formation experience than their provincial colleagues. Councils for the Flanders and Wallonia regions date from 1980, but for 15 years the two bodies consisted exclusively of elected members of the national parliament. In 1989 the metropolitan region of Brussels became the first region to directly elect its own parliamentary assembly, and in 1995 Flemish and Walloon voters had their first opportunity to choose representatives to autonomous regional parliaments. What Belgium's regional politicians and parties lack in government formation experience they make up for in functional competence and potential for profound system impact. When scholars characterize Belgium as "the first Western state to go into voluntary semi-liquidation, as it were, without a shot being fired" (Sharpe 1993, 32), it is upon the regions that the country's future is said to rest.

Subnational Government Structures

Since its creation in 1831, the modern Belgian state has developed from its original "unitary decentralized" form to a fully federalized arrangement. The Belgian Constitution after multiple revisions now establishes a hereditary monarchy within a parliamentary system, providing for the territorial organization of the country to include a federal authority with an executive (prime minister) and two legislative houses (Chamber of Representatives, Senate); three linguistic-cultural communities; three regions; 10 provinces, each with its own directly

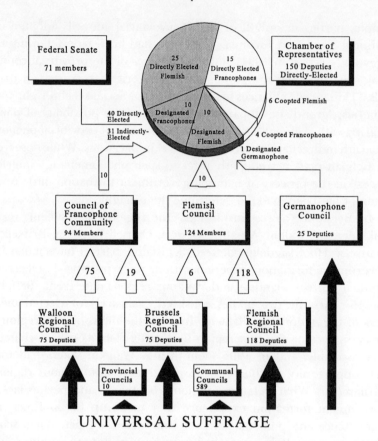

Figure 5.1 Belgian Political Institutions

elected deliberative council; and 589 communes (municipalities), each with its own council as well. The organization of the Belgian state is depicted in figure 5.1.

PROVINCES. The advantage in directing initial attention at the Belgian provinces is that, historically, they are the best and only example of intermediate-level territorial government in which politicians and parties playing the coalition game are clearly distinguishable from their counterparts in national parliament. This is so because before 1995 the regional and community councils for Flanders and Wallonia were chosen indirectly from among sitting national MPs.

Their status formalized by the Loi Provinciale of 1836 and by Article 108 of the Constitution confirming their power over "all matters of provincial interest,"[2] the provincial councils have intentionally mimicked, though in much reduced scope, the political structures existing in national government.[3] Their size depending on population, the provincial councils currently range from 50 seats (Luxembourg) to 56 (Walloon Brabant, Namur), 70 (Limburg), 75 (Flemish Brabant), 80 (Liège), and 84 (Antwerp, East Flanders, West Flanders, Hainaut). Each deliberative council is directly elected for six-year terms by mandatory universal suffrage, according to a proportional representation formula in which the basic electoral unit is the *arrondissement* (district). No provincial councilor may concurrently hold a mandate in the national parliament. Traditionally held on the same day as national parliamentary elections, provincial council and national parliamentary elections were "decoupled" for the first time with the provincial vote in 1994. This decoupling put an end to an important traditional feature of the life cycle of provincial legislatures, namely, their dissolution along with the national parliament.

At the outset of a new legislative session, each council elects by secret ballot a six-member provincial executive, or *députation permanente/bestendige deputatie*.[4] Party composition of the deputation is "usually the result of inter-party negotiations in the days following the elections" (Fitzmaurice 1983, 136). Permanent deputies, who receive salaries comparable to those of national senators, wield considerable executive power, even to the extent that one Luxembourg councilor claims, that "these six people can make the rain and sun in this province."[5] The allure of this prize is made even greater for political parties by the fact that provincial executives cannot "fall" or be dismissed by a vote of no confidence within the council. Calls for democratization by making the provincial executive more directly responsible to the council at large do exist and are particularly loud in some quarters.[6]

Historically, the work of the provincial assembly and its executive has been supervised by a putatively nonpartisan *gouverneur,* named by both the Crown and the minister of the interior and revocable at their joint request. This napoleonic holdover has during recent years waned in importance, ceding largely to the permanent deputation, and is also targeted for democratic reform. By eliminating the provincial governorship or by making it an elective office and thus politicizing the position, reformists hope to remove this vestige of central government *tutelle*.[7] Each provincial council also elects an internal bureau with a council president, a varying number of vice presidents, secretaries, and *questeurs/quaestoren* who represent the provincial opposition but whose number and influence depend ultimately on the good will of the majority. The bureau is chiefly responsible for preparing and managing council business, for interpreting procedural rules, and for resolving disputes that arise during plenary sessions.

Among the council's formal responsibilities are enforcement of laws and general decrees, allocation of expenditures to public works and commercial activities, distribution of national government subsidies, imposition of provincial taxes, creation of schools, industrial development, environmental management, and (historically) the election of provincial senators to the Belgian Senate.[8] Provincial councils meet at least once every two months, but the primary sitting takes place for two to eight weeks, beginning every October. Scheduled at that time is the "grande session budgétaire provinciale," during which parties debate and vote on a budget proposed by the provincial executive and supported by the provincial majority.

Budgetary debate is far from a dry, tedious process. The process gives opposition parties chances to snipe at the majority and to grandstand for the local media.[9] The ecologist parties in particular pursue this strategy with great effort and fanfare, employing their statutory right to question every item in the budget, literally line by line. To illustrate, during the October 1992 budgetary debates in Luxembourg province, the four-member opposition Ecolo party needled the Socialist-Liberal majority for "the terrible way they use our money."[10] The council chamber turned raucous when the Ecolos revealed that from a budget of 1.9 billion Belgian francs (approximately $57 million)[11] the majority had proposed 1.3 million francs ($40,000) for wine and cigars. The ecologists' efforts were received derisively by the majority parties in a boisterous exchange not unlike those that occur in the British House of Commons.

For most of Belgium's history, the provincial councils were instrumental in determining the political composition of the Belgian Senate. Provincial councilors elected approximately 50 of the 184 members of the Senate, with each province choosing at least 3 provincial senators.[12] Selection of provincial senators took place soon after an election during special council sessions in which parties presented lists either individually or as cartels. The remaining members of the Belgian Senate were then either directly elected (approximately 106) or "co-opted," the latter being a complex process in which a final group of senators was chosen together by the directly elected senators and the indirectly elected provincial senators. The reform of the Senate as realized by the latest federalization measures has substantially reduced the provinces' role in this selection process.

Belgium's institutional reform projects give cause to question the very continuation of the provinces as "political" and not just "administrative" institutions. For external observers especially, the country appears to have a penchant for "overgovernment." Debate over the future of the provinces arises periodically, the most serious threat coinciding with the so-called *pacte d'Egmont* and the Stuyvenberg accords in 1977 and 1978. At that time, the government of Prime Minister Leo Tindemans (CVP) envisioned putting an end to the provinces as genuine political institutions, and legislation passed in 1980 sharply curtailed the fiscal powers of provincial authorities. When center-left gave way to center-right in the coalition shift of 1981, however, the fortunes of the provincial institutions reversed. Laws passed in 1982 reestablished the fiscal powers of the provinces, and by 1984 the former minister of the interior, Charles Nothomb, proclaimed: "It is the end of the anti-provincial illusions" (Decoster 1987, 31).

Belgium's provincial politicians jealously guard their institutions, and calls for their suppression have only resulted in efforts toward their renewal. The creation of a tenth province in 1995 is but one manifestation of this renewal. Both Antwerp and Limburg have reacted to criticism of the provincial institutions by recently building ornate and expensive council chambers. The new provincial "palace" in Limburg, for example, is a 43,000-square-meter edifice, constructed at the cost of more than 2 billion Belgian francs ($66 million). Multiparty working groups have been formed in most provinces to "dust off and revitalize" the functioning of the institutions.[13] Recognizing a perceived "democratic deficit," provincial politicians now take stock of their institutional failings: "The provinces have paid the price for their own mistakes. Their principal defect is that of never addressing public relations. I believe the provinces are indispensable to the smooth functioning of the country. Of course, they must adapt to the new situation by establishing new rules and in defining the means of their administrative collaboration with each region."[14] The importance of council government in the Belgian provinces, as suggested by the Socialist Party's legislative leader in the Limburg Provincial Council, is in the end measured by popular perception: "The people on the street believe provincial politicians have the authority to influence their lives, despite whatever powers we may or may not actually have."[15]

REGIONS. Few observers question the authority and impact of Belgium's regional parliaments, their governments, or their cultural identities. Any visitor, indeed any researcher bothering to venture beyond the various directorates-general of the EU labyrinth in Brussels, today cannot miss the physical evidence of regional identity and enterprise. Excepting the tremendous outpouring of unionist sentiment upon the sudden death in August 1993 of Belgium's venerable monarch, King Baudouin, it is uncommon to find the national flag displayed in outlying areas. Instead, either the bright red rooster of Wallonia or the black lion of Flanders adorns most town squares, accompanied almost without exception by the familiar blue and gold of the European Union. One cannot take public transport (De Lijn in Flanders, Transport en Commun in Wallonia, STIB in Brussels) without noticing the placards claiming regional directorship. Visitors arriving in Ostende from Dover or Calais by ferry are likewise reminded of the inter-regional cooperation agreements between Kent (UK), Nord-Pas de Calais (France), Flanders, and Wallonia. Flanders sells itself to investors as the region of high-tech, science-based industry, attracting interest from numerous multinationals. Wallonia, alternatively, desperately attempts to attract investment in hopes of diversifying its economy and reversing its declining heavy industries (steel, textiles, construction). Brussels makes its pitch as the "capital region of Europe." The democratic manifestation of this emergent regional identity—and the agents behind much of the regional self-promotion—are the new parliamentary assemblies.

Flanders (58% of nation's population), Wallonia (32%), and Brussels (10%) inherit most of the competences deemed residual under the new constitution, including foreign trade, energy, employment, research and development, agriculture, and physical planning. To legislate and execute within these areas, regional parliaments are directly elected by mandatory universal suffrage for five-year terms. Parliamentarians select their own governments, the size of which varies across the three regions. The 75 members of the Walloon Parliament choose a minister-president and approve a cabinet of six ministers, the 124 members of the Flemish Parliament (118 of whom are directly elected from the Flemish Region and 6 of whom are appointed Dutch speakers from the Brussels-Capital Regional Parliament) elect a minister-president and approve a maximum of 10 cabinet ministers, and the 75 members of the Brussels Parliament select a minister-president and approve a cabinet of 4 ministers (2 francophones and 2 Dutch speakers) along with 3 secretaries of state (to include at least one Dutch speaker). None of the 268 regional deputies may now sit simultaneously in the regional assembly and the federal parliament, effectively ending a decade and a half of political redundancy at national and regional levels.

Party Participation in Coalition Governments

While the provinces today appear secondary to the newer regional institutions, the power and prestige associated with majority status in provincial government is real. This is especially true given the clientelism for which Belgian party politics is famous at all levels of the polity (Dewachter 1987; Dewachter and Clijsters 1982; Fitzmaurice 1983; Rudd 1986). The equation is simple: having no members in the governing deputation results in a party's having substantially less power and influence in provincial politics. Provincial elections, therefore, become minibattlegrounds for the parties and for the "second-tier" politicians who contest them.

The political parties that contest provincial elections and that are represented on the councils are subnational sections of the "national" parties. The linguistic parties from each of the three national political "families" (Socialist, Christian Social, Liberal) all currently have members in the provincial councils: Socialistische Partij (SP)/Parti Socialiste (PS), Christelijke Volkspartij (CVP)/Parti Social-Chrétien (PSC), Partij voor Vrijheid en Vooruitgang (PVV)/Parti Réformateur Libéral (PRL). The linguistic parties of the ecologist movement, Anders gaan leven (Agalev) in Flanders and Ecolo in Wallonia, have been consistent players in provincial politics since first gaining representation in 1981. Additionally, regionalist or "community" parties have pursued provincial office, including the Volksunie (VU) in Flanders and the Front Démocratique des Francophones (FDF) in Brabant. Recently, extremist parties have gained toeholds in the provincial councils, especially in Antwerp province, where in 1991 and again in 1994 the far-right, anti-immigrant Vlaams Blok (VlB) ranked as the second-largest party in the council. In the Walloon provinces the extremist parties do not fare as well, but the Front National (FN) and the equally vitriolic Agir have been able to gain a handful of seats, respectively, in recent elections (Downs, forthcoming).

In provincial government, single-party majorities are almost as rare as at the national level in Belgium. Of 109 postelection acts of government formation between 1961 and 1994, only 19 single-party majorities altogether have been formed in the Belgian provinces (table 5.1).

Hainaut province, where the Socialist Party long stood as the hegemonic power, boasts the most single-party majorities (6) during the
period. In two provinces, Brabant and Namur, there have been no
single-party majorities during the 30-year span. Of the remaining 90
cases, 73 (81%) have been two-party coalitions and 17 (19%) have comprised three or more parties. Quite striking is that 47 (52%) of the 90
coalition governments represent cases in which provincial parties
overtly chose not to duplicate the national majority-versus-opposition
alignment despite the numerical possibility of doing so.

Table 5.1 provides an important longitudinal picture of alliance behavior at one subnational level of the Belgian polity. What is evident
across three decades is clear variation in terms of patterns of party
coalition behavior, not only across parties but across provinces and
across time. Subsequent chapters attempt to identify reasons for such
variation, but the survey and interview data upon which the explanation is based are cross-sectional rather than longitudinal. It is therefore necessary to outline the historical context of evolving subnational
and national coalition patterns, a task achieved below by highlighting
key developments in five crucial time periods.

FROM SINGLE-PARTY GOVERNMENT TO THE POLITICS OF COALI-
TION (1961–73). This initial period is marked, first, by the transition
from predominantly single-party provincial governments to coalition
arrangements and, second, by a consistency in national-provincial coalition alignments as yet unequaled in subsequent legislative periods.
Of all the legislatures under consideration, the 1961-to-1965 term witnessed the creation of the greatest number (seven) of single-party provincial majorities. After the elections of March 1961, the Catholic party
collected a monopoly of power in all of the Flemish provinces and in
Luxembourg province as well. Socialists commanded an outright majority in Hainaut; and in Liège, where they held 43 of the 86 seats, the
PS received a "free" vote from the Communists to form the majority.[16]
The only coalitions were formed in Namur and Brabant, where the
centrist Christian Socials allied themselves with the Liberals on the
Right. Both provincial coalitions stood in contrast to the center-left
Lefèvre (PSC-BPS) national government (table 5.2).

The joint national-provincial elections of May 1965 were the first to
be truly colored by the regionalization issue and as such saw the entry
of "federalist" parties onto the political landscape. In the provinces the
trend away from single-party majorities had begun, their number

Table 5.1

Partisan Composition of Belgian Provincial Governments, 1961–1994*

	1961	1965	1968	1971	1974	1977	1978	1981	1985	1987	1991	1994
National Coalition	C+S	C+S	C+S	C+S	C+L+R	C+S+V+F	C+S+F	C+L	C+L	C+S+V	C+S	C+S
Province:												
Antwerp	C	C+L	C+S	C+S	C+S	C+S	C+S	C+S	C+S	C+S	C+S+L	C+S+L
Brabant	C+L	C+L	C+L	C+S+L	C+S+L	C+S+L	C+S+V+F	C+S+L	C+S+L	C+S+L	C+S+L**	
Vlaams Brabant												C+S+V
Brabant Wallon												S+L
East Flanders	C	C	C+S	C+S	C+S	C+S	C+S	C+L	C+L	C+L	C+L	C+S+L
Hainaut	S	C+S	S	C+S	C+S	S	S+R	S	S	S	C+S	C+S
Liège	S	C+S	C+S	C+S	C+S	C+S	C+S	S+L	S+L	S+L	S+L	S+L
Limburg	C	C	C	C+S	C+S	C+S	C	C+L	C+S	C+S	S+L+V	S+L+V
Luxembourg	C	C	C+L	C+S	S+L+R	S+L+R	C+S+L	S+L	S+L	S+L	S+L+V	S+L
Namur	C+L	C+L	C+S	C+S	C+S	C+S	C+S	C+S	S+L	S+L	S+L	S+L
West Flanders	C	C	C+S	C+S	C+S	C+S	C	C+S	C+S	C+S	C+S	C+S

Note: C = Christian Socials, S = Socialists, L = Liberals, V = Volksunie, F = Francophone Democratic Front, R = Walloon Rally.

*Underlined cases are those in which provincial coalitions congruent with national parliamentary alignments were numerically possible but were not formed.

**The Flemish Christian Democrats (CVP)—but not the francophone Christian Socials (PSC)—joined the Brabant provincial coalition in 1991.

Table 5.2
National Governments in Belgium since 1961

Prime Minister	Party Composition of Government*	Duration
Lefèvre	PSC-PSB	Apr. 1961–May 1965
Harmel	PSC-PSB	July 1965–Feb. 1966
Vanden Boeynants I	PSC-PLP	Mar. 1966–Feb. 1968
Eyskens IV	CVP-PSC-PSB	June 1968–Nov. 1971
Eyskens V	CVP-PSC-PSB	Jan. 1972–Nov. 1972
Leburton	CVP-PSC-PSB-PVV-PLP	Jan. 1973–Jan. 1974
Tindemans I	CVP-PSC-PVV-PLP	Apr. 1974–June 1974
Tindemans II	CVP-PSC-PVV-PLP-RW	June 1974–Mar. 1977
Tindemans III	CVP-PSC-PSB-FDF-VU	June 1977–Oct. 1978
Vanden Boeynants II	CVP-PSC-PS-SP-FDF-VU	Oct. 1978–Dec. 1978
Martens I	CVP-PSC-PS-SP-FDF	Apr. 1979–Jan. 1980
Martens II	CVP-PSC-PS-SP	Jan. 1980–Apr. 1980
Martens III	CVP-PSC-PS-SP-PVV-PRL	May 1980–Oct. 1980
Martens IV	CVP-PSC-PS-SP	Oct. 1980–Mar. 1981
Eyskens	CVP-PSC-PS-SP	Mar. 1981–Sept. 1981
Martens V	CVP-PSC-PVV-PRL	Dec. 1981–Oct. 1985
Martens VI	CVP-PSC-PVV-PRL	Nov. 1985–Oct. 1987
Martens VII	CVP-PSC-PVV-PRL	Oct. 1987–Dec. 1987
Martens VIII	CVP-PSC-PS-SP-VU	May 1988–Sept. 1991
Martens IX	CVP-PSC-PS-SP	Sept. 1991–Oct. 1991
Dehaene I	CVP-PSC-PS-SP	Mar. 1992–May 1995
Dehaene II	CVP-PSC-PS-SP	June 1995–

*In 1968 the Social Christian Party (PSC) split into the CVP and PSC; in 1972 the Liberal Party (PLP) split into the PVV and PLP; in 1978 the Belgian Socialist Party (BSP) split into the PS and SP; in 1979 the PLP became the Liberal Reform Party (PRL).

down to only three in 1965. Of the six coalitions, there were an equal number of center-left (Christian Socials–Socialists) and center-right (Christian Socials–Liberals) arrangements. The PS lost its majorities in both Liège and Hainaut, conceding executive posts to the PSC in each province. The PS-PSC coalition in Liège coincided with the conclusion of a 12-year provincial accord linking the two parties whenever election results would allow.[17] These arrangements, as well as a center-left coalition in East Flanders, mirrored the national coalition under Prime Minister Harmel. Budgetary crisis toppled the Harmel govern-

ment after little more than six months in office, leading to a reversal
of alliances and a new right-leaning Vanden Boeynants (CVP/PSC–
PLP) cabinet.

After almost two years of unpopular economic austerity measures
and mounting "community problems," the government resigned and
parliament was dissolved. The punctuating event in the crisis had been
the controversial creation of a French section at the University of Leu-
ven.[18] Elections in March 1968 and the negotiations that followed resulted in abandonment of the conservative national coalition and a
return to the center-left, this time headed by Prime Minister Gaston
Eyskens. Provincial majorities likewise moved to the left, with five
Christian Social–Socialist coalitions (three in 1965) and only two Christian Social–Liberal coalitions (three in 1965). After almost three and
a half years in office, the Eyskens government fell on 24 September
1971. Difficulties associated with the revision of the Constitution and
tensions over the status of certain linguistic and cultural trouble spots[19]
made the November elections especially combative; the results, however, prompted little change in the distribution of power. Refusing to
consider grand coalition with the Christian Socials and Liberals, the
Socialists gave the center parties no alternative but a reconstitution of
the same CVP/PSC-BSP coalition.[20] The "new" government had the
same prime minister and the same vice prime minister and was characterized by a "très grande continuité avec le gouvernement précédent,
à un degré rarement attein dans l'histoire politique de la Belgique" (a
great continuity with the preceding government, a degree rarely
achieved in Belgium's political history).[21] This continuity was further
reinforced in the provinces, as eight of the nine new council executives
were shared by Christian Socials and Socialists. In Brabant, where it
was impossible to duplicate the national arrangement, the three traditional party families formed a tripartite coalition, effectively blocking the largest party in the council and the election's clear winner—
the FDF-RW, with 25 seats—out of power. In protest against a majority
of Flemish preponderance (29 Dutch speakers out of 55), two members
of the Liberal group broke party ranks and publicly disavowed the new
alliance.[22] Coalition change also took place in Luxembourg province,
where the PS replaced the liberal PLP in the executive despite an accord signed on 17 April 1969 between the PSC and the PLP to maintain their 1968 coalition through two legislatures.

The political landscape in Belgium grew considerably more complicated in 1973. To resolve the "immobilisme" of the second Eyskens

government with regard to the mounting pressures of regionalization and constitutional revision,[23] a new tripartite cabinet coalition was formed on 26 January 1973, including the Socialists (PSB), both parties of the Christian Social family (CVP, PSC), and both parties of the Liberal family (PVV, PLP). The Leburton-Tindemans–De Clercq alliance was the first postwar Belgian government combining the three traditional parties, and it did so clearly to command the two-thirds majority necessary under parliamentary rules for reform of the Constitution. Still, the reform process moved nowhere, and the global economic crisis, especially the oil crunch and the devaluation of the U.S. dollar, only served to agitate the already bitter infighting among the rival government parties. The "grand" coalition collapsed after just one year.

REGIONALIST PARTIES GAIN ENTRY (1974–80). This second period is defined principally by the entry of regional linguistic community parties into governing arrangements at both national and provincial levels. With the fall of the Leburton government in January 1974, King Baudouin charged Leo Tindemans (CVP) with the task of forming a new government. Tindemans's initial failure prompted the dissolution of parliament—and the provincial councils—and the calling of new elections. After the March elections, Tindemans, again *formateur*, put together a short-lived minority national government (CVP/PSC–PVV/PLP). This right-leaning national government did not correspond with the coalition preferences of provincial parties. Not one of the nine provincial governments formed in March 1974 matched the Tindemans coalition. Christian Social parties in seven provinces opted for alliances with the Socialists, while the three traditional party families renewed their anti-FDF "blocking coalition" in Brabant. In Luxembourg province, Socialists, Liberals, and the Walloon Rally (RW) constituted a "coalition of minorities" and thrust the PSC out of its *vocation majoritaire* and into opposition. The participation of a federalist party, the RW, was the first in provincial government, and it anticipated the party's June entry into national government. The RW persisted longer in the Luxembourg majority than it did in Brussels, first refusing to support the government's budget and ultimately withdrawing its cabinet ministers in March 1977.

Elections in April 1977 saw gains for the Christian Socials, Socialists, and the Francophone Democratic Front in the Chamber of Representatives. The Liberals maintained their seats, while the Volksunie registered small losses. The RW's painful experiment as a party of government hurt it at the polls, where it lost 8 of its 13 seats in parliament. Tindemans, again in search of a coalition broad enough to deal effectively with the linguistic community divisions, succeeded in joining the two major party families in progression (CVP/PSC, BSP/PSB) with the two largest federalist parties, FDF and VU. The Socialists had vetoed any tripartite formula including the Liberals. The experimental arrangement in national government allowed for the two-thirds majority necessary for constitutional reform, and it comprised the largest parties in each of the country's three regions—CVP in Flanders, the PSB in Wallonia, and the FDF in Brussels. In provincial government there is no clear need for a two-thirds majority; hence, the results of coalition bargaining in the provinces were not likely to mirror those at the national level. Only in Luxembourg did a federalist party (RW) gain a share of the provincial executive. Still, the basic left-leaning nature of Belgian coalitions was upheld in six of the eight provinces. In Brabant the three traditional party families retained their anti-FDF alliance in spite of that party's arrival in national government.

Elections in December 1978 saw gains for three of the four existing national coalition partners. Only the Volksunie met with electoral defeat, losing six deputies and six senators. A 99-day crisis ensued, culminating in the formation of a CVP/PSC–SP/PS–FDF government with the necessary two-thirds strength to deal with continuing issues of state reform. In the meantime, provincial coalitions exhibited varying degrees of continuity with national arrangements. Even in the absence of a two-thirds decision rule, parties in Brabant's provincial council duplicated the CVP/PSC–SP/PS–VU-FDF coalition that had governed Belgium for more than a year. Outside its electoral base in Brabant, the FDF did not gain provincial council representation. Therefore, the center-left coalitions established in Liège, Namur, Antwerp, and East Flanders matched national trends. In Luxembourg province, where parties were gaining a reputation for nonconformity with national patterns, the three "great" parties (PSC, PS, PRL) agreed to share power after nine days of postelection negotiations.[24] In Hainaut province, where Socialists in some federation congresses voted by 80% against coalition with the PSC, an alliance with the RW was established to best express the "progressive will" of the population.[25]

Their impotence in government and mounting pressures from the CVP forced the FDF to exit the national cabinet coalition in 1980. The Christian Social and Socialist government left behind faltered and fell in April 1980. Rather than resort to new elections, Prime Minister Wilfried Martens (CVP) negotiated a tripartite arrangement with Socialists and Liberals, the third Belgian government to be headed by Martens. Martens III survived little more than four months, as primary issues of budgetary spending, unemployment, and social security rendered the alliance untenable. Martens IV, comprising Christian Socials and Socialists, endured five months, and yet another "new" government (CVP/PSC–SP/PS) tenuously survived five more months, this time led by Mark Eyskens (CVP).

ALTERNATIVES TO THE CENTER IN PROVINCIAL GOVERNMENT (1981–86). This third crucial period saw a major rightward shift in national alignments and the ouster of the center party in Wallonia in favor of coalitions of parties presumably "unconnected" on the left-right ideological scale. In the November 1981 general elections, the parties of the Christian Social family suffered their worst defeat of the postwar period, losing a combined 21 deputies and 17 senators. The Liberal parties, gaining a combined 15 deputies and 16 senators, registered the greatest victory. The big losers and the big winners formed the Martens V government. In the provinces, only two council majorities (East Flanders, Limburg) corresponded directly with the rightward shift. In three others (Namur, Antwerp, West Flanders), Christian Socials and Socialists rejected the national coalition reversal and maintained their center-left alliances. In Liège and Luxembourg provinces, Socialists and Liberals concluded unprecedented agreements to exclude the centrist PSC from provincial government.

In a break from past practice, the Martens V government invested in 1981 lasted its full legislative term. Elections in 1985 produced significant gains for the Catholic parties and only modest losses for the Liberals, thus allowing the coalition's continuation and the beginning of Martens VI. At the same time, the gap between patterns of provincial coalition policy and national coalition policy widened, with only one province (East Flanders) choosing to duplicate the national alliance. The three remaining Flemish provinces concluded center-left coalitions, and Liberals in three Walloon provinces (Liège, Luxembourg, Namur) rejected their national coalition partner (PSC) in favor of the national opposition (PS).

THE LEFTWARD WENDE (1987–93). The fourth period in our time line is notable initially for the leftward shift in power at the national level but also for the breakdown in previously solid party relations in the periphery. In October 1987 Martens VI temporarily stalled and was reconstituted as Martens VII (CVP/PSC–PVV/PRL), which itself lasted only until the early elections of December 1987. The elections were to produce real change in national coalition policy but none at all in the provinces. In each of the nine provinces, the majority formed following the 1985 elections was renewed in 1987. This occurred despite the conclusion in 1986 of an eight-year pact between the PSC and PRL to form coalitions in all institutions where election results allowed. By 1987 the alliance pact had ruptured, and Liberals in Liège, Luxembourg, and Namur made new deals with the Socialists (see chapter 7). The rupture was even more real in national government, as the Catholic parties in 1988 engineered a coalition change to include the Socialists and the Volksunie.

Coalition bargaining following the November 1991 elections saw a *formateur* attempt for the first time since 1958 to put together a Belgian government without the Catholic parties. In three Walloon provinces (Liège, Luxembourg, Namur), where the Christian Socials had first been blocked from power in 1981, "une coalition sans les sociaux-chrétiens" was realized in the form of PS-PRL governments. In Limburg the Socialist-Liberal-Volksunie coalition reduced the CVP to the ranks of the opposition for the first time ever in a Flemish province. In Brabant province the council parties reproduced a classic tripartite coalition, but with one profound difference—the PRL blocked the PSC's entrance to the permanent deputation. For the first time, a traditional party, the CVP, joined a provincial government without its linguistic partner, the PSC. This "accord historique" produced the country's first "asymmetrical" coalition. The anti-CVP/PSC coalitions in the Belgian provinces reflected public sentiment but were not realized in national government, where a center-left cabinet under Jean-Luc Dehaene (CVP) ultimately emerged.

COALITIONS IN THE FEDERAL STATE (1994–95). The postfederalization period in Belgian electoral and alliance politics ushered in several important changes: provincial elections detached from national elections, ten instead of nine provincial councils, and direct elections to autonomous regional parliaments. The provincial vote in October 1994 led to a renewal of the socialist-liberal axis in much of francophone Belgium and a continued, albeit marginal, erosion of Catholic dominance in the north. These developments took a back seat to the 1995 elections (table 5.3) and government formations in Flanders, Wallonia, and Brussels regions. Although Brussels had elected its first legislature and government in 1989, May 1995 signaled the democratization of Belgium's regions as a legitimate institutional tier of representative government. Following the elections, weeks of intense bargaining at multiple tables revealed the apparent interdependence of negotiations to form the federal and regional governments. In the event, the center-left parties in the Chamber of Representatives, the Flanders Parliament, and the Wallonia Parliament orchestrated matching coalition governments. Only in the Brussels region, with its bilingual legislature, did a more politically and linguistically inclusive alternative emerge.

General Patterns

It is evident from this broad historical overview that in Belgium single-party majorities are scarce at all levels of government. Indeed, Belgian parliamentary democracy is coalition politics. There is no question that examining coalition behavior in the Belgian provincial councils and regional assemblies, instead of simply in the national parliament, is an unconventional method of understanding the strategic behavior of the country's political parties. This fact, however, gives the approach part of its allure and value.

Repeated rounds of government formation at different levels of the polity demonstrate real diversity. Tables 5.1 through 5.3 attest to this fact. Parties in subnational legislatures appear, at least at first glance, to be responding in varying degrees at varying times to a range of motivations, such as concerns of coalition size, ideological connectedness, and coalition continuity; national party preferences; national coalition arrangements; and even sometimes the verdict of the electorate. Explaining this variance is an empirical matter and will be pursued in following chapters. The purpose of this initial overview of the Belgian case has been to establish the context in which coalitions occur, to confirm the existence of variance, and to describe the historical linkages between subnational and national coalition systems.

Germany

Despite a respectable number of case studies of coalition formation and collapse in the German states (see Broughton and Kirchner 1986;

Table 5.3

Partisan Composition of Directly Elected Belgian Regional Parliaments and Their Governments

Parties	Wallonia Parliament 1995 Seats (N = 75)	Votes (%)	Flanders Parliament 1995 Seats (N = 118)	Votes (%)	Brussels-Capital Parliament 1989 Seats (N = 75)	Votes (%)	Brussels-Capital Parliament 1995 Seats (N = 75)	Votes (%)
French-speaking socialists (PS)	30	35.2	—	—	18	22.0	17	21.4
Flemish socialists (SP)	—	—	25	19.4	2	2.7	2	2.4
Flemish Christian Democrats (CVP)	—	—	35	26.8	4	4.2	3	3.3
Francophone Christian Democrats (PSC)	16	21.6	—	—	9	11.8	7	9.3
Flemish-speaking liberals (VLD, was PVV)	—	—	26	20.2	2	2.8	2	2.7
Federation of French-speaking liberals and Francophone Democratic Front (PRL-FDF)	19	23.7	—	—	—	—	28	35.0
French-speaking liberals (PRL)	—	—	—	—	15	16.9	—	—
Francophone Democratic Front (FDF)	—	—	—	—	15	16.7	—	—
Volksunie (VU)	—	—	9	9.0	1	2.1	1	1.4
AGALEV	—	—	7	7.1	1	1.1	—	0.9
ECOLO	8	10.4	—	—	8	10.2	7	9.0
Vlaams Blok (VlB)	—	—	15	12.3	1	2.1	2	3.0
National Front (FN-NF)	2	5.2	—	—	2	3.3	6	7.5
French Speakers Union (UF)	—	—	1	1.2	—	—	—	—
Others	—	3.9	—	4.0	—	4.1	—	4.1
Government Formed	PS + PSC		SP + CVP		PS/SP + PSC/CVP FDF + VU		PS/SP + CVP + PRL-FDF + VU	

Culver 1966; Gunlicks 1977; Pridham 1973), little systematic attention has been devoted to analyzing the broader linkages between Land-federation coalitions. Nor has much research attempted to look, with an eye toward comparison, at the ways in which German state politicians and their parent party organizations cope with coalition environments. Do party leaders at the federal level want to impose the same coalition at all levels of government where election results permit, so as to avoid intraparty conflicts, ensure policy consistency, and engender harmony between federal coalition partners? Or do they actively encourage the formation of incongruent coalitions, perhaps to boost their leverage with federal coalition partners by increasing the credibility of the threat of coalition breakup? Or are federal party leaders not powerful enough to dictate the choices of recalcitrant state parties?

These questions are as old as the Federal Republic and take on added importance with the recent addition of five "new" Länder from the former German Democratic Republic (GDR). As in the case of Belgium, the following overview of institutional structures and historical development is not intended to supply every detail of every case of government formation at either the federal or the Land level. More directly, the task at hand is to describe the institutional settings in which coalitions form and to summarize basic trends in coalition outcomes for federal and Land governments.

Subnational Government Structures

For a much longer period than in Belgium, federalism has dominated the territorial administration and political division of Germany. The German state after 1949 is an amalgam of federal (*Bund*), regional (*Land*), county (*Kreis*), and municipal (*Gemeinde*) institutions. Germany's constitution or "Basic Law" (*Grundgesetz*) explicitly details the country's territorial organization, including deliberative assemblies at the national, regional, and local levels, as depicted in figure 5.2. At the national level are two parliamentary chambers: the *Bundestag* (lower house), directly elected by the German population, and the *Bundesrat* (upper house), appointed by and representing the interests of the respective Land governments. At the regional level reside separate parliaments (*Landtage*), each with its own executive. Finally, at the local and district levels, the German system provides for thousands of coun-

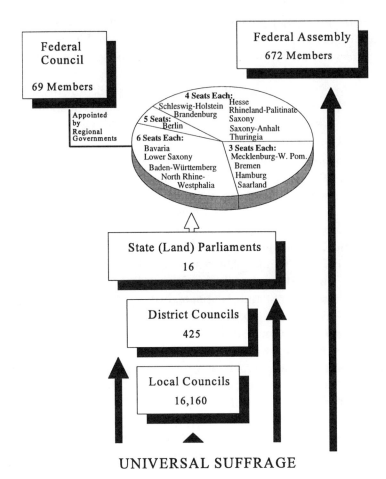

Figure 5.2   German Political Institutions

cils (*Gemeinderat, Stadtrat, Kreistag*) that have the authority to "regulate, under their own responsibility, all affairs of the local community, within the framework of the law."[26]

German "national" government exercises a wide degree of discretion in policy making. The federal chancellor (*Bundeskanzler*) and federal ministries (*Bundesregierung*) have constitutional jurisdiction to act exclusively in areas such as foreign affairs and defense, monetary policy, nationality laws, railways, air traffic administration, customs, postal services, and telecommunications. Wary, however, of vesting too much power in central authorities, the authors of the Basic Law established that "the exercise of state powers and the discharge of state functions rests with the Länder insofar as this Basic Law does not prescribe or permit other arrangements" (Article 83). Thus, the Länder hold certain reserved and residuary competencies—among them, education, law and order, cultural and religious affairs, and supervision over local government (Gerstenlauer 1995). Generally described by the term *cooperative federalism*, the German model "is characterised by competition, sometimes by controversy and confrontation, and eventually by bargaining. Neither element can force its will upon the other, rather the component units are forced into a scheme of co-operation" (Hrbek 1987, 32). Thus, the constitutional structures of German territorial division, much as in Belgium, do yield discernibly different national and subnational governmental arenas that, as will be described below, offer lucrative prizes for political parties.[27]

The component regional units of Germany's cooperative federalism are the individual Länder. Allied authorities created 11 West German Länder by 1949: Hamburg, Bavaria, North Rhine–Westphalia, Lower Saxony, Hessen, Rheinland-Palatinate, Bremen, Baden, Württemberg-Hohenzollern, Württemberg-Baden, and Schleswig-Holstein. West Berlin became an administrative unit with special status in 1950. By 1951 the three southwestern states of Baden, Württemberg-Hohenzollern, and Württemberg-Baden merged into the present Land of Baden-Württemberg. West Germany regained the Saarland in 1957, bringing the total number of Länder back to 11. These principal units of subnational government underpinned the West German state from its inception to its most recent transformation—the October 1990 reunification. With reunification came the incorporation of five Länder crafted from the territory of the former GDR: Brandenburg, Mecklenburg-West Pomerania, Saxony, Saxony-Anhalt, and Thuringia.

LAND GOVERNMENT. At the state or regional level resides "a complex balance of somewhat autonomous centres of power" (Lehmbruch 1978, 154). Each of the states has its own legislature, its own government, and its own constitution. Each government is headed by a chief minister (*Ministerpräsident*), who is accountable to the democratically elected parliamentary body. Each state party (*Landesverband*) has at some time asserted its local autonomy in relation to the formation of coalitions that differ from the arrangement prevailing in Bonn at the same time (Broughton and Kirchner 1986). This is the crucial factor that makes multiparty government in Germany's regional parliaments worthy of our attention.[28]

The Landtage (*Abgeordnetenhaus* in Berlin, *Bürgerschaft* in Bremen and Hamburg) range in size from 60 seats (Saarland) to 237 (North Rhine–Westphalia), corresponding to population size and to the statutes of the respective Land constitutions. Individual differences make general comparisons across the state parliaments more difficult than in the case of the uniformly structured Belgian provinces. Elections to the Landtage take place approximately every four or five years, but the legislative periods of the respective Landtage do not necessarily correspond with that of the Bundestag nor with those of each other. Moreover, the two-ballot electoral system (one vote for a constituency candidate, one for a party) that determines federal elections is not uniformly practiced by the Länder in their parliamentary elections. In North Rhine–Westphalia Landtag elections, for example, voters directly elect 151 deputies (MdL) in a "first past the post," single-member constituency system. With the same vote, however, the remaining 86 MdL are chosen via proportional representation from among those "Land reserve lists" gaining at least 5% of the overall vote.[29] Land parliament deputies may not concurrently hold mandates in the Bundestag.

Stakes in postelection coalition games are high in the Landtage. The minister president (*Bürgermeister* in the city-states of Hamburg, Bremen, and Berlin) is chosen by absolute majority from among the Landtag deputies in secret balloting. This chief executive then has the authority to appoint a cabinet of generally 9 to 15 ministers, each with a portfolio in some area such as finance, justice, education, or environment. In the absence of a single-party majority in the Landtag, multiple parties must negotiate the candidacy of the minister president and bargain over the distribution of cabinet ministries. Once invested, the minister president and the cabinet may be ousted from office by a constructive vote of no confidence. Here is one clear indicator of the differences between executives in the German Länder and those in the Belgian provinces.

In addition to the consequences of immediate importance to a particular Land, coalition outcomes also influence the balance of power in federal government. Much as the Belgian provincial and regional majorities have been able to determine the composition of the Belgian Senate, the majority party or parties in the German Landtage determine the political composition of the Bundesrat. The second chamber in Germany is composed of persons appointed by the individual Land governments, voting together as Land blocs and following the instructions of the Land governments. As most legislation requires passage in both the Bundestag and the Bundesrat, the Länder thus have a direct impact on federal policy. This becomes especially crucial when the majority in the Länder, and hence in the Bundesrat, does not match the federal majority in the Bundestag. A single change of coalition partners in a single Landtag can thus alter the balance of power in the Bundesrat and in the federal system altogether.

Party Participation in Coalition Governments

In federal Germany the construction of governments in both Bonn and in the Länder is largely a product of coalition politics. At both levels, the primary actors are the Christian Democratic Union/Christian Social Union (Christlich Demokratische Union/Christlich Soziale Union), the Social Democratic Party of Germany (Sozialdemokratische Partei Deutschlands), the Free Democratic Party (Freie Demokratische Partei), and the Greens (Die Grünen). In the first decades of the federation, smaller parties, including the German Party (Deutsche Partei) and the Association of Refugees and Disenfranchised (Gesamtdeutscher Block/Block der Heimatvertriebenen und Entrechteten), also made their way into governing coalitions. A formidable literature on German party dynamics generally concurs with Norpoth's (1982) observation that the pattern of coalition government in the FRG is one of "steady, effective, and at times creative government lacking the constant menace of crisis" (31; see also Broughton and Kirchner 1986; Hoffmann-Lange 1986; Johnson 1983; Klingemann 1985; Padgett 1989; Padgett and Burkett 1986; Pridham 1982; Pulzer 1982; Schmidt 1983; Smith 1989).

While there is no intention here to recapitulate the issues and cleavages that characterize politics in Bonn, the general evolutionary pattern of German coalition politics at the federal level does deserve initial attention. Table 5.4 provides the party composition and coalition status of federal governments since 1949. The immediate postwar period witnessed broad-based inclusive coalitions, followed by various minimum winning coalitions between the CDU and FDP, an oversized grand coalition from 1966 to 1969, and alternating periods of center-right CDU and center-left SPD alliances with the pivotal liberal FDP. To generalize, it may be said that SPD-dominated coalitions have tended to be "overloaded" with economic issues, including pro-labor and pro-welfare state measures, while CDU-dominated coalitions have tended

Table 5.4
Federal Coalitions in Germany since 1949

Parties in Government*	Period of Office	Factor Precipitating Change or Renewal
CDU/CSU–FDP–DP	Sept. 1949–Sept. 1953	Elections
CDU/CSU–FDP–DP– GB/BHE	Oct. 1953–Oct. 1955	Internal party split and defection
CDU/CSU–FDP–DP	Oct. 1955–Feb. 1956	Internal party split and defection
CDU/CSU–DP	Feb. 1956–Sept. 1957	Elections
CDU/CSU–DP	Oct. 1957–July 1960	Internal party split and defection
CDU/CSU	July 1960–Sept. 1961	Elections
CDU/CSU–FDP	Nov. 1961–Oct. 1963	Voluntary resignation
CDU/CSU–FDP	Oct. 1963–Sept. 1965	Elections
CDU/CSU–FDP	Oct. 1965–Oct. 1966	Coalition breakup
CDU/CSU–SPD	Dec. 1966–Sept. 1969	Elections
SPD-FDP	Oct. 1969–Nov. 1972	Elections
SPD-FDP	Dec. 1972–May 1974	Voluntary resignation
SPD-FDP	May 1974–Oct. 1976	Elections
SPD-FDP	Dec. 1976–Oct. 1980	Elections
SPD-FDP	Nov. 1980–Oct. 1982	No-confidence vote
CDU/CSU–FDP	Oct. 1982–Feb. 1983	Elections
CDU/CSU–FDP	Mar. 1983–Jan. 1987	Elections
CDU/CSU–FDP	Jan. 1987–Nov. 1990	Elections
CDU/CSU–FDP	Dec. 1990–Oct. 1994	Elections
CDU/CSU–FDP	Oct. 1994–	

Note: CDU = Christian Democratic Union; CSU = Christian Social Union; SPD = Social Democratic Party; GRÜNE = Greens; FDP = Free Democratic Party; GB/BHE = Refugee Party; DP = German Party.
*Bold type indicates possession of chancellorship.

to emphasize free-enterprise "social capitalism," religious and citizens' rights issues, and conflicts over law and order (Schmidt 1983).

In Land parliaments the party composition of coalition governments has demonstrated greater variation. While the CDU has traditionally dominated governments in such states as Baden-Württemberg, Rhineland-Palatinate, Schleswig-Holstein, and the Saarland, it has done so by allying on frequent occasions with its liberal partners, the FDP, but also at times with its avowed adversaries, the SPD. Only in Bavaria, where the CSU has long been hegemonic, has the Christian Union largely avoided coalition compromises and enjoyed uninter-

Table 5.5
Partisan Composition of German Land Governments since 1961

Year, Federal Coalition	Baden-Württemberg	Bavaria	Berlin	Bremen	Hamburg	Hessen	Lower Saxony	North Rhine-Westphalia	Rhineland Palatinate	Saarland	Schleswig Holstein
1961	CDU+FDP+					SPD+FDP			CDU+FDP		
CDU/CSU	GDP	CSU+BP/				SPD+GDP		CDU+FDP			CDU+FDP
+FDP		SVP	SPD+FDP	SPD+FDP			SPD+FDP		CDU+FDP		
	CDU+FDP										
1965		CSU	SPD+FDP		SPD	SPD	CDU+SPD	SPD+FDP	CDU+FDP		CDU+FDP
CDU/CSU				SPD+FDP							
+SPD	CDU+SPD										CDU+FDP
1969		CSU			SPD+FDP	SPD+FDP	SPD	SPD+FDP			
SPD+FDP			SPD	SPD					CDU		CDU
1972	CDU	CSU			SPD+FDP	SPD+FDP	SPD+FDP				
SPD+FDP	CDU		SPD+FDP	SPD				SPD+FDP	CDU	CDU	CDU
1976		CSU			SPD	SPD+FDP	CDU		CDU		CDU
SPD+FDP			SPD+FDP	SPD			SPD	CDU	CDU+FDP		
1980	CDU	CSU	CDU			SPD	CDU			CDU+FDP	
SPD+FDP				SPD							
1983			SPD		SPD+		SPD+		CDU		CDU
CDU/CSU	CDU	CSU	CDU+FDP		GRÜNE		GRÜNE			CDU	
+FDP		CSU				CDU+FDP		SPD		SPD	
1987	CDU			SPD	SPD+FDP	CDU+FDP			CDU+FDP		SPD
CDU/CSU			SPD								SPD
+FDP											SPD
1990		CSU		SPD+FDP	SPD	SPD+	SPD+	SPD	SPD+FDP	SPD	
CDU/CSU	CDU+SPD		CDU+SPD	+GRÜNE		GRÜNE	GRÜNE				SPD
+FDP											
1994		CSU			SPD+	SPD+	SPD	SPD+	CDU+FDP	SPD	
CDU/CSU	CDU+FDP		CDU+SPD	CDU+SPD	STATT	GRÜNE		GRÜNE			
+FDP											

Note: CDU = Christian Democratic Union; CSU = Christian Social Union; GDP = German Party; SPD = Social Democratic Party; Grüne = Greens; STATT = "Instead" Party (Dissident CDU); FDP = Free Democratic Party; BP/SVP = Bavarian Party.

rupted single-party majority government. The Social Democrats have controlled Land governments in Bremen, Hamburg, Hessen, and North Rhine–Westphalia, coalescing most often with the Free Democrats but also engaging in experimental alliances with the emergent Greens. Table 5.5 lists Länder governments and coalitions from 1961, which marks the beginning of the "stable period" of the party system (Roberts 1989).

As has been shown to be the case in Belgium, in Germany an important dimension of subnational governments is their frequent incongruence with the partisan composition of national governments. Unlike the Belgian case, however, such patterns in Germany have attracted a certain degree of scholarly attention. Roberts (1989), for one, categorizes state-level coalition governments that differed during some period of their term with respect to the inclusion or exclusion of one or more major parties in comparison to the Bonn coalition. The catalog yields three primary periods of national/subnational coalition incongruence, including FDP-SPD Länder coalitions while the FDP was in coalition with the CDU/CSU in Bonn (1949–56, 1961–66); FDP-CDU Länder coalitions, or support for CDU minority governments, during the Bonn SPD-FDP coalition (1969–82); and inclusive all-party Länder governments predating the 1966–69 CDU/CSU–SPD "Grand Coalition" in Bonn. Updating Roberts's list, it is useful to add the SPD-FDP alliances, the so-called traffic light SPD (red)–FDP (yellow)–Grünen (green) coalitions, the CDU-SPD grand coalitions that have emerged at the Land level during the Kohl CDU-FDP federal government, and the SPD–Statt Partei government in Hamburg. While not incongruent as such, the SPD-Green coalitions in such states as Lower Saxony, Hesse, and Hamburg deserve attention for their potential "experimental" value.

For purposes of historical background, it is useful to summarize the evolution of coalition systems at both the state and federal levels. Without breaking the overview into separate federal legislative periods, it suffices to adopt the conventional four-part division of German electoral periods, which recognizes an era of center-right domination (1961–66), the "grand coalition" interlude (1966–69), an era of center-left domination (1969–82), and finally the recent span of Christian Democratic–Liberal hegemony (1982–).

CENTER-RIGHT DOMINATION (1961–66). The period of center-right dominance spans the entire fourth Bundestag legislature and the beginning of the fifth legislature, both of which were marked by solid CDU/CSU–FDP majorities (309 of 499 seats from 1961 to 1965, 294 of 496 seats from 1965 to 1966). The Christian-Liberal alliance, headed by Chancellor Konrad Adenauer, took shape, strangely enough, following an election campaign in which the FDP and its federal chairman Dr. Erich Mende had explicitly promised voters that it would *not* join an Adenauer cabinet (Kloss 1990). Rewarded by the electorate for this hardline stance with an impressive 5% gain over its 1957 totals, the FDP nonetheless did accept a junior position in a new Adenauer government. Despite this "betrayal of trust" (Culver 1966, 312) and its severe electoral consequences in subsequent state elections, in the Länder the Liberals managed to duplicate the Bonn alliance in varying forms in 5 of the 11 governments. Parliamentary parties in Rhineland-

Palatinate and Saarland matched the Bonn alliance perfectly, while in Baden-Württemberg, Bavaria, and Schleswig-Holstein, the Refugee Party (BHE) gained a share of government power as a third partner.

Elsewhere, FDP coalitions with the Social Democrats in Bremen, Hamburg, and Lower Saxony stood in stark contrast to the Bonn government. These coalitions clearly predated the Social-Liberal federal alliance that would be built later in the decade. While these state governments were thus "incongruent" with the federal coalition, only in a few cases had strict "congruence" been a mathematical possibility. This was certainly the case in both Bremen and Hamburg, although in both states the SPD could have governed alone but chose instead to govern with the Free Democrats as junior partners. In Lower Saxony the CDU and FDP could have formed a governing majority, indeed a minimum winning majority; nevertheless, the Liberals negotiated a coalition with the largest party in the Landtag, the SPD. In West Berlin the CDU-SPD grand coalition that had governed the city-state since 1955 collapsed in 1963, but as in Lower Saxony, the Socialists shared power with the FDP despite owning an outright parliamentary majority.

Although they reneged on their electoral promises at the federal level, there is little in the five-year period to suggest that the Free Democrats were flagrantly disloyal to their coalition partners in Bonn, except that they were easy prey for a Social Democratic Party intent on proving itself as a successful party of government and as a reasonable alternative to the Christian Democrats. There is also little to support the notion of minimum-size coalitions being the most preferable ones to parties in state parliaments. In addition, with the case of Berlin, the precedent for a national unity government—a CDU-SPD coalition—had already been set.

GRAND COALITION (1966–69). The period of "Große Koalition" in Bonn had been foreshadowed in the Länder. This formula had been attempted not only in Berlin (1955–63) but also in various arrangements in Bavaria (1945–54), Bremen (1951–59), Hamburg (1945–46), Hessen (1945–51), Lower Saxony (1946–51, 1957–59, 1965–70), North Rhine–Westphalia (1946–50), Rhineland-Palatinate (1946–47, 1947–51), Saarland (1956–61), and Schleswig-Holstein (1946–47). When the FDP left the national Erhard (CDU) government and the coalition with CDU/CSU amid the economic recession of 1966, the Christian Union parties and the Social Democrats agreed to unite under the chancellorship of Kurt-Georg Kiesinger (CDU), then minister-president of Baden-Württemberg. The oversized coalition produced a surplus majority of 198 seats in the fifth Bundestag, and it should be noted that the FDP could have chosen coalition with the SPD over its eventual decision to go into opposition.[30]

During the 1966-to-1969 period of CDU/CSU–SPD power sharing, there were six Landtag elections resulting in coalition governments, five in 1967 and one in 1968. Parties in both Baden-Württemberg and Lower Saxony reproduced the coalition policy of the Bonn parties, with the SPD abandoning the FDP in Lower Saxony and the CDU abandoning the FDP in Baden-Württemberg. Alternatively, the SPD in Bremen and West Berlin reconstituted alliances with the Liberals in 1967, whereas CDU parties in Rhineland-Palatinate and Schleswig-Holstein reaffirmed their coalitions with the FDP the same year. Here is striking evidence of divergent coalition behavior among the same parties at roughly the same time but across different Länder.

THE LEFT ASCENDANT (1969–82). A series of SPD-FDP coalitions in Bonn succeeded the grand coalition, stretching from the sixth to almost the end of the ninth Bundestag legislatures, and effectively ended 20 years of Christian Democratic dominance. The first Brandt (SPD) government (1969–72) secured a slim five-seat majority in parliament following the 1969 federal elections. The second Brandt government (1972–74) could seemingly have expanded this margin to 22 seats, but defections over foreign policy gave the SPD-FDP coalition a weak voting majority in the Bundestag. In both of these cases, a CDU/CSU–FDP government had been possible given the distribution of Bundestag seats, and in 1969 the SPD-FDP coalition propelled the Christian Democrats into opposition despite the latter's plurality of parliamentary seats. Schmidt's (SPD) chancellorship from 1974 to 1982 maintained the Social Democrat–Liberal alliance, although the 1976 federal election reduced the coalition's Bundestag majority to a tenuous four seats.

During the 13-year period, there were some 38 Landtag elections, most of which produced single-party majorities. In 11 instances, however, two-party governing coalitions were formed in postelection bargaining. Ten of the 11 (Hamburg in 1970 and 1974; Hessen in 1970, 1974, and 1978; Lower Saxony in 1974; North Rhine–Westphalia in 1970 and 1975; West Berlin in 1975 and 1979) matched the SPD-FDP coalition in Bonn. In two of these cases (Hamburg in 1974, Hessen in 1970), a CDU-FDP government had been the minimum winning combination but was chosen in neither case. Moreover, Social Democrats in Hamburg following the 1970 election held an absolute majority but were still willing to accept the Free Democrats as coalition partners. Only in Saarland did an explicitly "incongruent" coalition form following an election. This occurred after the April 1980 Landtag election when the FDP joined Werner Zeyer's CDU in coalition, despite the feasibility of allying with the SPD.[31] Elsewhere, the FDP had tolerated CDU minority governments in West Berlin and in Lower Saxony, perhaps in order to "balance" the federal position of the party (Broughton and Kirchner 1986).

The era of Social Democratic–Liberal dominance in federal government appears to have been mirrored to a large extent in the Länder, but not completely. The SPD managed to control five Länder—Bremen, Hamburg, Hessen, North Rhine–Westphalia, and Berlin—either alone or in coalition with the FDP, yet the CDU remained the strongest in five others—Baden-Württemberg, Rhineland-Palatinate, Saarland, Schleswig-Holstein, and Bavaria (CSU). The SPD-FDP combination proved to be the preferred power-sharing arrangement and thus appears to have followed the lead of the federal coalition system. This particular observation should not neglect the inverse, namely, that the SPD-FDP federal coalition had already been widely tested in the Länder before 1969. Both parties had already been partners in government at one time or another since 1946 in 7 of the 11 Länder.

GREENS AND REUNIFICATION ALTER THE EQUATION (1982–). Most accounts of the Social Democrat–Liberal federal government agree that the coalition fell apart in 1982 largely on account of mounting economic problems and deteriorating personal relationships between Chancellor Schmidt and the FDP's Hans-Dietrich Genscher (Broughton and Kirchner 1986; Schmidt 1983). With the so-called economic liberals of the FDP's right wing gaining sway within the party, the Free Democrats resigned from the Schmidt cabinet and by October 1982 had formed a workable majority coalition with their old partners the Christian Democrats under Helmut Kohl. Center-right Kohl governments had by 1996 thus survived more than a decade and almost four Bundestag legislatures in power.

With the emergence of Die Grünen onto the electoral landscape, the relatively simple and stable three-party coalition system grew more complex. The Greens bargained their way into Land governments in Hesse (1985–87, 1991, 1995), Lower Saxony (1990), Bremen (1990), and North Rhine–Westphalia (1995), while in the process usurping the FDP's traditional role as *the* coalition party. In Hesse the first case of a coalition involving the Green Party occurred when, from 1985 to 1987, Holger Börner's SPD chose coalition over minority government by concluding an agreement—or "red-green experiment"—with the Greens (Padgett 1989). In four other cases—Hesse (1987–91), Lower Saxony (1986–90), Rhineland-Palatinate (1987–91), Berlin (1985–89)—the CDU and FDP matched the Bonn coalition. Incongruent coalitions formed in Hamburg (1987) and Rhineland-Palatinate (1991), where the Free Democrats joined SPD governments despite their supposed allegiance to the CDU in federal government. The SPD-FDP coalition in Hamburg, beginning in 1987, marked the first case of an incongruent coalition after the change of government in Bonn in 1982. In addition, in both Berlin (1991) and Baden-Württemberg (1992), election outcomes led to reconstitutions of the old CDU-SPD coalitions, giving voice as well as substance to those calling for a new grand coalition in federal government to deal with the problems of reunification. This most recent period has also seen the first "traffic light" (SPD-FDP-Grüne) coalition, which occurred in Bremen in 1990,[32] as well as the first, albeit failed, serious attempt at forming a "black-green" CDU-Grüne coalition in Baden-Württemberg (1992).

East-West reunification has added new players and new possibilities to party government in Germany. The first elections to democratic parliaments in the eastern Länder in 1990 resulted largely in a duplication of traditional alliance patterns in the West (table 5.6). The Christian Democrats, benefiting from Chancellor Kohl's success at ending four decades of national partition, captured power outright in Saxony and imported Kurt Biedenkopf to serve as minister-president. In Mecklenburg-West Pomerania, Saxony-Anhalt, and Thuringia, Kohl's party managed to forge cabinet coalitions with the Free Democrats. Only in Brandenburg did the CDU join the ranks of the opposition, coming up short against Manfred Stolpe's SPD-FDP–Bündnis 90 (Greens) coalition. Four years later, the FDP was completely banished from the ranks of state government in the eastern Länder, falling under the 5% threshold owing to the strength of the Party of Democratic Socialism (PDS, former Communists). The Free Democrats' demise has hurt the CDU, which although retaining its conservative bastion in Saxony was forced in 1994 into coalitions with the SPD in Mecklenburg-West Pomerania and Thuringia. The Social Democrats, wary of alliance with ex-

Table 5.6
Partisan Composition of Governments in "New" German States

Landtag	Government, 1990	Government, 1994
Brandenburg	SPD + FDP + Bündnis 90 (Grünen)	SPD
Mecklenburg–West Pomerania	CDU + FDP	CDU + SPD
Saxony	CDU	CDU
Saxony-Anhalt	CDU + FDP	SPD + Grünen
Thuringia	CDU + FDP	CDU + SPD

Communists and avoiding grand coalition where possible, opted for the red-green formula in Saxony-Anhalt to complement their unshared rule in Brandenburg.

General Patterns

This overview of the historical development of coalition systems at both the Land and federal levels provides background and establishes variance. State-level coalitional strategy has not invariably followed federal-level coalitional strategy. Parties in the Landtage have seemingly followed minimum winning types of rationality on some occasions but on others have chosen to form governments that include surplus members (in terms of both parties and seats). These divergent patterns suggest that it is worth investigating in the German case the broader questions that drive our analysis: Where are the fundamental decisions of participation in state government coalitions made—at the national or the subnational level? On what bases are these decisions reached? And how much influence is brought to bear on state party leaders by the federal party leadership? In the German case, just as in that of Belgium, simple reference to formal theory does not immediately provide adequate explanation. Criteria of minimalist rationality can account for the formation of only some of Germany's state-level coalition governments.

France

Regional-level coalition government in France lacks some of the formal tradition of Belgium and Germany, given that directly elected assemblies at this level date only from the mid-1980s. France is, however, a crucial case. Long one of the most centralized countries in Europe, indeed once the "archetype of a centralised country" (Hainsworth and Loughlin 1989, 149), recent French governments have sought to "rationalize and reform the complex structure of centre-periphery relations" (Mazey 1989, 42). In particular, the Socialist government of Prime Minister Pierre Mauroy and President François Mitterrand moved in 1982 to establish directly elected regional councils with full revenue-raising powers and significant legislative capacity. Because of France's divisive party system, the creation of conseils régionaux as important decision-making bodies with executive offices beholden to the assembly at large has made multiparty coalitions in many regions likely if not absolutely necessary.

In a country where national strategies have traditionally determined local tactics and where dissident party members are often expelled, the emergence of regional council coalitions has presented party leaders and individual representatives with a novel set of circumstances. Voting results in 1986 left most of the 21 mainland councils without a single-party majority.[33] The extremist Front National, largely considered "untouchables" at the national level, found themselves holding the balance of power in many regions and were rewarded for their support with a share of power alongside mainstream Gaullists and Giscardians. Following the 1992 regional elections, Socialists tried to salvage their presence in regional government by patching together alliances with the Communists and the ecologist parties, largely to no avail. Coalition politics in the French regional assemblies, in short, is like that in the German Landtage and in Belgium's meso-level parliaments: an important political reality showcased repeatedly during the act of government formation.

Subnational Government Structures

Until the reforms instituted by the Socialist regime in the early 1980s, the unitary French state of the Fifth Republic concentrated formal political authority in national government institutions—namely, the president, the prime minister, and Parliament. This produced the characteristic depiction of the French state as a "centralized, structured, hierarchical system" (Meny 1988, 130). Local administrative units in the form of 96 metropolitan *départements* with departmental councils (*conseils généraux*) and 36,000 communes with communal councils (*conseils municipaux*) largely did the bidding of a government-appointed prefect, who has been described as both "a kind of impe-rialist 'governor'" of true Jacobin heritage and a "mediator" who rep-resents the central government (Hainsworth and Loughlin 1989, 150).

Only in 1972 did a French government add regional institutions to the territorial division of the state. The 1972 decentralization act created a regional prefect and a regional council, neither of which was directly elected. National deputies and senators automatically became regional representatives. The act also resulted in increased regional autonomy, but the 22 regions (including Corsica) had no intervening economic power and remained clearly subservient to the preexisting levels of government—nation, department, and commune (Schmidt 1990). Throughout the 1970s, the regions and their councils "were widely criticized as being undemocratic, powerless and inadequately financed" (Mazey 1986, 297).

With the arrival of Mitterrand and the Socialists in 1981, the pace of decentralization quickened. Prime Minister Mauroy's interior min-ister in charge of decentralization, Gaston Defferre, placed in motion a series of 33 laws and 219 decrees between 1982 and 1985 aimed at reforming the system of territorial administration in France. The re-forms established that departmental and regional executives would be elected by their respective elected councils and that the regional coun-cils would henceforth be elected by direct suffrage. This move would eliminate the *tutelle* of the prefects, who had to give up their positions as territorial executives. Further, the reforms provided regions with their own budgets and bestowed on them significant powers to inter-vene in the economic field. The region thus became a distinct, fourth level of French government, with its own autonomous deliberative council, its own executive, and its own budget. The basic components of the post-1982 French state structure are presented in figure 5.3.

REGIONAL GOVERNMENT. Since independent regional assemblies have existed only since the date of their first election in 1986, the exact nature and true identity of regional government are still in formation. The councils themselves range widely in size from 43 seats (Franche-Comté) to 209 (Ile-de-France), corresponding to population size in the regions. Elections to the regional councils for fixed terms take place every six years, the first having occurred in March 1986 and the second in March 1992. The 1986 regional elections were held in conjunction with the national legislative elections; Mitterrand and the Socialist au-thorities, however, changed this practice for the 1992 regional elec-

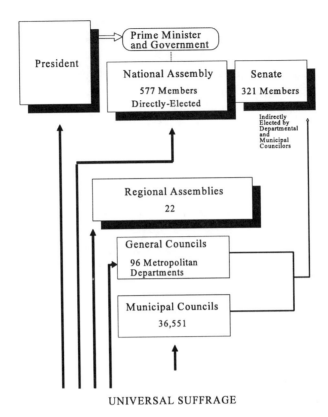

Figure 5.3   French Political Institutions

tions, which took place a year in advance of the Assemblée Nationale elections. A proportional system has been employed in both regional elections, and the regional balloting, unlike balloting in national elections, is limited to one round.

As in both Belgium and Germany, postelection maneuvering for the prizes of regional office is intense. A week following regional elections, the new assembly convenes to elect a president who will serve a six-year term as the region's chief executive. A candidate can be elected regional premier in one of three rounds of voting. Where a single party holds an absolute majority in the council, its candidate for president may easily ascend to the office of regional presidency in the first round. In the absence of such a single-party majority, however, the politics of coalition ensues. To be successful in forming a majority, a candidate in the second round must piece together an alliance with another party, whose candidate would then stand down, or bargain with individuals to desert their own party's candidates in secret balloting. If no absolute majority emerges after a second round of voting, the candidate able to produce a relative majority in the third and final round is elected president.

The winning majority, whether a single party or a multiparty coalition, must then elect an executive bureau or cabinet. The actual executive cabinet is a group of between 4 and 16 vice presidents, the party composition of which usually—but not always—mirrors the party composition of the majority that elected the regional president. In addition, a body of secretaries (*commission permanente*) is elected, generally representing all other parties on the council. The regional president and the vice presidents thus constitute the clear executive power in the council and as such are the real prizes for political parties participating in the coalition game.

Party Participation in Coalition Governments

In large measure, the key players in the regional coalition game are the same as those that pursue and participate in French national government. The principal actors at both levels include the Socialist Party (Parti Socialiste, PS), the neo-Gaullists (Rassemblement pour la République, RPR), the Giscardian French Democratic Union (Union pour la Démocratie Française, UDF), the Communists (Parti Communiste Française, PCF), the National Front (Front National, FN), and the two ecologist parties (Les Verts and Génération Ecologie, GE). The Left-Radicals (Mouvement des Radicaux de Gauche, MRG) are closely affiliated with the PS and during the 1986-to-1995 period stood under the "majorité présidentielle" umbrella. On the Right, the UDF is itself a federation of parties, including the Christian Democrats (Centre des Démocrates Sociaux, CDS), the Social Democrats (Parti Social-Démocrate, PSD), the Republicans (Parti Républicain, PR), and the Radicals (Parti Radical, Rad). Another party contesting elections at both levels under the label of "diverse droite" is the Centre National des Indépendants et Paysans (CNI). Smaller parties, such as Jean-Pierre Soisson's France Unie (FU)—representing the non-Socialist forces of the presidential majority—and the antiecologist Chasse, Pêche, Nature et Traditions (CPNT), have also found their way into the regional assemblies.

The sheer number of parties in the French system distinguishes it clearly from the German system and even from the complex Belgian party system. However, with a two-ballot electoral system and a much smaller degree of proportionality determining parliamentary party strengths at the national level in France, the effective number of parties or party "blocs" seeking power in Paris is reduced. This is not the case in the outlying regions, where single-party majorities are highly exceptional, where two-party coalitions are themselves not especially abundant, and where multiparty coalitions are the norm. Thus, we can ask of coalition activity in France's regional assemblies: What factors motivate and constrain coalition building? What is the nature of national party policy toward regional alliances? What pressures do national party leaders bring to bear on their regional colleagues? And to what extent do patterns of regional collaboration influence cooperation in Paris?

In addition to answering these questions, by devoting attention to coalition politics in the French regional assemblies it is possible to correct the unfortunate tendency to view France (more appropriately, the French Fifth Republic) as a case unworthy of inclusion in studies of coalition government. Because the French president holds formal constitutional powers over the prime minister, "France has continued to be a problem case for coalition analysts" (Laver and Schofield 1990, 225) and is omitted from most cross-national studies of coalition government (see Browne and Franklin 1986; De Swaan 1973; Dodd 1976; Luebbert 1986; Taylor and Laver 1973). Most studies of coalition behavior tend to lose interest in France after the coalitional frenzy of the Fourth Republic and the onset of a supposed bipolarization in the Fifth. Granted, the rules of the game at the national level in France distinguish it from other systems: Article 8 of the Constitution gives the president power to appoint a prime minister and, on the latter's advice, to appoint and dismiss the other members of the government; Article 9 provides for the president to preside over the Council of Ministers; and Article 12 gives the president authority to dissolve the National Assembly, after consultation with the prime minister and the presidents of the two houses of Parliament. Rules matter. For our purposes, however, what is important is that national-level and regional-level governments are normally products of bargaining among multiple parties in the absence of outright parliamentary majorities.

Table 5.7 lists French national governments since 1959. Three recent periods stand out as particularly illustrative of coalitional activity: 1981–84, 1986–88, and 1993–95. In 1981 the admission of the Com-

Table 5.7
Presidents, Prime Ministers, and National Governments in France since 1959

President	Prime Minister	Dates	Parties in Government
De Gaulle	Debré (UNR)	1/59–4/62	UNR, MRP, Independents, Radical Socialists
	Pompidou (UNR)	4/62–12/62	UNR, MRP, Independents
	Pompidou (UNR-UDT)	12/62–1/66	UNR-UDT, Independent Republicans
	Pompidou (UNR-UDT)	1/66–4/67	UNR-UDT, Independent Republicans
	Pompidou (UNR-UDT)	4/67–5/68	UNR-UDT, Independent Republicans
	Pompidou (UNR-UDT)	5/68–7/68	UNR-UDT, Independent Republicans
	Couve de Murville (UDR)	7/68–6/69	UDR, Independent Republicans
Pompidou	Chaban-Delmas (UDR)	6/69–7/72	UDR, PDM, Independent Republicans
	Messmer (UDR)	7/72–4/73	UDR, CDP, Independent Republicans
	Messmer (UDR)	4/73–3/74	UDR, CDP, Independent Republicans
	Messmer (UDR)	3/74–5/74	UDR, CDP, Independent Republicans
Giscard d'Estaing	Chirac (UDR)	5/74–8/76	UDR, MRG, Independent Republicans
	Barre (UDR)	8/76–3/78	UDR, CDS, Radical Socialists, Independent Republicans
	Barre (UDR)	3/78–5/81	UDR, CDS, Radical Socialists, Independent Republicans
Mitterrand	Mauroy (PS)	5/81–6/81	PS, MRG
	Mauroy (PS)	6/81–3/83	PS, MRG, PCF
	Mauroy (PS)	3/83–7/84	PS, MRG, PCF
	Fabius (PS)	7/84–3/86	PS, MRG, PSU
	Chirac (RPR)	3/86–5/88	RPR, UDF-PR, UDF-CDS
	Rocard (PS)	5/88–6/88	PS, MRG, UDF, Independents
	Rocard (PS)	6/88–5/91	PS, MRG
	Cresson (PS)	5/91–7/92	PS, MRG, FU
	Beregovoy (PS)	7/92–4/93	PS, MRG, FU
	Balladur (RPR)	4/93–5/95	RPR, UDF
Chirac	Juppé (RPR)	5/95–	RPR, UDF

Note: UNR = Union pour la Nouvelle République; UDT = Union Démocratique du Travail; MRP = Mouvement Républicain Populaire; UDR = Union des Démocrates pour la République; PS = Parti Socialiste; CDS = Centre des Démocrates Sociaux; MRG = Mouvement des Radicaux de Gauche; RPR = Rassemblement pour la République; UDF = Union pour la Démocratie Française; DU = France Unie; PR = Parti Républicain; PSU = Parti Socialiste Unifié; PDM = Progrès de Démocratie Moderne; CDP = Centre Démocratie et Progrès

munist Party (PCF) into government, "prepared by negotiations between the PCF and PS leaders" (Wilson 1989, 69), temporarily bridged an ideological gulf between two parties whose campaigns "were almost as critical of their allies as of their opponents" (Machin 1989, 61). In 1986, the peculiar setting of "cohabitation" freed the government formation process of presidential control, thus forcing Jacques Chirac to consult with party leaders of the right-wing coalition over the party composition and ministerial assignments for his government. In both cases, "Consultations between the executive and party leaders [took] place during the formation of new governments" (Wilson 1989, 69). Similarly, with the devastating defeat of the Socialists in the 1993 legislative elections, cohabitation again returned, forcing Chirac, Giscard, and new Prime Minister Eduard Balladur to divide the spoils of cabinet portfolios among the RPR and UDF victors.

The important point here is not that the systemic characteristics of government formation in France mirror those of Belgium or Germany, or of multiparty systems in general. Clearly, the national government formation process in France differs in certain respects from that of most parliamentary democracies. The bottom line, instead, is that political parties in France—parties with distinct identities, and parties that compete electorally with their partners—combine to form majority governments.

These combinations, in turn, are not always duplicated in the regions. Table 5.8 lists regional governments in France since 1986. As is clear, the regions belong overwhelmingly to the parties of the Right. The demise of the French Left, undeniable by the time of the 1993 legislative elections, is evident as early as the 1986 regional elections. Even on the Right, neither the Gaullist RPR nor the Giscardian UDF— which in a sizable number of constituencies did have candidates standing against one another—chose to govern alone. Coalition building has been the rule in most regions. Regional coalitions, whether among the Communists and Socialists on the Left or among the Gaullists, Giscardians, and lepènists (FN) on the Right, contradict party alliances at the national level in France. So, too, do the regional governments that include the ecologists (Verts, GE) or the antiecologist reactionary CPNT.

The evolution of coalition patterns in the French regional assemblies is easily divided into two periods, the first coinciding with the 1986-to-1992 regional legislative term and the second coinciding with the 1992-to-1998 term.

THE EXTREME RIGHT AS KINGMAKERS (1986–92). When 27.8 million French voters went to the ballot boxes on 16 March 1986, they possessed an opportunity for the first time to elect representatives to autonomous regional councils. François Mitterrand's Socialist government was five years into its first *septennat*, Gaston Defferre's blueprint for decentralization was reality, and the bipolar structure that had characterized recent party politics was rapidly coming apart. The so-

Table 5.8

Partisan Composition of French Regional Governments, 1986 and 1992

Region	1986[a]	1992[b]
Alsace	UDF + RPR + DVD	UDF + RPR + DVD + FN*
Aquitaine	UDF + RPR + DVD + FN	UDF + RPR + DVD + CPNT*
Auvergne	UDF + RPR + DVD	UDF + RPR + DVD
Bourgogne	UDF + RPR + DVD	FU + PS + GE + VERTS*
Bretagne	UDF + RPR + DVD	UDF + RPR + DVD*
Centre	UDF + RPR + DVD	UDF + RPR + DVD*
Champagne-Ardenne	UDF + RPR + DVD*	UDF + RPR + DVD*
Corse	UDF + RPR + DVD + FN*	UDF + RPR + DVD
Franche-Comté	UDF + RPR + FN	UDF + RPR + DVD
Ile-de-France	UDF + RPR + DVD*	UDF + RPR + DVD*
Languedoc-Roussillon	UDF + RPR + DVD + FN	UDF + RPR + DVD*
Limousin	PS + PC	PS + PC + DVG + GE*
Lorraine	UDF + RPR + DVD*	UDF + RPR + DVD
Midi-Pyrénées	UDF + RPR + DVD	UDF + RPR + DVD + CPNT
Basse-Normandie	UDF + RPR + DVD	UDF + RPR + DVD
Haute-Normandie	UDF + RPR + DVD + FN	UDF + RPR + DVD + FN
Nord-Pas de Calais	PS + MRG + PC	VERTS + PS*
Pays de la Loire	UDF + RPR + DVD	UDF + RPR + DVD
Picardie	UDF + RPR + DVD + FN	UDF + RPR + DVD + CPNT*
Poitou-Charentes	UDF + RPR + DVD	UDF + RPR + CPNT
Provence-Côte d'Azur	UDF + RPR + DVD + FN	UDF + RPR + DVD*
Rhône-Alpes	UDF + RPR + DVD	UDF + RPR + DVD + CPNT + VERTS + GE*

Note: UDF = Union pour la démocratie française; PS = Partie socialiste; GE = Génération Ecologie; RPR = Rassemblement pour la République; PC = Parti communiste; DVD = Diverse Right; MRG = Mouvement des radicaux de gauche; FU = France unie; DVG = Diverse Left; CPNT = Chasse, pêche, nature et traditions; FN = Front national; VERTS = Greens.

*Indicates minority government.

[a]National parliamentary majority: UDF + RPR + DVD.

[b]National parliamentary majority: PS + MRG + FU.

called Union of the Left that propelled both the Socialists and the Communists into power in 1981 had broken down. Tensions on the Right, where the RPR-UDF alliance remained, were only slightly more muted. Farther right, Jean-Marie Le Pen's Front National was fresh off a solid performance in the 1984 regional assembly elections in Corsica. When the results of the March joint regional/legislative elections were tallied, votes for regional party lists so closely paralleled those for parliamentary parties vying for the National Assembly that few observers considered the regional elections worthy of independent analysis.

Immediately following the elections, Jacques Blanc, atop the UDF's list in Languedoc-Roussillon, signed a written agreement with eight Front National councilors to secure his election as president of the regional council. The UDF, along with its ally the RPR, had gained only 31% of the popular vote in the Mediterranean region. Without the added support of the FN (12%) and the CNI (9%), Blanc could not have found the necessary votes from the 65 councilors to gain the region's top executive prize. In return for the FN's support, the UDF rewarded Le Pen's forces with a coveted vice presidency and three seats on the executive bureau. In Paris, party leader Jacques Chirac, who had for years accused the Socialists of unholy alliances with the Communists, busied himself with the task of publicly denouncing the Front National and its "simplistic, anti-immigrant, pro-guillotine stances" (Machin 1989, 62), while turning a blind eye to Languedoc-Roussillon, Aquitaine, Franche-Comté, Haute-Normandie, and Picardie, where similar deals had been cut (Hainsworth and Loughlin 1989; Mazey 1986; Perrineau 1986, 1987).

In addition to these developments on the Right, the PS-MRG-PCF alliance continued to function, albeit poorly, at the regional level despite the collapse of the left-wing coalition at the national level (Schmidt 1990). The PCF supported Socialist candidates for regional president at the second round in Limousin and in Nord-Pas de Calais, these being the only two regions successfully preserved by the Left. In the case of Limousin, the regional party had actually been instructed by its national central committee *not* to cooperate (Mazey 1986). Elsewhere, the regional Communists took a much harder line against their old allies the Socialists, with PCF-PS alliances being "non-existent" (Hainsworth and Loughlin 1989, 159).

The French regional assemblies in 1986 were clearly important arenas for coalition bargaining in which partnerships frequently departed from the patterns in Paris. The new national parliamentary majority, a RPR-UDF government under Prime Minister Chirac cohabiting with the Socialist President Mitterrand, excluded the 35 Front National deputies. Nevertheless, by entering into explicit or tacit alliances with the mainstream Right in a handful of regions, the FN could claim a giant leap forward in its quest for national legitimacy.

MINORITY GOVERNMENT (1992–). Unlike the 1986 elections, the 22 March 1992 regional elections took place independent of national legislative elections. As such, the results of France's first election in three years had been awaited as a kind of barometer of political opinion at the midway point of Mitterrand's second seven-year presidential term. On the Left, the Socialists had tried to mobilize voters by warning about the dangers of letting the FN gain a permanent foothold in French politics. On the Right, the RPR and UDF, blaming the Socialists for economic slowdown, rising unemployment, urban blight, and an excess of Third World immigration, had promised to impose a "quarantaine républicaine" on the Front National and to reject any alliances with the extremists. Voting tallies registered the worst defeat for the Socialists since the party's modern inception in 1971, but the Socialists' losses did not translate directly into gains for the traditional Right. Le Pen's Front National registered impressive gains, as did Antoine Waechter's Verts and Brice Lalonde's Génération Ecologie, making all three parties powerful arbiters in the ensuing government formation process.

In 1986, 14 regional presidencies had been decided in the first round of voting; in 1992, conversely, only 4 presidential majorities emerged as easily in the first round. In 1986, only 4 elections of regional presidents had reached the third round; in 1992, conversely, a total of 16 contests were decided in the final round. In 1986, parties in 17 regional assemblies succeeded in establishing clear postelection governing majorities, and in only 3 cases did the failure to do so result in relative majorities (i.e., minority governments). Roughly the opposite occurred in 1992: in only seven regional assemblies did the three-stage bargaining process yield absolute majorities, whereas 14 councils wound up with minority governments that would be dependent subsequently upon producing voting coalitions in order to pass a budget or generate legislation. The differences between 1986 and 1992 are stark, and if coalition had been the order of the day in 1986, it was even more so in 1992.

The conservative parties remained true, in places, to their promise not to share power with the FN. In Aquitaine, Languedoc-Roussillon, Picardie, Provence-Alpes-Côte d'Azur, and Rhône-Alpes, for example, the RPR-UDF forces accepted minority government over the support of the Front National, which would have assured clear and safe majorities for the Right. Elsewhere, the formation of conservative regional governments was clouded by accusations of collusion with the FN, this being the case in Alsace, Franche-Comté, and Haute-Normandie. Only in Alsace and Haute-Normandie, however, did the FN obtain a regional vice presidency. In lieu of coalitions with the FN, the conservatives formed coalitions with André Goustat's antiecologist reactionary party, CPNT, which had obtained 29 council seats across 13 regions. The CPNT thus gained a share of power in four regional governments. Alternatively, the Right courted even the ecologists, as in Rhône-Alpes, where Charles Millon (UDF-PR) attempted to shore up his weak "majority" (64 seats out of 157) by awarding vice presidencies to the Verts and GE.

The Socialists' options were more limited, and their success was minimal. In the traditional regional bastion of Limousin, Robert Savy (PS) managed to put together an alliance of Socialists, Communists, and the Génération Ecologie that produced a relative majority and gave the presidency to Savy. In Nord-Pas de Calais, an even greater Socialist stronghold, the PS national government minister, Michael Delebarre, failed to negotiate the support of the PCF and was forced to enter an unprecedented coalition with the Verts under the presidency of Marie-Christine Blandin, a relatively unknown 38-year-old professor of natural sciences and member of Greenpeace.

The events in Lorraine and Bourgogne regions, however, proved even more controversial. In each region, a non-Socialist minister in Prime Minister Edith Cresson's cabinet government succeeded in gaining the regional presidency; in both cases, however, charges of alliance with the FN proved destabilizing. In Lorraine, a coalition of Socialists, Communists, and Greens helped elect Jean-Marie Rausch (France Unie) regional president in the third round. Subsequent charges that Rausch had negotiated the support of the FN broke the coalition and forced Rausch to resign his post two days after the election. In Bourgogne, a similar coalition elected Jean-Pierre Soisson (France Unie), Cresson's civil service minister, and again the supposed support of one or more FN councilors spawned charges and countercharges. Soisson, protesting suggestions from his own prime minister that he had knowingly colluded with the far Right, resigned his national ministerial portfolio while keeping the regional presidency in an attempt to construct the foundations of a "laboratoire de l'ouverture."[34]

Coalition building after the 1992 regional elections proved to be "a feverish political journey, full of surprises."[35] Among the national-level consequences were a shake-up in the cabinet and the subsequent replacement of Prime Minister Edith Cresson with Pierre Beregovoy. The foundation for Michel Rocard's "big bang," or alliance among Socialists, reformed Communists, centrists, and ecologists, had also been laid with regional experiments such as the one in Nord-Pas de Calais. For their part, the RPR and UDF could reclaim some but not all of the honor lost through their 1986 alliances with the extreme Right. Although excluded from most of the official majorities of which it had been a part since 1986, the Front National found that it could still reap the benefits of the majority formation process simply by inflicting disorder on it.

General Patterns

As in both the Belgian and German cases, regional sections of national political parties in France find themselves bargaining—and rewarding—their national-level adversaries. There is, as well, variance in the behavior of parties across the two time points and across the regions. Why did the PCF support the PS in some regions but not in others? Why did the Green parties support the Left in some coalition situations and the Right in others? Why did the conservative parties establish power-sharing arrangements with the extreme Right in 1986 but back off from the practice in 1992? Similarly, why did the Right's quarantine of the FN break down in some cases? These questions suggest that regional-level coalition behavior can provide the impetus to reintegrate the French case into coalition studies.

Cross-Country Comparisons

Clearly, the intermediate-level legislatures and executives in Belgium, Germany, and France are not uniform in their structures. Each, however, has a distinguishable executive body, a directly elected representative assembly, and some power to tax, spend, and pass legislation— that is, each has meaningful political relevance. In addition, the Belgian provincial/regional assemblies, the German state parliaments, and the French regional councils each exhibit interesting coalition dynamics. Of course, some aspects of coalition behavior in the respective institutions are a function of the basic, static structural environments in which they occur. Table 5.9 draws together relevant comparative institutional and procedural aspects of subnational government in each of the three countries.

It is, for one thing, easier to spot variation at one time point in the French regional councils than in the Belgian provinces because there

Table 5.9

Institutional and Procedural Dimensions of Subnational Assemblies and Government Life Cycles

	Belgium		France	Germany
	Provincial Councils	Regional Parliaments	Regional Councils	State Parliaments
Number	10	3	22	16
Size range in seats	50–90	75–118	43–209	60–237
Average number of parties in assembly (1994)	5.7	7.3	7.9	3.9
Length of legislative period	6 years	5 years	6 years	4–5 years
Dismissed with national parliament	No (Yes, before 1994)	No	No	No
Directly elected	Yes	Yes	Yes	Yes
Elections concurrent with national parliamentary elections	No (Yes, before 1994)	Yes—first elections No—subsequent elections	Yes—1986 No—1992	No
Possible to hold concurrent mandate in national parliament	No	No	Yes	No
Executive	Governor/ permanent deputation	Minister-president/ cabinet of ministers	President/ bureau of vice presidents	Minister-president/ cabinet of ministers
Executive elected by formal investiture vote in assembly	Governor—no, central government appointee Permanent deputation—yes	Yes	Yes	Yes
Executive chosen by secret ballot	Yes	Yes	Yes	Yes
Executive revocable by formal no-confidence vote in assembly	No	No	No	Yes

133

are simply so many more assemblies in France. Conversely, it is more difficult to generalize about longitudinal patterns in the French case because there have been only two regional elections, whereas change can be measured more accurately in Belgium and Germany. Further, it should be noted from these basic descriptive data that the universe of possible coalition combinations is likely to be larger in the French regions, where on average almost eight parties are represented in the councils, as compared to just four in the German state parliaments.

Additionally, these data suggest from the outset that in terms of cross-national comparisons, national-subnational linkages should be strongest in France, where it is possible to hold concurrent mandates as a regional councilor and a national deputy. This fact, however, does little to explain within-nation variance. Along similar lines, concerning the so-called "nationalization" of local electoral systems, it should be kept in mind that provincial elections in Belgium have historically taken place on the same day as national legislative elections. A final matter to be considered is the termination of subnational coalitions, which in the German Länder can take place between elections after a formal vote of no confidence. There is no such provision for a midterm dismissal of the executive coalition in Belgium, and in France regional governments usually change only with elections or the resignation of a regional president. This makes the possibility of midterm coalition change greatest in Germany.

Across all cases, it is evident that political parties are powerful intermediaries between electorates and governmental authority at subnational levels. When provincial, regional, or state elections make it possible for any one of a number of different governments to materialize, each representing a different combination of parties, then the choices made by parties during the government formation process are clearly important. Outcomes reflect choices. That these choices are made largely in secret does not lend much transparency or accountability to the process.

In establishing rules, structures, and history, it has been an important aim to confirm the existence of variation in coalition outcomes within each country. Since this study is explicitly comparative in purpose and in method, the concluding section of this chapter is a compilation of comparative coalition outcomes, presented in keeping with the descriptive intentions of the chapter but also serving as a useful segue into the analytical chapters that follow. A series of pie charts illustrate coalition behavior across levels of government according to the following criteria: type of government formed, coalition size in seats, number of parties in coalition, congruence with national coalitions, ideological "connectedness" of coalitions, and responsiveness to the verdict of the electorate (inclusion of largest legislative party; inclusion of winners/losers).

Government Types

Figure 5.4 compares the types of governments formed across national and subnational assemblies in Belgium, France, and Germany. It is clear from these data that in all three countries coalition government is a fact of political life. Of the 263 cases of subnational government formation examined, 188 (71.5%) resulted in some form of power-sharing arrangement between two or more political parties. The incidence of multiparty government is even greater at the national level in the three countries, where all 62 governments have been multiparty coalitions. At the subnational level, only in the German Landtage does single-party government occur more frequently than coalition government.

Coalition Size in Seats

Formal theoretical assumptions about coalition formation frequently suggest that the most likely outcomes are those that minimize the membership size of coalitions, specifically the number of seats or individual parliamentarians contained within the coalition. While the object here is not to apply a stringent test of such assumptions, for descriptive purposes it is useful to note that many, if not most, governing coalitions, at both levels of government in Belgium, France, and Germany, do contain excess members (figure 5.5). Post hoc observation of these coalition outcomes suggests that simple reliance on certain assumptions about coalition size with respect to individuals will not yield a powerful or accurate explanation.

Of 188 coalition governments responsible to territorial assemblies, 123 (65.6%) contained excess individual members, whereas 65 (34.6%) contained the minimum required, of which 27 actually mustered less than the required minimum winning threshold (assuming a 50% + 1 winning rule). Applying size assumptions to Belgian national government runs into problems in that the literal winning threshold (50% + 1) for government formation is not always the de facto winning threshold. Constitutional revision, in which recent Belgian governments have been mired, requires a two-thirds parliamentary majority.[36] Conse-

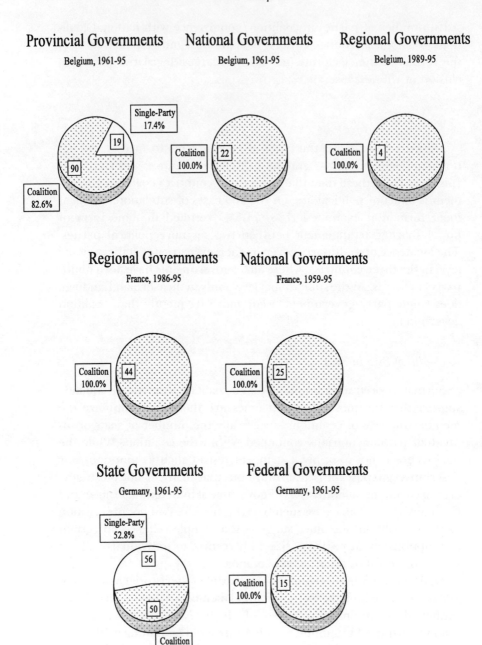

Figure 5.4 National and Subnational Government Types

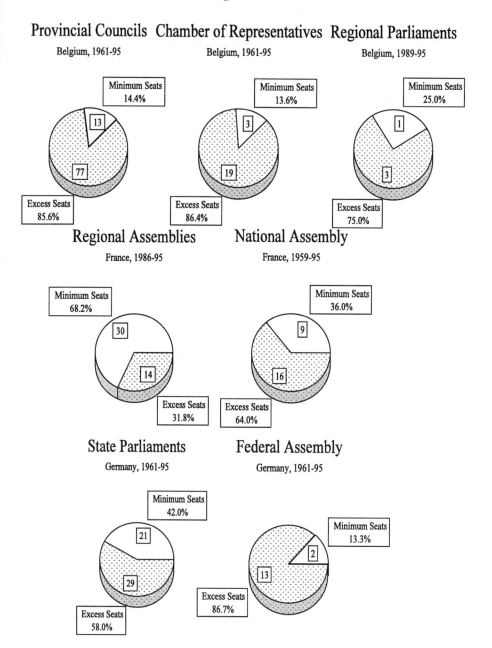

Figure 5.5   Size of Governing Coalition in Parliamentary Seats

quently, an overwhelming 86.4% of Belgian governments since 1961 have contained "excess" members. Formally, almost all German federal governments since 1961 have contained more than the minimum number of deputies required. However, periodic defections during the course of a legislative period have shrunk many postelection coalition majorities. While French parties do largely adhere to minimum size conditions in regional government, even to the extent of preferring minority arrangements over larger, safer majorities, such has not been the case in national government, where 64% of the Fifth Republic's cabinet governments have contained spare members.

Number of Parties in Coalition

Perhaps a better initial gauge of the size characteristics of coalitions is the number of political parties agreeing to participate in an eventual government (figure 5.6). If parties are disciplined units, then while coalitions may contain excess individuals, they may still contain only the minimum necessary number of parties. The data indicate that most coalitions in all but French national government contain only the minimum number of parties needed to form a majority. Approximately four of every five governing coalitions invested by subnational parliaments across all three countries combined do meet formal expectations about minimum numbers of parties.

Congruence with National Coalitions

Data from coalitions in the Belgian provinces and regions, the French regions, and the German Land parliaments reveal that parties in each subnational assembly do stray from national coalition arrangements (figure 5.7). Apparently in spite of some of the structural and procedural differences between subnational government and party systems in the three countries, this basic fact characterizes all three countries. The propensity to form incongruent coalitions is greatest in the Belgian provinces. This tendency is still present but weaker in France, where somewhat fewer than half (43.2%) of the power-sharing arrangements in regional executives deviated from existing national alliances. In the German Länder, two of every five governments since 1961 have failed to match the majority-versus-opposition alignments existing in federal government. This suggests important exceptions to the policy of congruence or matching (*Gleichschaltung*).

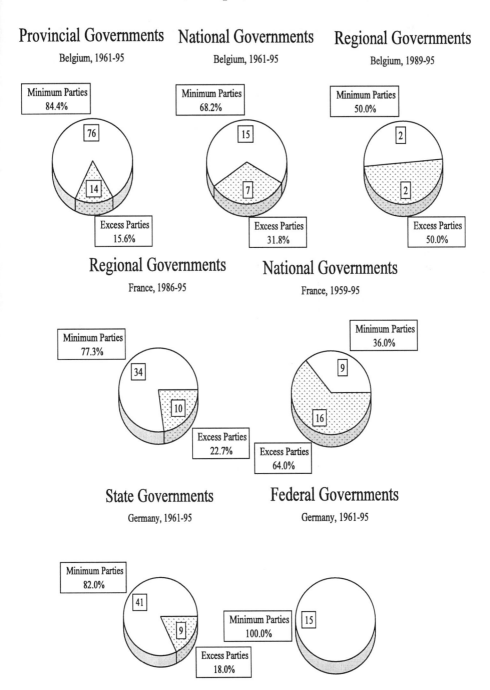

Figure 5.6 Number of Parties in Governing Coalitions

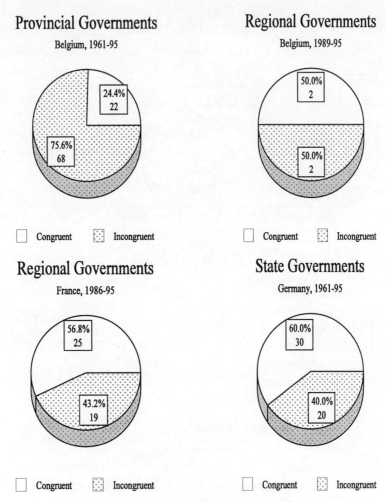

Figure 5.7 National-Subnational Congruence of Governing Coalitions

"Connectedness" of Coalitions

A fourth dimension that deserves initial comparison is the extent to which the parties participating in a governing coalition are "connected" in an ideological or policy sense. Using standard left-right placements of parties in each country,[37] it is possible to observe that connectedness is indeed a characteristic of coalitions at both levels of government (figure 5.8). Christian Social parties at the center of the Belgian party system have historically formed national governments

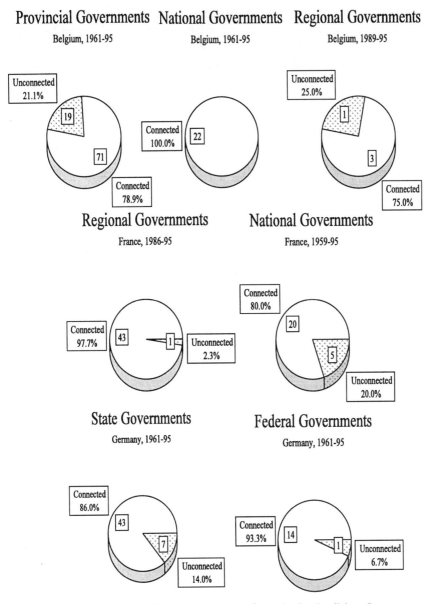

Figure 5.8 Ideological "Connectedness" of Parties in Coalition Governments

with Socialists to their immediate left or Liberals to their immediate right. In the provinces, however, Socialists and Liberals often bypass the center and construct unconnected, nonideological "red-blue" coalitions. In French national government, cohesive party blocs on the left and right of the political spectrum generally accede to government power, although radical socialists have joined conservative cabinets and conservatives have participated in Socialist cabinets on several occasions. While postelection "presidential" coalitions in the French regions are frequently unconnected, with right-wing extremists supporting Socialist presidential candidates and ecologists supporting conservatives, the actual power-sharing, executive coalitions generally do overwhelmingly tend to be connected. The much simpler party system in Germany and its more restricted set of coalition alternatives make connected coalitions at both levels of government especially likely. If we follow Castles and Mair (1984), Inglehart and Klingemann (1987), and Sani and Sartori (1983) in considering the FDP to be located strategically between the SPD and CDU/CSU, then all but the "grand" CDU-SPD coalitions and the SPD's singular experiences governing Hesse with the German Party (GDP) and Hamburg with the Statt Partei may be considered connected.

Responsiveness to the Verdict of the Electorate

A more practical concern is the extent to which postelection coalition bargaining actually results in government that reflects the verdict of the electorate. Granted, elections that result in no party's holding an absolute majority of seats do not send clear messages to the parties faced with forming a government. Parties can, presumably, still try to interpret the vote. The responsiveness of parties to electoral verdicts can be measured indirectly through (1) the presence in government of the party holding a plurality of parliamentary seats and (2) the presence in government of at least one party whose vote share is equal to or greater than its vote share at the preceding election.

The charts in figure 5.9 accordingly compare the inclusion in winning coalitions of the party initially strongest in resources (i.e., votes and seats) across national and subnational levels of government. Of the 188 subnational governments formed, a substantial 44 (23.4%) failed to include the strongest single legislative party. In approximately one of every four cases, then, electoral strength paradoxically translates into governmental weakness. This apparent denial of electoral

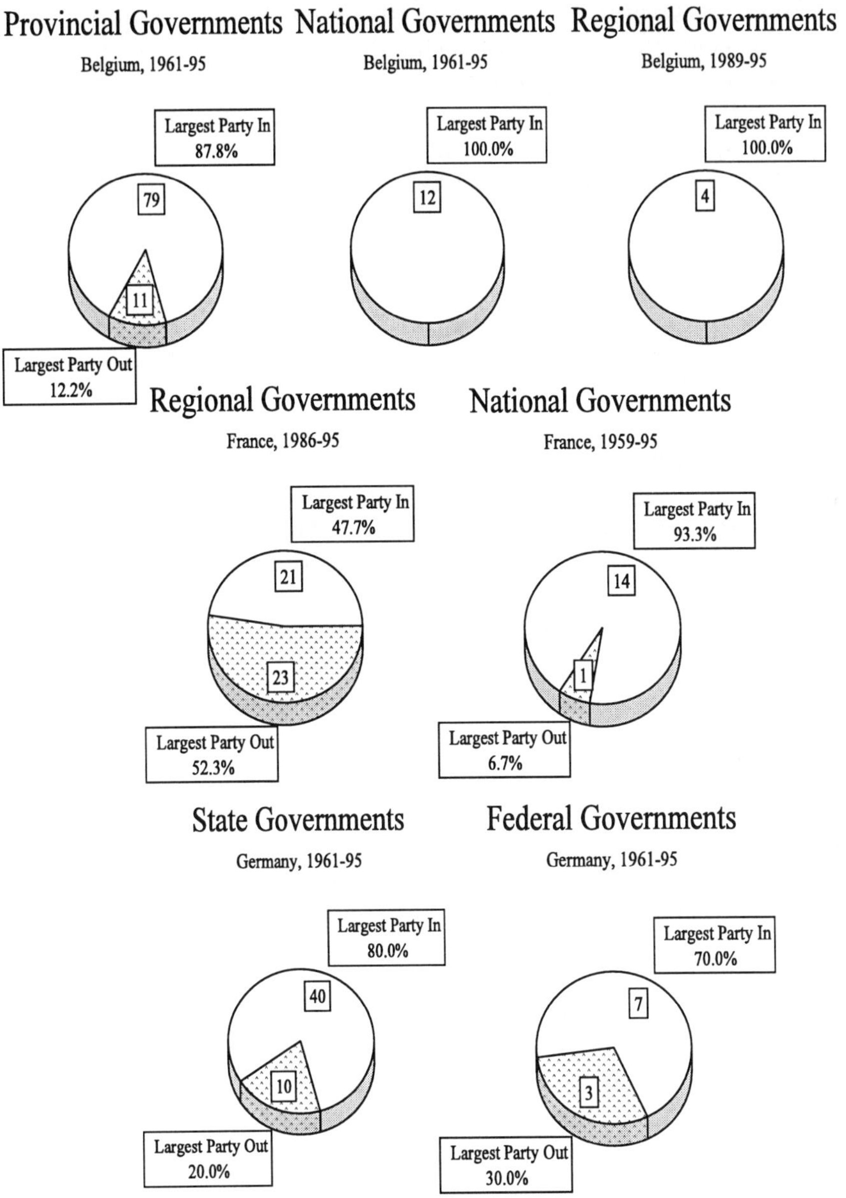

Provincial Governments   National Governments   Regional Governments

Belgium, 1961-95   Belgium, 1961-95   Belgium, 1989-95

Largest Party In
87.8%

Largest Party In
100.0%

Largest Party In
100.0%

79

12

4

11

Largest Party Out
12.2%

Regional Governments   National Governments

France, 1986-95   France, 1959-95

Largest Party In
47.7%

Largest Party In
93.3%

21

14

23

1

Largest Party Out
52.3%

Largest Party Out
6.7%

State Governments   Federal Governments

Germany, 1961-95   Germany, 1961-95

Largest Party In
80.0%

Largest Party In
70.0%

40

7

10

3

Largest Party Out
20.0%

Largest Party Out
30.0%

Figure 5.9 Membership of Largest Legislative Party in Governing Coalition

verdicts occurs also in national government, though to a lesser extent. If we exclude midterm coalition changes and focus only on coalitions formed in the immediate aftermath of elections, we find that only four national governments in our sample denied the largest parliamentary party a share of the ministerial portfolios. Such "coalitions of minorities" appear most likely in Germany. Given the data at hand, then, parties in subnational legislatures appear more inclined than their national counterparts to gang up on the party supported by the plurality of the voters. This pattern is one not likely to go unnoticed by democratic theorists or by voters.

A second outcome of coalition bargaining that can indicate responsiveness to electoral verdicts is whether parties in territorial assemblies construct governments of "winners" or "losers." Evidence indicates that "coalitions of losers" are not unusual at either the subnational or the national level (figure 5.10). Better than one in five subnational coalition governments includes only parties that have lost vote shares since the previous election. In the Belgian provinces, a substantial 27% of coalition governments have contained only election "losers." These are the kind of data that tend to give pause to those considering the "democratic" merits of coalition government.

Summary

This chapter has sought to introduce the actual politics of coalition as it has played out in the intermediate-level subnational assemblies of three European countries. The chapter, in short, places our study in proper historical and institutional context. In doing so, it has also revealed a substantial amount of meaningful political behavior worthy of explanation, not the least of which is the apparent propensity of parties at provincial and regional levels to form coalition governments incongruent with those in existence nationally. The most important behavioral patterns revealed by our inventory of subnational governments are recorded in table 5.10.

Addressing basic behavioral patterns has revealed several important findings. It is evident, first, that the translation of electoral strength into governmental power is not automatic at subnational levels. Second, it is apparent that minority or relative majority government can be a preferred alternative of parties competing in the subnational arena. Oversized subnational governments are common as well, fur-

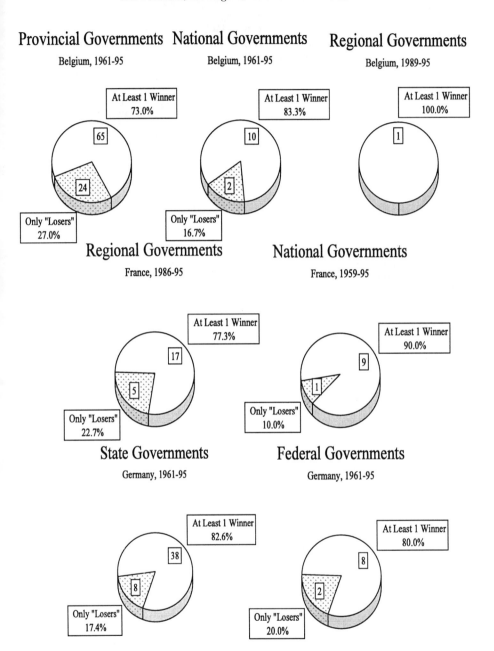

Figure 5.10   Composition of Postelection Coalition Governments, by Electoral Success

Table 5.10

Government Formation in Belgian, French, and German Subnational Assemblies:
Comparisons of Coalition Outcomes

Institution	Belgium (1961–95)		France (1986–92)	Germany (1960–94) West	East
	Conseil Provincial/ Provincieraad	Conseil Régional/ Gewestraad	Conseil Régional	Landtag	
N of units analyzed	9–10	3	22	11	5
N of governments formed	109	4	44	96	10
Government types (%)					
Single-party majority	15	0	0	49	30
Single-party minority	2	0	0	5	0
Coalition majority	83	100	61	46	10
Coalition minority	0	0	39	2	60
% of coalition governments excluding party with plurality of seats (%)	12	0	52	22	10
% of coalition governments including only election "losers"	27*	0**	23	17	0
% of coalition governments incongruent with national governments-vs.-opposition alignments	76	50	43	39	43
% of coalition governments whose members are ideologically "unconnected"	21	0	0	12	29
% of all governments including more parties than required to "win"	16	50	23	19	14
Cooperative or "grand" coalitions including #1 and #2 parties (%)	60	25	25	9	29

*Excludes coalitions formed in new provinces of Vlaams Brabant and Brabant Wallon after 1994 elections.

**Only comparison here is between governments formed after 1989 and 1995 regional assembly elections in Brussels.

ther indicating that a size principle is not absolute. There is, in short, variation in coalition outcomes. Outcomes reflect *choices,* not necessarily electoral verdicts, obligatory duplications of national arrangements, or strict adherence to zero-sum competition. Having established variation, the task of subsequent chapters is to test the theoretical relationships posited in chapter 3 in order to impose some analytical order on the range of behavior exhibited by parties competing for power in territorial parliaments.

Chapter Six

Do Electoral Verdicts Matter?
The Effects of Competition
on Strategic Choice

The election? It can mean nothing. In forming a new majority, anything goes.

—Regional Councilor,
Nord-Pas de Calais (France)

The people speak, then we act.

—Regional Councilor,
Lorraine (France)

Ideally, the act of government formation in territorial parliaments should serve to commission and legitimize the direction of public policy in a province, region, or state. In this single act lies any newly elected assembly's first and most overt expression of "opinion-policy congruence" (Page, 1994). Where election results play little or no role in determining the choice of government, however, the veracity of this legitimizing function tends to come into question. In such cases, a fundamental principle of representative democracy—that the government, at whatever level of the polity, should enjoy the support of the electorate—may, to some, seem lost. The extent to which this elemental linkage between representatives and voters, the "electoral connection," actually compels or constrains regional parliamentarians and provincial councilors at the occasion of their first major postelection decision is the subject of this chapter.

Bogdanor (1983) writes that "elections do not choose governments, they alter the power relations between the parties. . . . The formation of a government, then, is the process of artificially constructing a ma-

147

jority" (272). Characterizing the government formation process as "artificial" is as accurate at subnational levels as it is at the national level. At both levels, political parties, not voters, ultimately decide the composition and character of a government. Identifying the factors that influence the manufacturing of governing majorities is our task, and to that end we focus here on the relative influences of electoral competition, electoral accountability, and electoral change. Following chapter 3's theoretical discussion and drawing upon a mix of historical, interview, and survey data, the challenge is to determine whether key characteristics of electoral environments (namely, their instability and localism) shape the ways in which representatives view the responsibilities of government formation. If electoral context "matters," then the opportunities and constraints produced by varying environments may help explain why, for example, local sections of the same national political party choose different coalition strategies in different provinces, regions, and states.

Dilemmas of Electoral Accountability, Responsiveness, and Transparency

Indirect or artificial selection of governments highlights a host of normative dilemmas inherent in most parliamentary systems. The existence of such dilemmas frames our inquiry. To illustrate the level of controversy and the direction of elite thinking about certain aspects of government formation and multiparty coalitions, evidence may be found first in the responses of sitting provincial and regional councilors to a set of explicitly normative statements (table 6.1). In personal interviews with elected representatives in Belgium, France, and Germany conducted during the September 1992–September 1993 period, politicians were asked to react to carefully worded statements regarding electoral accountability, disclosure of coalition intentions, government formation by secret ballot, publication of coalition agreements, alliances with extremist parties, and the formation of "coalitions of losers."

The responses are presented here purely for descriptive and suggestive purposes. What is important is that the data suggest some clear and consistent patterns as well as some tensions among politicians as they reflect upon the responsibilities of forming new governments. For instance, while a majority of those interviewed in each country

Table 6.1

Representatives' Responses to Normative Dilemmas of Coalition Government

		Agree (%)	Disagree (%)
Item 1. Coalition Decisions and Electoral Accountability	"Voters should hold individual politicians and their parties accountable for the legislative and power-sharing alliances they form following an election."		
	Belgium (N = 44)	63.6	36.4
	France (N = 31)	67.7	32.3
	Germany (N = 22)	77.3	22.7
	Total	68.0	32.0
Item 2. Disclosure of Coalition Plans during Campaign	"Parties should be required to reveal their coalition preferences during an election campaign in order to give voters a better basis upon which to choose."		
	Belgium (N = 44)	27.3	72.7
	France (N = 31)	41.9	58.1
	Germany (N = 22)	36.4	63.6
	Total	34.0	66.0
Item 3. Government Formation by Secret Ballot	"Selection of a governing executive by secret ballot should be eliminated, as it makes representatives accountable to neither the voters nor the party."		
	Belgium (N = 43)	32.6	67.4
	France (N = 30)	13.3	86.7
	Germany (N = 22)	45.4	54.6
	Total	29.5	70.5
Item 4. Publication of Coalition Agreements	"Coalition agreements should be made available to the public in written form."		
	Belgium (N = 44)	47.7	52.3
	France (N = 31)	48.4	51.6
	Germany (N = 19)	63.2	36.8
	Total	51.1	48.9
Item 5. Coalition Building and "Extreme" Parties	"It is the responsibility of all democratic parties, no matter the differences normally separating them, to govern together against an extreme party, even if the extreme party has won a plurality of votes and seats in a fair, democratic election."		
	Belgium (N = 44)	70.5	29.5
	France (N = 31)	32.3	67.7
	Germany (N = 19)	73.7	26.3
	Total	58.5	41.5
Item 6. Representation and "Coalitions of Losers"	"A governing coalition that contains only parties that have lost votes and seats since the previous election is a "losers' coalition" and is an evasion of the electorate's verdict."		
	Belgium (N = 44)	22.3	77.3
	France (N = 31)	19.4	80.6
	Germany (N = 20)	50.0	50.0
	Total	37.9	62.1

answered that voters *should* hold them accountable for decisions of coalition participation (item 1), a rather surprising one-third envisioned
no "electoral connection." Some parties campaign openly on the basis
of specified coalition intentions, while others campaign on promises
not to collaborate with a certain other party or parties. But generally
voters are in the dark about what parties intend to do once the votes
are counted. Two-thirds of the subnational parliamentarians disagreed with the proposition that parties should divulge coalition preferences and intentions during election campaigns (item 2). This, many
politicians explained, would tie their hands during negotiations. As for
postelection issues, several representatives felt that formal investiture
of new governments by secret ballot (item 3) decreases accountability
and eliminates transparency; still, the clear majority wanted to pre-
serve this procedural rule because it enhances rather than detracts
from the "democraticness" of the government formation process. The
deals upon which investiture votes are won are frequently struck beyond the reach of journalists—if not behind closed council chamber
doors, then literally anywhere, from restaurants to restrooms. The
question of whether the texts of signed coalition agreements, once successfully negotiated by party leaders, should enter the public domain
(item 4) generates a real split in thinking among provincial and regional politicians.

One dilemma often faced by parties in regional or local assemblies
before their colleagues in national parliament is how to deal with extreme, fringe, or new parties that emerge from the grass roots. Should
the threatening party be isolated, or should it be incorporated into the
power structure in order to uncloak it as incapable of effective governance? This dilemma is especially tricky when the so-called pariah
party gains a plurality of votes and seats in a democratic election (item
5). When a question regarding the duty of "democratic" parties to
form blocking coalitions against "extreme" parties was asked systematically of 94 elected subnational assembly members, the responses
proved indicative of the ways in which mainstream parties in the respective countries approach the dilemma in practice. In both Belgium
and Germany, the preference has been to isolate insurgent parties perceived as extreme (Vlaams Blok and Front National in Belgium, the
Republicans and the Party of Democratic Socialism in Germany). Conversely, in France there has been considerable collaboration between
mainstream center-right parties and the Front National of Jean-Marie
Le Pen.

Similarly, there is frequent criticism that parties are insensitive to shifts in electoral support and that they use the coalition process to evade electoral verdicts. Here the politics of mutual self-preservation is said to win out over responsiveness to popular will. When asked straightforwardly whether governments composed strictly of parties that have lost votes and assembly seats since the previous election are "losers' coalitions" and thus rejections of the electorate's wishes (item 6), almost two-thirds of the 95 politicians interviewed disagreed. What matters, many argued, is simply meeting the 50% + 1 threshold for winning in the assembly. Others, especially the German Landtag deputies, place higher value on choosing combinations of parties that reflect not only the *level* of public support but the *direction* as well.

For our purposes, what matters is the admission from a large number of key players in the power game that these dilemmas exist. The apparent vagaries of the "electoral connection" prompt closer examination. One method for testing the strength of this connection lies in assessing the impact of two variables: *electoral volatility* and *electoral localization*. These two variables represent, as outlined in chapter 3, the extent of competitiveness, uncertainty, and instability present in subnational electoral environments. Competitiveness, to restate the argument, should increase the risks of coalition building, heighten the pressures of accountability for strategic choices, and restrict the number of feasible coalition alternatives. Competition, uncertainty, and instability should, in other words, restrict coalition choice. Under conditions of competitive uncertainty, politicians and parties faced with strategic dilemmas should recognize the presence of an electoral constraint and thus should be expected to behave in ways different than they would if they enjoyed the relative security of stable vote shares and "nationalized" elections. In short, electoral competition should constrain the degree to which parties can make decisions independent of the preferences of the local electorate.

To investigate these possibilities, this chapter first provides measures of electoral volatility and electoral localization, respectively, in the provinces and regions of Germany, Belgium, and France. These measures yield distinct groupings of electoral environments within each country. Once regions and provinces have been dichotomized according to volatility and localization, the chapter proposes combining the two measures to produce a typology of electoral environments in the three countries. This done, hypotheses are tested linking electoral conditions with individual-level attitudes and with actual coalition out-

comes. The evidence suggests how individuals and groups endowed
with political responsibility weigh the costs and benefits of alternative
strategies according to the electoral environments in which they must
act. From these data, electoral uncertainty and instability emerge as
powerful constraints on individual representatives' perceptions of strategic freedom. However, indications that *individual perceptions* of risk
and accountability often fail to translate into predictable forms of *collective behavior* suggest that although electoral verdicts may "matter," it
may be organizational constraints (i.e., party-legislator links) rather
than electoral constraints (i.e., voter-legislator links) that matter most.

Electoral Volatility

Measuring volatility is a fairly straightforward endeavor. Previous work
by Denters (1985) and Pedersen (1983) provides rough guides, although Pedersen's indicators examine volatility only in national party
systems. Electoral volatility is the "average of the absolute inter-election
differences between the voting shares of particular . . . political parties" in subnational elections across an established period of time (Denters 1985, 306). In this way, greater volatility is indicated by larger net
changes in voting shares. A region, state, or province's mean volatility
is the average change across successive elections for all or a select number of parties. If the posited relationships between electoral context
and coalition behavior are to hold, then larger net changes and greater
volatility should be sufficiently obvious to politicians and party leaders
to act as a constraint on strategic behavior, including coalition choice.
The formulas for volatility that we use are:

$$\text{Volatility}_{\text{Party}} = [\Sigma|P_{a(t)} - P_{a(t+1)}| + |P_{a(t+1)} - P_{a(t+2)}| + |P_{a(t+n)} - P_{a(t+n\ldots)}|]/E,$$

where $P_{a(t)}$ = the voting share of party a in subnational election at time
t, and E = number of elections, and where:

$$\text{Volatility}_{\text{Subnational Unit}} = [\text{Volatility}_{\text{Party }A} + \text{Volatility}_{\text{Party }B\ldots n}]/P,$$

when P = number of parties.

Data from provincial and regional assembly elections allow for measurements of volatility in each of the three countries.[1]

Electoral Volatility in the German Länder, Belgian Provinces, and French Regions

Observers of coalition politics in Germany frequently suggest that "major trends in electoral change can be observed at state level before they occur in the federal party system" (Müller-Rommel 1989, 117). The question here, however, is to what extent volatility differs geographically, and the corresponding expectation is that such differences may have consequences for alliance building in the respective Land parliaments. Using the indicator proposed above, the average volatility of West German state party systems is measured from the early 1960s (table 6.2).[2] Levels of electoral change are measured for two periods, the pre-Greens period (1961–77) and the Greens period (1978–95). For the sake of consistency, the measure includes interelection differences in vote shares for the CDU, SPD, FDP, and Die Grünen, excluding minor parties and others consistently falling under the 5% threshold. While the method of computation is somewhat different and the time period extended, these findings generally concur with those of Müller-Rommel (1989) and Padgett (1991). Measuring volatility in the German Länder thus produces evidence, at least on the surface, of more unstable electoral systems, as in the city-states of Bremen, Hamburg, and Berlin, and more static electoral systems, as in Bavaria and North Rhine–Westphalia.[3]

The same measure can be applied to the Belgian provinces. Table 6.2 presents the mean volatility of each of the nine pre–federal era provinces for the period 1961–91.[4] The 30-year span is divided in two parts (1961–76, 1977–91), covering elections both before and after the first participation of "community" parties in coalition governments. The observation that leaps out immediately is that volatility has been greatest in the Walloon provinces, whereas it has been more moderate in Flanders. Namur, for example, has considerably greater instability than East Flanders. In practical terms, this has meant that each of the parties (e.g., PS, PSC, PRL, Ecolo) competing for the 285,000 votes in Namur on average either gains or loses 12,800 votes between elections. If the Socialist Party in Namur had gained 12,800 votes in 1991 over its 1987 total, the party would have secured an absolute majority in the provincial assembly. Instead, the PS actually lost 13,800 votes and four seats, primarily to the Ecolos (+15,000), thus necessitating a coalition with the liberal PRL. In other words, major and consistent fluctuation in provincial voting patterns has meant that coalitional politics

Table 6.2

Electoral Volatility in Germany, Belgium, and France

German Länder	Period I, 1961–77 (%)	Period II, 1978–95 (%)	Land Average (%)	Number of Election Periods	Müller-Rommel Rank,* 1956–83	Padgett Rank,** 1975–90
Bremen	4.5	4.6	4.5	8	1	1
Hamburg	4.6	4.3	4.4	10	4	2
Berlin	4.2	3.3***	3.7	7	—	—
Saarland	3.7	3.5	3.6	7	3	3
Baden-Württemberg	4.6	2.1	3.4	8	2	8
Hessen	3.9	2.5	3.0	9	6	5
Rhineland-Palatinate	2.6	3.1	2.9	7	7	4
Lower Saxony	2.9	2.4	2.7	8	5	7
Schleswig-Holstein	2.1	2.9	2.6	8	10	6
North Rhine–Westphalia	2.5	2.2	2.4	7	9	10
Bavaria	2.4	1.8	2.0	8	8	9
German Average	3.4	3.0	3.3	7.9		

*Müller-Rommel (1989), 119.

**Padgett (1991), 6.

***Appropriate time period is 1978–89. No meaningful comparison of 1990 Land election in united Berlin can be made to previous Land elections.

154

Belgian Provinces	Period I, 1961–76 (%)	Period II, 1977–91 (%)	Province Average (%)	N of Election Periods
Namur	5.2	3.6	4.5	10
Hainaut	4.2	3.0	3.7	10
Liège	4.3	2.9	3.7	10
Luxembourg	4.2	3.0	3.7	10
Limburg	3.5	2.8	3.2	10
Antwerp	3.3	3.0	3.2	10
West Flanders	2.8	3.1	2.9	10
East Flanders	2.5	3.1	2.8	10
Brabant	3.3	2.1	2.7	10
Provincial Average	3.7	3.0	3.4	10
Brussels Region			1.2 (1989–95)	1

French Regions	Period 1986–92 (%)	French Regions	Period 1986–92 (%)
Lorraine	9.6	Ile-de-France	8.0
Rhône-Alpes	9.4	Pays-de-la Loire	7.8
Provence-Alpes Côte d'Azur	9.4	Alsace	7.6
Franche-Comté	9.2	Centre	7.5
Champagne-Ardenne	9.2	Bretagne	7.3
Haute-Normandie	8.6	Basse-Normandie	7.2
Aquitaine	8.5	Corse	6.8
Picardie	8.3	Nord-Pas de Calais	6.8
Poitou-Charentes	8.3	Midi-Pyrénées	6.0
Languedoc-Roussillon	8.3	Limousin	5.8
Bourgogne	8.0	Auvergne	4.9
		French Average	7.8

has taken place in the midst of a changing environment. Much less fluctuation has characterized voting for the Brussels Regional Parliament, for which a measure of volatility across the span of its two elections is provided.

Changes in vote shares among the parties in the new French regions are on the whole significantly greater than in both Belgium and Germany. Average net volatility across two time points (1986 and 1992), as presented in table 6.2, suggests that instability is pronounced in many of the regions but markedly less pronounced in others. Lorraine and Rhône-Alpes, for example, are characterized by much greater volatility than Limousin and Auvergne. Here in France, as in Germany and Belgium, we find clear evidence of relative differences in electoral environments across regions.

Electoral Localization

The degree of electoral localization is considered to be the extent to which average absolute interelection mutations in party vote shares in a subnational arena deviate from average absolute interelection mutations for the same parties in the national arena. In this way, greater localization is indicated by greater subnational-national *differences* in the mutations. Greater nationalization is indicated when changes in subnational election results mirror those occurring across successive national elections. If changes in partisan support differ across levels, this is likely to be a clue that voters are basing their decisions on different criteria (i.e., local and national). Conversely, if changes in partisan support across levels mirror one another, then local factors are likely to be playing less of a role. The measurement of localization used here is:

$$\text{Localization}_{\text{Party}} = [\Sigma |(Sa_t - Sa_{t-1}) - (Na_t - Na_{t-1})| + |(Sa_{t-n} - Sa_{t-n\ldots}) - (Na_{t-n} - Na_{t-n\ldots})|]/E,$$

where $Sa_t - Sa_{t-1}$ = change in voting share of party a between subnational elections at times t and $t-1$; $Na_t - Na_{t-1}$ = change in voting share of party a between national elections at times t and $t-1$; E = number of elections; and where:

$$\text{Localization}_{\text{Subnational Unit}} = [\text{Localization}_{\text{Party } A} + \text{Localization}_{\text{Party } B \ldots n}]/P,$$

when P = number of parties.

The measure should equal 0 when changes in subnational election results mirror perfectly those for parties in the national arena. The larger the localization measure, conversely, the more important are subnational deviations from national patterns.

Electoral Localization in the German Länder, Belgian Provinces, and French Regions

Changes in party vote shares in the Land elections between 1961 and 1995 are neither perfect reflections nor complete distortions of changes in party vote shares in federal elections. There is instead variation, "a marked heterogeneity from one Land to another" that "may be taken as an indication of the impact of local factors in Land elections" (Padgett 1991, 4). The calculations presented in table 6.3 indicate that voting patterns across the states do deviate from federal averages to markedly greater and lesser degrees. The small city-states of Bremen, Hamburg, and Berlin are among those Länder whose election results are less attributable statistically to federal trends and thus appear to have idiosyncratic patterns of voting behavior. Conversely, changes in election results in North Rhine–Westphalia, Lower Saxony, and Rhineland-Palatinate more closely mimic global German trends. Illustrative of these patterns on a small scale are the fates of the CDU in "localized" Bremen and "nationalized" North Rhine–Westphalia. With a net change for the CDU between the 1987 and 1990 Bundestag elections at 0.1%, change in support for the North Rhine–Westphalia CDU followed directly at 0.2%; however, the Bremen CDU over the same period weathered a massive 10% change. It may further be noted that the average percent vote for independent candidates and purely "local" parties in the state elections of Bremen, Hamburg, and Baden-Württemberg (i.e., the "localized" states) is more than three times greater than that for Lower Saxony, North Rhine–Westphalia, and Rhineland-Palatinate (i.e., the "nationalized" states). That Baden-Württemberg is among the more localized electoral systems seems initially surprising, given its size and presumed national importance, but it is a fact confirmed by previous studies: "Baden-Württemberg falls into the same category of states with a distinctive political culture, and idiosyncratic patterns of voting behaviour" (Padgett and Burkett 1986,

Table 6.3

Electoral Localization in Germany, Belgium, and France

German Länder	Period I, 1961–77 (%)	Period II, 1978–95 (%)	Land Average (%)	Number of Election Periods	Average % Vote for "Local" Lists, 1961–95
Bremen	3.0	3.7	3.4	8	3.4
Hamburg	3.0	2.9	3.0	10	4.1
Baden-Württemberg	2.7	2.3	2.5	8	4.7
Berlin	2.6	2.3*	2.4	7	3.3
Saarland	3.1	1.8	2.4	7	1.8
Hessen	2.8	2.0	2.4	9	4.5
Schleswig-Holstein	2.3	2.3	2.3	8	2.3
Bavaria	2.1	1.1	1.6	8	2.4
Lower Saxony	1.2	1.7	1.5	8	2.7
North Rhine–Westphalia	1.8	1.3	1.5	7	0.3
Rhineland-Palatinate	1.0	2.2	1.5	7	1.8
German Average	2.3	2.1	2.2	7.9	2.8

*Appropriate time period is 1978–89. No meaningful comparison of 1990 Land election in united Berlin can be made to previous Land elections.

Belgian Provinces	Period I, 1961–76 (%)	Period II, 1977–91 (%)	Province Average (%)	Number of Election Periods	Average % Vote for "Local" Lists
Namur	3.6	2.9	3.2	10	3.5
Luxembourg	2.8	3.1	3.0	10	2.9
Antwerp	1.9	1.8	1.8	10	2.8
Hainaut	1.8	1.9	1.8	10	3.0
Limburg	2.2	1.6	1.8	10	1.4
West Flanders	2.0	1.4	1.7	10	1.4
Liège	1.6	1.5	1.6	10	2.3
Brabant	2.0	1.1	1.5	10	2.1
East Flanders	1.5	1.3	1.4	10	0.9
Provincial Average	2.2	1.8	2.0	10	2.3
Brussels Region			0.9	1 (1989–95)	1.4

French Regions	Period 1986–92 (%)	Average % Vote for "Local" Lists
Alsace	5.4	4.3
Basse-Normandie	4.9	3.6
Lorraine	4.7	1.6
Champagne-Ardenne	4.5	5.2
Rhône-Alpes	4.5	2.2
Provence-Alpes Côte d'Azur	4.4	12.7
Limousin	4.4	2.6
Franche-Comté	4.3	1.5
Haute-Normandie	4.0	5.4
Poitou-Charentes	3.7	3.3
Aquitaine	3.5	12.2

French Regions	Period 1986–92 (%)	Average % Vote for "Local" Lists
Nord-Pas de Calais	3.3	10.1
Picardie	3.3	6.7
Languedoc-Roussillon	3.3	5.2
Ile-de-France	2.9	0.5
Bourgogne	2.9	4.3
Pays-de-la-Loire	2.8	2.1
Bretagne	2.6	0.6
Corse	2.6	15.1
Centre	2.5	0.8
Auvergne	1.6	3.3
Mid-Pyrénées	1.5	4.4
French Average	3.5	4.9

276). For present purposes, then, this statistical procedure lends cre-
dence to the assumption of differentiation in regional voting traditions
in Germany.[5]

The provincialization of election results in Belgium is somewhat
more difficult to discern. This is due in significant part to the simul-
taneous occurrence of provincial and national elections. Nevertheless,
changes in provincial voting results do not vary strictly according to
national patterns (table 6.3). The francophone province of Namur
stands out as the most distinctive province, followed by Luxembourg,
the province physically and historically most distant from the Belgian
capital. Although most things in Belgium resist the label *nationalized,*
the province of East Flanders should still qualify given the degree to
which elections there consistently follow larger Flemish and Belgian
trends. So, too, should the Brussels region, where voting patterns have
demonstrated little local distinctiveness.

It is possible to offer a limited measure of localization (i.e., regionalization) in the election results of France's 20 regions. This calculation
measures interelection changes in party vote shares between the 1986
and 1992 regional elections. These results are then compared with
interelection changes in party vote shares for the two closest national
parliamentary elections, those having occurred in 1986 and 1993. As
the data in table 6.3 reveal, election results in many of the French regions have a distinctive local flavor, with regional-level party gains and
losses being detached from national-level party changes to a far
greater extent than in Belgium and Germany. The degree of localization in small and historically contested Alsace in the northeastern
periphery of the French hexagon, for example, is more than three
times that of Auvergne, located at the country's center.

A Typology of Subnational Electoral Systems in Germany, Belgium, and France

Our statistical measures of objective conditions—such as instability
and idiosyncrasy of voting behavior—may have tapped into a pool of
influences (physical size, historical identity, distance from center, oc-
cupational structure, economic conditions) that can combine to create
different regional voting patterns. For our purposes, it suffices to note

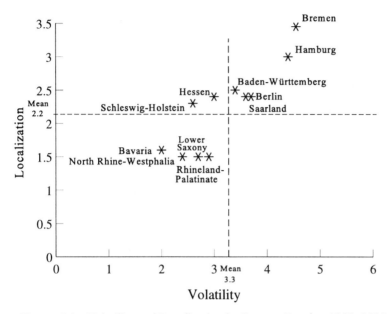

Figure 6.1   Volatility and Localization in German Länder, 1961–1995

the actual presence of *variation,* variation that may condition several strategic behaviors, of which coalition building is but one.

Given these two measures, each country's subnational units may be classified by cross-comparing a state, province, or region's cumulative scores for both volatility and localization (figures 6.1 through 6.3). Doing so reveals clear variation and the existence of separate clusters of subnational electoral arenas. Within their respective systems, Bremen, Namur, and Lorraine are characterized by consistently high levels of electoral instability; conversely, voting patterns in Lower Saxony, Brabant, and Midi-Pyrénées are comparatively and consistently more stable. Likewise, voting shifts in Hamburg, Luxembourg, and Alsace demonstrate greater independence from national shifts than do those in Rhineland-Palatinate, Liège, and Auvergne.

These measures provide solid empirical evidence of differential electoral conditions across the territorial divisions of Germany, Belgium, and France. As such, they should facilitate investigation into "conditional" coalition behavior. The empirical classification scheme also enables us to characterize the relative constraints under which our survey respondents find themselves, since the territorial assemblies constituting the sample represent different combinations of electoral

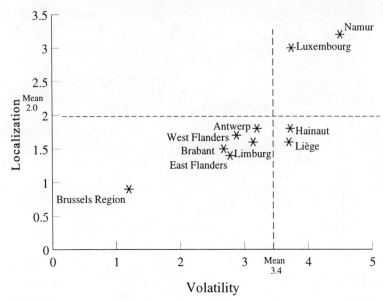

Figure 6.2 Volatility and Localization in Belgian Provinces, 1961–1991, and Brussels Region, 1989–1995

volatility and localization. Given that the survey instrument was cross-sectional and the classification scheme longitudinal, however, effort was made to ensure that the same relative disparities in volatility and localization held true for the most recent election period in the locality. Controls for electoral environment were also corroborated by survey items tapping respondents' own perceptions of volatility and localization; provincial and regional means for these items correlated strongly and positively with our objective, cumulative measures of high/low volatility and localization/nationalization.[6]

In a very basic way, the typology of electoral environments thus achieves an important goal: it establishes a contextual framework that allows for the specification of certain likely electoral constraints on the strategic behavior of subnational parliamentarians. This is a necessary precondition for testing whether the electoral milieu in which parties find themselves actually influences the development of strategic policy and the making of coalition choices. These measures obtained, the question that must be addressed is whether the two variables of electoral volatility and electoral localization, either separately or in combination, intervene to condition the ways in which politicians and parties approach coalition situations.

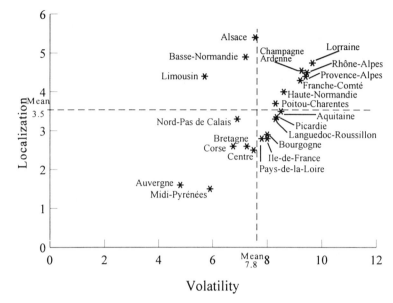

Figure 6.3   Volatility and Localization in French Regions, 1986–1992

Do Volatility and Localization
Have an Impact on Coalitions?

When politicians and parties believe that what they do in the hours, days, and weeks following an election has a direct impact on future election outcomes, then their strategic choices are constrained by the necessity of appearing reliable and credible to the local electorate. In less competitive situations, however, politicians can, without serious worry about damaging their election result, pursue a more unrestricted set of coalition possibilities. This section tests the influence of volatility and localization on individual-level strategic assessments as well as on aggregate-level coalition outcomes.

Hypothesis: Volatility Heightens Risk and Accountability

If electoral conditions (e.g., proximate and unstable competition) really do influence and constrain what rational politicians may be expected to do, then some relationship between volatility and actor appreciation of coalition accountability and decision-making responsibility should exist. Basic tenets of democratic theory anticipate that electoral competition increases the need for "responsible," reelection-minded representatives and parties to appear consistent and reliable to their electorates. In other words, increased competition for electoral support presumably heightens the risks of strategic choices, elevates the stakes of coalition games, and magnifies the accountability that political actors (individually and/or collectively) feel for their actions. This should be true especially for coalition preferences and decisions, as they are among the most outward signals of governing intent and political motivation. Whether such sensitivity to electoral pressures exerts any influence in the realm of coalition politics is the initial empirical matter to be addressed here.

To test for contextual influence, initially on micro-level rationality, we can compare subnational legislators' perceptions of coalition accountability, concern for local public opinion, and consideration of the electoral consequences of strategic decisions under different electoral conditions. Combining the objective measures of volatility presented above with responses to select items in the survey questionnaire sent to Belgian, German, and French representatives, we can instructively put to the test the null hypothesis that has heretofore guided general theories of coalition formation, namely, that context does not matter.

The questionnaire asked representatives:

"Will voters at the next election hold you and your party accountable for a coalition you may have sought with another party or parties to influence the distribution of government posts or to promote a policy?"

The resulting frequencies reveal that a majority (59.8%) of the subnational deputies sampled do anticipate electoral consequences to follow from their coalitional activity. French (67% or 164), German (61% or 104), and Belgian (51% or 87) respondents indicated that they believe that the voters in their respective regions, states, and provinces hold them accountable for power-sharing arrangements or other forms of cross-party collaboration. However, these majorities are by no means absolute, revealing that substantial numbers of representatives (40.2%) actually perceive *no* accountability to voters for their decisions of government formation and interparty cooperation. These percentages remain consistent when controlling for party participation in an actual governing coalition.

Table 6.4
Level of Coalition Accountability, by Volatility
of Electoral Environment (%)

Level of Coalition Accountability	Volatility of Electoral Environment		
	High	Low	N
High	68.8	43.3	355
Low	31.2	56.7	239
N	384	210	

$\chi^2 = 4.71$, $df = 1$, $p < 0.030$.
Kendall's Tau-b $= 0.10$, $p < 0.05$.

The primary purpose here, however, is to learn if concern over coalition accountability may vary according to different electoral environments. Table 6.4 presents respondents' answers to the question on coalition accountability, dichotomized by respondent location in environments of either high or low electoral volatility. The evidence provides an important first clue supporting the "context matters" thesis. A substantial two-thirds of the councilors and deputies competing in electoral environments that objectively and consistently demonstrate high levels of electoral change acknowledged the connection between coalition behavior and electoral success. Conversely, fewer than half of the representatives whose electoral milieu may be deemed "low volatility" sensed the presence of such an accountability dynamic. This initial discrepancy in responses is statistically significant, supports the underlying logic of the hypothesis, and thus warrants further investigation.

If politicians operating in unstable environments perceive greater strategic risk than do those operating in stable environments, then to what extent do they allow environmental pressures to influence their choices? Free in theory to maximize individual and collective goals by cutting deals with any number of potential partners once elected, players in the coalition game are formally bound by few rules except that of "winning." Some have revealed their coalition intentions during a campaign and in party conferences, but many have not. In the post-election trading and bickering over personalities, portfolios, and policies, most of which transpires outside council chambers and beyond

Table 6.5
Concern for Public Opinion in
Decisions of Coalition Composition,
by Volatility of Electoral Environment (%)

Influence of Land/ Regional/Provincial Public Opinion	Volatility of Electoral Environment	
	High	Low
Very influential	20.1	8.2
Somewhat influential	59.6	55.6
Not at all influential	20.3	36.2
N	334	207

$\chi^2 = 7.19$, $df = 2$, $p < 0.104$.
Kendall's Tau-c $= 0.11$, $p < 0.12$.

the reach of journalists, it is unclear how interpretations of the "verdict of the electorate" figure into decisions of government participation, choices of partners, and the direction of joint public policy.

Table 6.5 presents responses to the following survey question:

"In the process leading to the formation of a new coalition, you and your party are likely influenced by many considerations in your approach to negotiations. How influential is [provincial/regional/Land] public opinion in determining your party's strategy?"

The councilors and deputies answered by indicating "very influential," "somewhat influential," or "not at all influential." Even given a tendency of elected officials to inflate the extent to which popular will drives their behavior, the response pattern fits theoretical expectations regarding the intervening influence of electoral context. Of the 334 subnational representatives competing under conditions of high volatility, 20.1% indicated that public opinion is very influential in formulating coalition strategy, whereas only 8.2% of the 207 respondents in low-volatility arenas so indicated. At the same time, 36.2% from low-volatility environments responded that public opinion was not at all important, compared with a smaller 20.3% from the high-volatility category. In both cases, the majority of respondents indicated public opinion to be "somewhat influential" in strategic choice. That the climate of provincial, regional, or state public opinion influences coalition behavior to a greater extent in more competitive, unstable electoral

Table 6.6
Perceived Importance of Vote-Maximizing
Capacity of Coalition Strategy,
by Volatility of Electoral Environment (%)

Importance of Winning Votes with Coalition	Volatility of Electoral Environment	
	High	Low
Great	12.2	5.8
Moderate	50.3	48.1
Little or none	37.5	46.1
N	328	208

$\chi^2 = 7.05$, $df = 2$, $p < 0.029$.
Kendall's Tau-c $= 0.08$, $p < 0.13$.

environments is apparent. What should not be overlooked, especially for its substantive, if not normative, implications, is that in both types of electoral environments, there are more representatives answering that public opinion is "not at all influential" than there are those answering that it is "very influential."

Addressing the influence of public opinion taps into political sensitivity to popular will. A more direct measure of motivation can be achieved by asking representatives about the vote-maximizing intentions of certain approaches to coalition situations. Table 6.6 reports findings for the following survey item:

"Please characterize the following as a motivation for your party when seeking a coalition with another party or parties: Gaining votes at the next election."

The gap here is not huge, but it is consistent with theoretical expectations. Forward-looking vote maximization is twice as important a motivation among competitors in high-volatility situations as among their colleagues in more stable electoral contexts. Indeed, close to half of the respondents in the latter category answered that a coalition's capacity to win votes at the next election was of little or no importance in either its selection or its rejection.

Individually, the data presented in tables 6.4 through 6.6 are important, if initially unspectacular. Taken together, the patterns apparent from the data suggest a positive relationship between electoral context and individual-level perceptions of strategic risk and coalition accountability. Consistent with the hypothesis, these findings successfully link environment with important motivational concerns. According to these individual-level attitudinal data, then, it seems justifiable to proceed under the assumption that volatility may in fact increase the perception among politicians that electoral fortunes are linked to coalition choices. Recognizing this makes it possible to regard electoral context as a potential constraint on behavior.

Hypothesis: Localization Heightens Risk and Accountability

When changes in election results at the subnational level are consistently tied to those at the national level, politicians developing strategy at the lower levels should be freed somewhat from the pressures to appear consistent and reliable to the local electorate. Conversely, the more fluctuations in party vote shares in the subnational arena distinguish themselves from those at the national level, the greater such pressure is likely to be. Under conditions of "localized" (or "provincialized," "regionalized") rather than "nationalized" election environments, politicians are more likely to collectively recognize competition as a threat to the attainment of office and thus are less likely to remain indifferent to local preferences in developing strategy.

As with the examination of our first hypothesis, the prime concern here is to test whether objective electoral conditions—in this case, contextual traditions of localization—condition actor perceptions of the coalition game, its stakes, and especially its electoral consequences. At issue are whether officeholders' recognition of coalition accountability, their reliance on public opinion as a guide to strategic alternatives, and their vote-seeking motivations increase as the resemblance of subnational elections to those at the national level decreases. Using the same survey items as were employed in the analysis of the previous hypothesis, it is possible to take one further step toward establishing that context "matters" when otherwise self-interested politicians are faced with collective action problems.

Table 6.7 presents responses to the "accountability," "public opinion," and "vote-seeking" survey questions, this time dichotomized by respondent location in electoral environments that may be deemed either "localized" or "nationalized." Consistent with expectations, a greater proportion of respondents competing in localized environments feel that voters will ultimately hold them and their parties ac-

Table 6.7
Concern for Preferences of Local Electorate
in Decisions of Coalition Composition,
by Localization of Electoral Environment (%)

	Localization of Electoral Environment	
	High	Low
Level of Coalition Accountability*		
High	63.9	57.2
Low	36.1	42.8
N	208	386
Influence of Land/ Regional/Provincial Public Opinion**		
Very influential	13.5	10.2
Somewhat influential	58.9	48.8
Not at all influential	27.6	41.0
N	207	334
Importance of Winning Votes with Coalition***		
Great	11.5	7.9
Moderate	58.6	43.2
Little or none	29.9	48.9
N	208	328

*$\chi^2 = 1.18$, $df = 1$, $p < 0.28$; Kendall's Tau-b $= 0.09$, $p < 0.07$.
**$\chi^2 = 5.80$, $df = 2$, $p < 0.21$; Kendall's Tau-b $= 0.08$, $p < 0.05$.
***$\chi^2 = 11.9$, $df = 2$, $p < 0.01$; Kendall's Tau-b $= 0.11$; $p < 0.05$.

countable for coalitional activity in the subnational assembly. Also matching theoretical expectations is the pattern revealed by responses to the question on public opinion. While only 27.6% of the respondents representing localized electoral systems relegated provincial/regional/ Land public opinion to the "not at all influential" category, 41% of the respondents from more nationalized electoral systems did so. Finally, the motivation of securing votes via coalition choices also appears to

Table 6.8
Perception of Coalition Accountability,
by Dominant Themes of Subnational Electoral Politics (%)

Level of Coalition Accountability	Determining Forces of Subnational Electoral Politics		
	Provincial/ Regional Issues and Personalities	National Issues and Personalities	Administrative Concerns; Not Party Politics
High	62.2	39.4	21.1
Low	37.8	60.6	78.9
N	275	198	19

$\chi^2 = 21.85$, $df = 2$, $p < 0.000$.
Kendall's Tau-c $= 0.21$, $p < 0.04$.

vary according to electoral localization. Similar percentages of respondents labeled "gaining votes at future elections" as a very important motivation; however, substantially more respondents in nationalized electoral milieus (48.9%) indicated that vote getting was a marginal if nonexistent motivation for them, compared with 29.9% in localized environments. Together, these results suggest that, like volatility, localization creates pressures of which representatives do seem to be aware. In raising the risks and stakes of the coalition game, the onus of making "responsible" choices intervenes in the politician's and the party's pursuit of goals and rewards.

An additional questionnaire item serves to corroborate these findings as well as the validity of the aggregate measure of localization. Respondents were first asked to characterize the determining forces of elections in their respective province, region, or state. They were given the opportunity to answer that elections are decided "more by national themes, personalities, and parties," "more by [provincial/regional/Land] themes, personalities, and parties," or "more by administrative concerns and not party politics." As the results in table 6.8 demonstrate convincingly, only among those indicating that "local" issues, personalities, and parties ultimately decide elections did a majority of respondents perceive any real accountability links in the coalition process. Here, again, is more evidence of differential constraints.

One final method of establishing the relationship between localization and constraints on coalitional activity is presented in figure 6.4. Here objective measures of average electoral localization of provinces, regions, and Länder included in the survey population are plotted

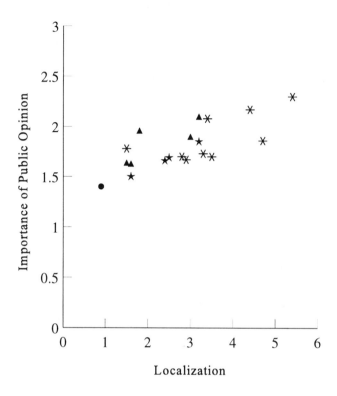

Figure 6.4 Perceived Importance of Local Public Opinion in Determination of Coalition Strategy, by Localization of Electoral Environment

against area response means for the question addressing the influence of public opinion in determining party strategy in coalition situations. The results clearly indicate a positive relationship between the contextual condition of electoral localization and respondent affirmation of a role for public opinion in the formulation of coalition strategy. These data, too, provide tangible evidence that localization can be an important intervening variable between preferences and choices. The findings make it possible to contend that localization, like volatility, can be a constraint on behavior. The weight of the evidence suggests that context does matter, and that it does so in systematic ways.

The question remains, however, whether attitudes, perceptions, and recognition of strategic risk and democratic responsibility, once increased by unstable and localized electoral conditions, necessarily translate into recognizably different patterns of behavior. If they do, then there will be reason to believe that an electoral explanation of subnational coalition politics is appropriate and useful. If they do not, then a weak link in popular representation at the subnational level will be highlighted. If, further, the influence of elections on coalition patterns is especially ambiguous, then there will be cause to explore separate organizational and motivational factors in search of a more suitable explanation. In any event, tests of individual-level *attitudes* cannot be used in isolation to generalize about coalition *behavior.* The survey data cannot by themselves discern whether representatives, individually and collectively, will actually act in accordance with their recognition of coalition accountability. It is therefore necessary to go beyond the individual level of analysis to examine the connections between electoral conditions and coalition outcomes. Aggregate-level data will allow some indication of whether higher levels of electoral volatility and/or localization are associated with certain types of coalition outcomes.

Behavioral Companions to Micro-Level Rationality

The most direct means of addressing the behavioral companions to the micro-level rationality thus far exposed is to examine actual outcomes of government formation in subnational assemblies. An ample amount of such behavioral data can be put to use from a set of 176 subnational governments formed in the aftermath of elections in Belgium ($N = 82$), Germany ($N = 50$), and France ($N = 44$). Each outcome was coded according to the type of coalition formed, along with the volatility and localization measures for each election. Each coalition was assigned a series of binary codes (0, 1), corresponding to its composition: minimum number of parties, ideological "connectedness," party with the most seats included, inclusion of one or more "winning" parties, whether the winning coalition represented a change from the previous arrangement, congruence with the national coalition, and whether the coalition was "cooperative" (i.e., whether it allied the two initially strongest parties).

If volatility and localization do have an impact on coalition behavior, either separately or in conjunction, these variables should be associated in some clear and meaningful fashion with certain types of coalition outcomes. With increased volatility and localization, we might expect to find, for example, that parties more often pursue and form power-sharing coalitions that minimize ideological heterogeneity, thus reducing the amount of postelection compromising that could damage a party's image with voters. Along these lines, heightened risk should reduce the likelihood of coalition experimentation. As competition increases, moreover, parties should be more likely to seek governing coalitions that contain only the minimum number of partners necessary to "win." With the rewards and resources of government status in greater demand and their possession more uncertain, parties as rational agents should be less likely to engage in any unnecessary acts of cooperation with their competitors. They may also have greater incentives to react to electoral change and instability with short-term adversarial strategies, such as seizing power from the initially strongest party. Such strategy would, however, run the risk of retaliation and exclusion from coalitions at future iterations of the government formation process. Vote-maximizing coalition behavior under conditions of high volatility and localization may also manifest itself in coalitions that include at least one "winner." Where, further, forming coalitions congruent with national alliance patterns would represent rejection of local electoral cues and local balances of power, incongruent coalitions should be more likely to form. All told, the hypothesized picture is one of parties pursuing goals through coalitions in unstable environments, full of strategic risk, by adopting adversarial strategies that minimize the electorally deleterious risks of compromise and domination by coalition partners.

Conversely, where electoral environments are relatively stable and the driving forces behind partisan change are national rather than local, we should expect to find a wider assortment of coalition outcomes. Here parties not only are free simply to duplicate previous arrangements (i.e., strategic inertia) or to replicate the national balance of power but also are less constrained in attempts to form ideologically unconnected coalitions, to experiment with untried alliances, or to engage in more long-term cooperative strategies, primarily those that link the two strongest parties in a kind of "grand coalition."

A useful test of these basic propositions is to compare the frequency of certain outcomes according to varying levels and combinations of electoral volatility and electoral localization. Table 6.9 presents the results of this comparison, highlighting patterns of coalition outcomes in opposing electoral systems, namely, those in high volatility/localized environments and those in stable/nationalized environments. The percentages of provincial, regional, or Land government coalitions meeting each of the seven criteria are listed, along with correlation coefficients measuring strength and direction of association between each criterion and each outcome's electoral context (i.e., level of volatility, level of localization, and a multiplicative measure of the interactive effects of the two variables combined).

Results of this analysis provide some evidence that context matters. As electoral constraints increase, parties seem to pursue adversarial strategies (e.g., coalitions that minimize cooperation between the strongest rivals or that exclude the dominant party). Electoral constraints also appear to restrict the incentives for parties to engage in political inertia by maintaining the coalition status quo; this finding is important, for it indicates responsiveness to electoral cues. There is also useful evidence to the effect that congruence with national alignments, like coalition inertia, is more difficult to maintain under the pressures of electoral constraints. In addition, there is some behavioral support for the notion that context intervenes to influence the formation of ideologically homogeneous governing partnerships. Contrary to the expected direction of this relationship, however, it appears that in these three countries, parties competing under electoral constraints are more likely to react with "unconnected" coalitions than are their counterparts in unconstrained environments. This may mean that parties prefer "strange bedfellows" over opposition status in volatile electoral markets or that ideological cleavages and distances between parties as they are perceived in national politics do not apply directly in the provincial or regional context. Most likely, what these data suggest is that parties in contentious, risky electoral environments, faced with dilemmas of short-term survival rather than of long-term partnership, behave more as office seekers than as ideological or policy purists.

In terms of statistical robustness, these data are rather a mixed bag. By themselves they are not definitive. However, together with the survey evidence presented earlier, they are suggestive of the existence of linkages and intervening contextual mechanisms that work to constrain and influence the choices rational actors make in coalition situations.

Application and Discussion

Cross-national evidence presented in this chapter suggests the existence of relationships among electoral conditions, coalition outcomes,

Table 6.9

Coalition Outcomes, by Condition of Subnational Electoral Environment

	Exclude Strongest Party	Include Only Losers	Contain Excess Parties	Excess Ideological Distance	Incongruent with National Alignments	Coalition Change	Include #1 and #2 Parties
				% Coalitions Exhibiting Characteristics			
				Belgium			
Volatile/localized	30	31	15	45	75	33	40
Stable/nationalized	6	22	17	6	59	23	74
Vol*Loc r	0.05	0.27***	− 0.12	0.11	0.23***	0.27***	− 0.23**
Vol r	0.04	0.30***	− 0.10	0.13	0.23***	0.32***	− 0.32***
Loc r	0.01	0.19**	− 0.10	0.02	0.27**	0.26**	− 0.19*
				Germany			
Volatile/localized	14	16	45	21	36	57	16
Stable/nationalized	9	29	7	7	33	57	7
Vol*Loc r	0.25*	− 0.16	0.14	0.25*	0.07	− 0.04	0.05
Vol r	0.22*	− 0.16	0.01	0.04	0.16	0.08	0.07
Loc r	0.30**	− 0.06	0.14	0.26*	− 0.08	0.01	− 0.05
				France			
Volatile/localized	57	29	14	43	43	57	0
Stable/nationalized	42	33	0	17	17	50	0
Vol*Loc r	0.34*	− 0.10	0.05	0.27*	0.02	0.03	—
Vol r	0.07	− 0.22	0.14	0.17*	0.10	0.22	—
Loc r	0.41*	0.01	0.22	0.22*	0.10	0.14	—

$*p < 0.10$, $**p < 0.05$, $***p < 0.01$.

and representatives' strategic assessments. To some degree, the relationships measured on the individual level are stronger than those measured at the aggregate, behavioral level. This is in some small part probably an inherent artifact of the survey measurement instrument itself. It is, however, also likely that in large part the perceptions, assessments, and attitudes of individual officeholders are constrained by more than just electoral cues. The set of variables that most probably play an equally important intervening role are those regarding the organizational context of coalition building. These variables will be addressed in the following chapter. At present, it remains to venture a final assessment of the utility of explaining coalitional dynamics based upon electoral cues. Such an assessment ultimately rests on just how much of the story of actual coalition behavior we can tell on the basis of the apparent responsiveness of parties in subnational assemblies to variable electoral markets. Practical applications of the electoral model can be pursued by making paired comparisons of coalition behavior in provinces, regions, or states of contrasting electoral contexts.

Coalition Outcomes in Contrasting Belgian Provinces

Two provincial polar opposites in Belgium are Namur and West Flanders. From the beginning of the 1960s through the early 1990s, electoral competition in Namur has been intense compared to that in West Flanders. In Namur, the average change per election in party vote shares during this period is 4.5%, higher than the 2.9% average volatility for West Flanders across the same 11 provincial elections. Moreover, differences in national-provincial mutations in party vote shares across elections are comparatively greater in Namur (3.2%) than in West Flanders (1.7%). Figure 6.5 demonstrates differences between the two provinces caused by the joint presence of volatility and localization. Have these different conditions in any way manifested themselves in different patterns of provincial government coalition formation?

In Namur, 11 provincial elections have produced 11 provincial coalitions. During the 30-year period, there have been three different types of provincial majority and two coalition alternations. Christian Socials (PSC) and Liberals (PRL) shared power from 1961 to 1968, and in 1968 the PSC switched partners and allied with the Socialists (PS) until 1985. Subsequently, the PS and PRL constituted provincial governments after the 1985, 1987, and 1991 elections. In West Flanders, 11 provincial elections have produced eight coalition governments.

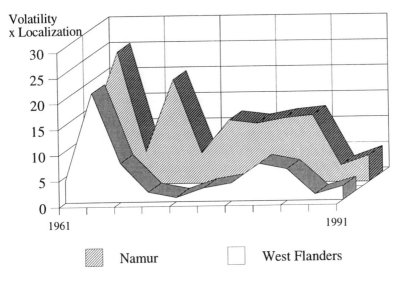

Volatility x Localization

1961   1991

Namur   West Flanders

Figure 6.5   Electoral Constraints in Two Provinces

During the period, there has been but *one* coalition formula: Christian Democrats (CVP) and Socialists (SP). These two parties alone divided provincial power from 1968 to 1978, and one term of CVP single-party government (1978–81) gave way again to a center-left alliance during the period since 1981.

Every West Flanders coalition has linked the first- and second-ranking parties in the council in a provincial version of the "grand" coalition model. Conversely, in Namur, coalitions have joined the strongest and the weakest parties (1961), the first- and third-strongest parties (1965, 1968, 1985–91), the two strongest parties (1971–81), and two of three equally powerful parties (1968). Each West Flanders provincial coalition has included the center party (CVP) and a party immediately adjacent to it on an ordinal policy/ideology scale (SP). Alternatively, in Namur, the 1985, 1987, and 1991 majorities may be said to be ideologically "unconnected" in that they pair Left (PS) with Right (PRL) but skip over the center (PSC).

To a discernable degree, then, patterns of coalition behavior in Namur and West Flanders do vary. Inertia is the strongest single explanation for the consistency of the center-left arrangement in West Flanders, and the relative freedom from electoral pressures there has allowed Christian Democrats and Socialists to develop a long-term, cooperative arrangement that serves their mutual power interests but denies Liberals, ecologists (Agalev), or nationalists (Volksunie, Vlaams Blok) any hope of gaining entry. As in West Flanders, in Namur, Christian Socials and Socialists have also been the two strongest parties in provincial parliaments after every election since 1961. Contrary to what has occurred in West Flanders, however, these two parties have agreed to share power on only 5 of 11 occasions. Instead of a long-term cooperative strategy, coalitions have been built on the basis of more short-term competitive strategies. The differences in electoral environments between the two political arenas have to be considered important factors influencing the discrepancy in behavior.

Coalition Outcomes in Contrasting German Länder

Statistical analysis of coalition outcomes in the German Land parliaments supplied some limited support for assuming that certain types of state governments will form given the presence or absence of certain variable electoral conditions. That these findings are not stronger seems to support Cerny's (1990) characterization of the "rare occasions in the FRG that an election outcome remove[s] an incumbent government" (219–20).

It remains instructive to compare coalition governments chosen by Land parliaments in states marked by substantially different levels of electoral stability and localism. One useful comparison may be made between Hamburg, a small state with a tradition of erratic and localized voting, and Lower Saxony, the second-largest state and one with relatively stable and "nationalized" voting patterns. The electoral conditions under which parties in the respective states compete are conspicuously different (figure 6.6), and coalition outcomes in the two Länder differ accordingly.

Hamburg has experienced some of the greatest electoral "earthquakes" in postwar German state politics. Volatile voting patterns have been a familiar feature of elections in the city-state, especially since 1974. In losing the absolute majority it had held since 1957, the SPD in March 1974 surrendered 14 seats and a full 10% of its 1970 parliamentary strength. Filling the gap, the CDU increased its vote share by a substantial 8% and gained 10 new seats in the Bürgerschaft. Votes for the perennial "buffer" party, the FDP, increased by almost 4%, giving the Liberals four additional deputies. Although a CDU-FDP coalition would have secured a safe majority, the election's undisputed

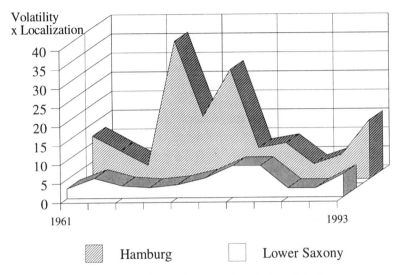

Figure 6.6 Electoral Constraints in Two Länder

loser—the SPD—managed to maneuver around the electorate's verdict and secured a partnership with the FDP in the senate.

Similarly, in 1982 the SPD once again relinquished 10% of its vote, with the CDU gaining 6% and with the Green Alternative List (GAL) bursting onto the scene with 8% of the vote and nine seats. Holding the plurality for the first time in Hamburg, the CDU nevertheless could bring itself neither to form a Grand Coalition with the Social Democrats nor to contemplate any sort of alliance with the new Greens. The SPD, itself not prepared to venture into a full-fledged red-green experiment, attempted to break the stalemate with a minority government to be "tolerated" by the GAL—a government that ultimately lasted less than six months and that had been marked by more acrimony than tolerance (Kitschelt 1989b). Hamburg's voters, forced by the unwillingness and inability of the parties to establish any system for cooperation, were summoned back to the polls and asked to abandon their original verdict.

Rendering the SPD a safe majority in December 1982, Hamburg's mercurial voters nevertheless once again turned against the Social Democrats in dramatic fashion at the November 1986 election. This election handed the plurality back to the CDU and increased the GAL's strength to an unprecedented 10.4%. Maintaining their uncompromising strategies, the parties yet again failed to construct a viable

majority government. Another short-lived SPD minority government
fell, and new elections in May 1987 passed judgment on five years of
chaos by returning the FDP to the Bürgershaft and to government for
the first time since the 1974–78 legislature. That the SPD chose the
Liberals as partners rather than the GAL, which held the same number
of seats, is indicative of an adversarial strategy vis-à-vis both the GAL
and the CDU (by breaking the "Bonn model").[7]

The tradition of adversarial strategies in Hamburg can be seen
as a function of electoral conditions,[8] especially when the pattern of
coalition behavior in this small, volatile arena is compared with that
in a much larger, more stable, and relatively more "nationalized"
arena. In Lower Saxony, for example, state elections are more often
than not fought and won on national issues rather than the local concerns of a smaller state such as Hamburg (Braunthal 1983; Culver
1966; Kloss 1990; Pridham 1973). Moreover, in Lower Saxony the
electoral peaks and valleys of competing parties are noticeably less
pronounced.

While the SPD in Hamburg weathered on average a ±7% change
in support at every Land election since 1961, the Social Democrats in
Lower Saxony experienced fluctuations of only ±3%. Similarly, the
CDU and FDP in Hamburg have oscillated with ±4% and ±2.5%
swings, respectively, while in Lower Saxony these figures are reduced
to ±3% and ±1.5%. At the same time, interelection vote shifts in
Lower Saxony have proven more likely to follow patterns for the parties
at Bundestag elections. For example, the average difference in changes
in support for the SPD at Lower Saxony Land elections and changes
in support for the SPD at national elections is only 0.76%, while in
Hamburg the gap is substantially greater at 4.1%. In comparison to
Hamburg, then, Lower Saxony is a low-volatility, nationalized electoral
market.

Examination of coalition outcomes in Lower Saxony accordingly reveals cases of "cooperative" coalition building to an extent unmatched
in Hamburg. Whereas grand coalition in Hamburg never proved to
be a feasible option (even when the alternative was minority government), in Lower Saxony the CDU-SPD formula came to fruition in
1965 even before its introduction at the federal level. Similarly, Greens
and Social Democrats in Lower Saxony succeeded in concluding a governing alliance in 1990, a feat their more contentious colleagues in
Hamburg could not pull off three years earlier. If electoral success
really "reinforces noncooperative strategies" (Kitschelt 1989b, 255),

then the modest volatility in Lower Saxony has to be seen as one factor facilitating cooperation where none occurred in the more explosive Hamburg electoral system.

Coalition Outcomes in Contrasting French Regions

Understanding the electoral context in which coalition players develop strategy in the French regions can likewise shed some light on the forces that condition government formation and alliance politics in that country. One substantively interesting set of decisions that may be explained in part by recognizing the electoral environments in which coalition bargaining took place concerns the PCF-PS "union de la gauche." Choices between adversarial and cooperative strategies were not uniform across the regions after the elections in either 1986 or 1992. In this regard, it is useful to compare the fate of the Communist-Socialist axis in Limousin, Nord-Pas de Calais, and Provence-Alpes-Côte d'Azur.

In both 1986 and 1992, the Communist Party's delegation to the Limousin regional council chose to support the Socialist Party and its candidate for regional premier, Robert Savy. True to the once-strong tradition of "désistement républicain," the PCF in 1986 withdrew from the presidential contest after the first round of voting and combined its eight-strong group with the 15 PS councilors, securing a three-seat majority for the Left at the second round. Similarly, in 1992, with the PCF-PS union in disarray throughout the country and the central committee of the Communist Party instructing its regional representatives not to cooperate with the Socialists, the Communists nonetheless renewed their support for Savy and so allowed the PS to retain one of its last regional bastions.[9]

Cooperation on the Left in Limousin contrasted sharply with the confrontational strategies adopted elsewhere, such as in Nord-Pas de Calais and in Provence-Alpes–Côte d'Azur. Having contributed to the creation of a regional government headed by the PS in 1986, the PCF in 1992 stunned and embarrassed the Socialists in Nord-Pas de Calais by refusing to support a majority ruled by the national government minister Michel Delebarre. This decision facilitated a virtual seizure of power by the Verts, a party of just 8 persons in a council of 113. In Provence-Alpes–Côte d'Azur, a coalition of Left parties (Socialists and Communists) and ecologists—a veritable "majorité de progrès"— would have forced the Right in 1992 to either ally with the FN or lose its grip on power in the important southern region. In the event, no

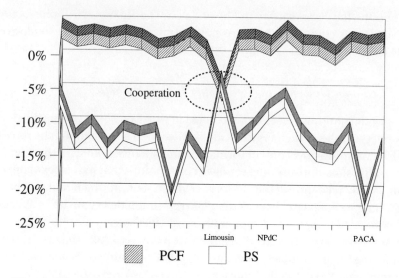

Figure 6.7 Relative Change in Support for PCF and PS, 1986–1992 Regional Elections

such majority emerged. Instead, the Communist group led by Guy Hermier rejected the overtures of another minister in the Socialist government, Bernard Tapie, and so handed regional power back to the Right and to its candidate for regional president, Jean-Claude Gaudin (UDF-PR).

One means of explaining the variation in PCF-PS strategies between Limousin, on the one hand, and Nord-Pas de Calais and Provence-Alpes–Côte d'Azur, on the other, is offered by the electoral conditions under which the respective party groups found themselves. In all three regions, the PCF and PS had each held especially strong positions in 1986. In 1992, however, the parties' fortunes altered dramatically (figure 6.7). In Limousin, the Communists lost 9.5% of their 1986 vote, the *largest* setback for the party in any region. The Limousin Socialists, although squandering 5% of their previous electoral support, nevertheless weathered the *smallest* net 1986–92 change for the PS in all the regions. Indeed, excluding the fortunes of the PCF, Limousin's voters altered their 1986 preferences very little in 1992. If electoral failure reinforces a party's propensity to pursue survivalist strategies—that is, cooperation—then the PCF's stinging defeat in Limousin probably proved to be a key influence in the party's decision to maintain its union with the PS.

The PCF's losses in Nord-Pas de Calais (NPdC) and Provence-Alpes–Côte d'Azur (PACA) were the reverse of Limousin: the Communists gave up just 2.8% of their preexisting support in NPdC and only 2.5% in PACA. At the same time voters in NPdC denied the PS 9.3% of its 1986 total, and in PACA the Socialist Party's 1986 total (25%) was almost entirely wiped out and replaced in 1992 by Tapie's Energie Sud list at 21%. The fortunes of the parties in the regions were reversed, and so too were the strategies of the Communists. The PCF's bargaining power had clearly been stronger in NPdC and PACA than in Limousin. Thus, it proved easier for Alain Bocquet's Communists in NPdC and Guy Hermier's group in PACA to play the role of an "opposition de gauche" and to keep their distance from a Socialist Party whose popularity had just absorbed crushing blows in the two respective regions. According to Hermier, "The Communists are not for sale," and Bocquet proclaimed, "We will not participate in the shady deals. We reject coalitions of circumstance for majorities of circumstance."[10] In Limousin, however, it was Raymond Labrousse's PCF and not Savy's PS that suffered the staggering setback. There the risks of noncooperation proved greater, and given his party's position as the loser among otherwise stable parties, Labrousse resigned himself and his party to the position that in Limousin a continuation of the Union of the Left and a Left majority in the regional assembly was justifiable to "compensate for the possible negative effects of national politics."[11]

There are, then, some useful insights into actual coalition outcomes gained through understanding the constraints placed on decision makers by electoral conditions. The German and French cases also raise the important caveat that the relative electoral success or failure of individual parties—not just the objective, aggregate condition of electoral volatility—can explain why subnational branches of the same political party choose different coalition strategies in different provinces, regions, or states. This caveat prompts the final hypothesis of the chapter.

*Hypothesis: Electoral Success Reinforces
Noncooperative Strategies, while Electoral
Failure Reinforces Cooperative Strategies*

Documented strategies of Social Democrats and Greens in Hamburg and Lower Saxony, or Communists and Socialists in Limousin and Nord-Pas de Calais, provide ready and clear empirical support for this hypothesis. A more limited test of these propositions using the available survey data is presented in table 6.10. The questionnaire asked all respondents to indicate frequency of personal participation in a variety of cooperative coalition-building acts with members of other political parties, including various acts of government formation, passage of budgets, and passage of legislation. Responses to these questions were added, and the cumulative pattern was coded as either "cooperative" or "noncooperative." All respondents were coded as either "winners" or "losers," according to whether their party had either won or lost percentage shares of the vote at the most recent election. If electoral success really "reinforces noncooperative strategies" (Kitschelt 1989b, 255), then it was expected that "winners" would report less cooperation than "losers," who must salvage their influence on the political process via coalition tactics.

The Belgian respondents fit the expected relationship convincingly, both in strength and in direction. If winning strengthens bargaining positions and thus reduces incentives to cooperate, then logical sense can be made of these data. Two-thirds (64.2%) of the Belgian councilors belonging to electorally successful parties reported noncooperative approaches to postelection government formation and postformation legislative activity. This compares with the much smaller 26.7% of electoral winners who reported similar adversarial behavior. This pattern, clear and statistically powerful in the Belgian case, does, however, wash out in the German and French cases. The French data are informative, nonetheless, as majorities of *both* winners and losers report noncooperative approaches to regional politics. Given that French regional volatility is on the whole more intense than in Belgium and Germany, this finding matches expectations that competition will produce adversarial strategies. That Belgium appears to stand apart on this measure also complements earlier findings that linked electoral cues with coalition behavior to a greater extent in Belgium than in Germany or France. This might lead us to believe that in subsequent analysis intervening organizational factors play a greater role in the latter two countries than in Belgium.

Summary

Returning to the question with which this chapter began—"Do electoral verdicts matter?"—it is possible to venture a qualified "yes." Vol-

Table 6.10
Reported Cooperation with Other Parties,
by Change in Party Bargaining Strength (%)

Cooperation	Membership in Winning or Losing Parties	
	Winners	Losers
Belgium*		
Noncooperative strategies and behavior	64.2	26.8
Cooperative strategies and behavior	35.8	73.2
N	67	71
Germany**		
Noncooperative strategies and behavior	46.5	48
Cooperative strategies and behavior	53.5	52
N	86	50
France***		
Noncooperative strategies and behavior	56.8	60.7
Cooperative strategies and behavior	43.2	29.3
N	95	84

*$\chi^2 = 12.83$, $df = 1$, $p < 0.000$; Kendall's Tau-b $= 0.36$, $p < 0.093$.
**$\chi^2 = 1.26$, $df = 1$, $p < 0.265$; Kendall's Tau-b $= 0.05$, $p < 0.078$.
***$\chi^2 = 0.98$, $df = 1$, $p < 0.389$; Kendall's Tau-b $= 0.05$, $p < 0.095$.

atility and localization both increase the tendency of politicians to view coalition decisions as acts that may influence their chances for election and reelection. For voters, this finding can bolster faith that even in coalition systems, imposing change at the ballot box can heighten the accountability politicians feel for their party's coalition decisions and thus can influence the allocation of subnational power. Holding politicians accountable for their coalition decisions is a key aspect of democracy in multiparty systems. Whether politicians act on their democratic responsibilities is a different matter, however.

The immediate implications of these findings should be apparent. Coalition behavior is not so simple that it can be reduced to expectations of unconstrained decision making. Electoral environment appears to influence behavior. The modest strength and patchy consistency of the findings for the behavioral companions to individual-level perceptions nevertheless hints that forces outside the immediate electoral context may also play an influential role. It could be argued, for instance, that political inertia is a powerful influence in some provinces, regions, or states, leading parties to simply continue remaking old alliances as a means of mutual self-preservation. A more instructive explanation, however, may lie in the organizational or internal party dimension of coalition behavior. Recognizing that coalition governments at subnational levels are not completely detached from those in national government means recognizing that party strategies in both arenas may also be linked. Accordingly, chapter 7 examines the question of organizational constraints.

Chapter Seven

Loyalists and Radicals: Coalitions and Intraparty Politics

> In matters of major importance for the party, we must usually do as we are told by Bonn. A party leader can expect that his instructions will be followed at all levels of political power.
> —Free Democrat Landtag Deputy,
> Rhineland-Palatinate

> The Rheinland-Pfalz statement refers to the practice which is naturally followed, and that is to consult. I do think that after analyzing a situation there is hardly ever a conflict between the national leadership and the Länder leadership over what kind of government, what kind of coalition, should be formed.
> —Officer,
> FDP Federal Headquarters

Do parties in subnational parliaments choose solutions to questions of coalition participation according to local preferences or according to the wishes of their national party leaders? If by themselves electoral conditions can explain only some of the variation in strategic attitudes and coalition behavior, how compelling is an alternative explanation based on internal party conditions? One variant of the democratic ideal maintains that the act of majority formation in the territorial parliaments of liberal democracies should be decided by those persons and those groups elected by, and responsible to, the citizenry. When, however, the decisions allocating provincial or regional power are made outside the immediate bargaining arena—that is, at the center—then the democratic ideal presumably languishes. In such cases, subnational party groups take on the guise of passive trustees of national party policy rather than that of responsible delegates serving their constituents.

Of the linkages between territorial deputies and their parent party organizations, Duverger (1954) writes: "The problem of their reciprocal relations is of great importance: democracy requires that parliamentary representatives should take precedence over party leaders and the members of the electorate over the members of the party. . . . In practice the opposite often takes place: in many parties there can be seen a tendency of party leaders to give orders to the parliamentary representatives. . . . The domination of the party over its elected representatives constitutes a form of oligarchy" (182). The particular concern of this chapter is the extent to which organizational oligarchy conditions and constrains parties' choices at the occasion of their first important postelection decision: government formation.

Investigating coalition behavior in subnational legislatures requires that we peer into the "black box" of vertical intraparty decision-making processes. To not do so would be to accept on faith the premise that parties are unconstrained unitary actors as regards coalitions and to risk overlooking significant variation in attitudes and strategic behavior. Focusing on the relationship between intraparty decision making and coalition choices at the subnational level thus raises a variety of pertinent questions that can be studied in a systematic and comparative way: At what organizational level of the party are decisions of coalition strategy formulated? What is the nature of national party involvement and influence in subnational coalition bargaining? Can national leaders assume the deference and adherence of party groups in subnational assemblies with regard to coalition strategy, or can the process of coalition building in subnational institutions be a source of internal party conflict? Finally, does the competitiveness of the subnational electoral environment influence the degree to which organizational constraints condition coalition bargaining? Recounting some finer details of one specific case of government formation, such as that presented below, illustrates how important questions about vertical party relations are for the politics of coalition.

Case Testing Coalition Loyalty and Party Discipline: Belgium's "Pacte de Huit Ans"

On the last day of January 1986, Gérard Deprez, president of Belgium's Parti Social-Chrétien (PSC), and Louis Michel, president of the

Parti Réformateur Liberal (PRL), signed an eight-year accord linking their two parties in coalition at all levels of power where the two together could make up a majority and where there were no other pre-existing agreements to the contrary. The contract translated into a pledge that the two parties would stand together, either in power or in opposition, in the French Community Council, the Walloon Regional Council, and the provincial councils of Brabant, Hainaut, Liège, Luxembourg, and Namur. This arrangement, announced amidst great pomp and dubbed the "pacte d'amour" by Belgium's media,[1] corresponded directly with the national government of the day, a center-Right (CVP/PSC–PVV/PRL) cabinet under CVP Prime Minister Wilfred Martens. In establishing coalition uniformity across all levels of government, Deprez and Michel hoped to solidify their hold on power and by doing so to relegate Wallonia's Socialists to a position of unprecedented political weakness.

General elections in December 1987 would provide the first test of this explicit attempt at linking national and subnational coalitions. The Christian parties suffered the biggest electoral setback, together losing seven seats in the national parliament. Their Liberal coalition partners, on the other hand, succeeded in maintaining all 48 of their seats in the Chamber of Representatives. Together, the existing parties of government could still command an eight-seat parliamentary majority if the Deprez-Michel accord were honored and the then six-year-old coalition reconstituted. The PSC and PRL could also faithfully implement their pact in the French Community Council and the Walloon Regional Council, although in the latter the two parties could not by themselves form a majority but could do so with help from smaller parties such as Ecolo and the Francophone Democratic Front.

Extending the pact to certain of the provinces would be possible as well. Election results immediately indicated that this would be especially easy in Luxembourg province, where the PSC and PRL together held 35 of the 50 council seats, and where the Deprez-Michel pact could finally put an end to the PSC's decade-long absence from power.[2] In Brabant, the Christian and Liberal parties enjoyed a one-seat majority, although the bilingual status of the province would encourage a continuation of traditional Socialist/Christian/Liberal tripartism. In "red" Hainaut, however, voters ensured yet another absolute majority for the Socialists. In Liège, the election results also made a coalition without the Socialists mathematically impossible. In Namur, where the PSC and PRL could feasibly constitute a one-seat majority, a well-publicized PS-PRL accord dating from 1985 precluded extension of the multilevel PSC-PRL pact to the province. The first real test of the global PSC-PRL accord, then, would be in Luxembourg province.

Only a day after the election, news breaking out of the provincial capital of Arlon stunned and embarrassed PSC and PRL leaders in Brussels. The Luxembourg PRL, meeting late into the night, had decided to *reject the eight-year pact orchestrated by its own party president* and instead to construct a power-sharing alliance with the Parti Socialiste (PS). Scrambling to remedy and reverse the situation, national PRL leaders, including party chief Michel and Vice Prime Minister Jean Gol, immediately issued a démarche to their colleagues in Luxembourg insisting that they renege on their agreement with the Socialists. In refusing, the Luxembourg Liberals explained that they were obligated by a *secret* accord, dated 14 October 1985, to maintain the PS-PRL provincial coalition and that this accord predated the 1986 PRL-PSC "pacte de huit ans." The PS-PRL coalition, the defiant Luxembourg Liberals decided, would stand.[3]

Despite Louis Michel's protestations that the Luxembourg accord had been secret even to him, the ramifications of the provincial decision were not lost on PSC chief Deprez. Deprez judged that the accord between PRL and PS in Luxembourg was an intentional rupture of the PSC-PRL pact signed in 1986: "The PRL negotiators affirmed at the time that the pact would be applied to the province of Luxembourg. I state that the Luxembourg PRL have dishonored the signature of the national leaders of the PRL and have put an end unilaterally to the PSC-PRL pact."[4] The alliance that was to last for eight years did not last for two. Subsequent to the events in Luxembourg province, the PSC abandoned the PRL and joined forces with the PS to share executive power in both the French Community Council and the Walloon Regional Council. Ultimately, indeed six months after the general elections, the Christian parties succeeded in engineering a major coalition reversal in national government by wooing the Socialists and Flemish Volksunie into a cabinet headed yet again by Wilfred Martens. The Liberals in Wallonia were thus rudely and completely banished from all but provincial power. Provincial infidelity bore high costs.

The PSC-PRL pact of 1986 had been an overt attempt by national party leaders to impose the same coalition formula at all levels of government. For PSC president Deprez, one of the principals, the effort was in retrospect ill conceived: "The eight-year pact was stupidity. It was an idea of Jean Gol and Louis Michel. At the time my first preoccupation was to make a coalition without the Socialists at the regional level. I wanted to demonstrate that it was possible to rule Wallonia without the Socialists. Jean Gol, however, was afraid that if we excluded the Socialists they would later seek revenge and retaliation against one or another party. Gol said he would accept a coalition without the Socialists at the regional level, but that he would have to ask for a pact for eight years. In my party the provincial lobby made sure the agreement was extended to the provincial level."[5]

For Deprez and the PSC, a strategy of global coalition with the Liberals would therefore have served to show that the PS did not have a monopoly on power in Wallonia. For the PRL, this demonstration may not have been as important as the apparent security given by the pact to a weary center-Right national coalition. Nevertheless, by agreeing to an eight-year deal, both parties assumed loyalty and compliance on each other's part and on the part of their own constituent party groups in the respective subnational assemblies. Deprez states: "I know that Jean Gol and Louis Michel and the staff of the PRL were not informed of the agreement in Luxembourg. I know that they were totally surprised when they received evidence of the PS-PRL coalition. But given that the PRL could not then satisfy what was in the pact, I decided the pact was broken. This single act gave me the free hand to enter negotiations for the composition of the national government and to begin speaking of ending an increasingly unpopular coalition. It was a convenient political crisis."

Here, then, is a useful example of the coalition choices of subnational party groups confounding the overt desires of national party leaders. These choices, made by provincial assembly members under pressure from national party figures at the highest level, ultimately proved responsible for the subsequent termination of the center-Right national coalition and the dramatic leftward *Wende* of 1987, even if only as a pretext for the PSC's ending of an increasingly untenable coalition.

The Luxembourg case is also suggestive of several important patterns in national-subnational coalition behavior. It first suggests that national political party leaders do on occasion attempt to concoct multilevel coalition strategies, imposing the same coalition partnership on constituent party groups across levels of government. The case also illustrates that even in matters of such extreme strategic importance, party leaders cannot count on the compliance and loyalty of subnational groups. Finally, the aftermath of the Luxembourg rupture of the PSC-PRL pact demonstrates that spoiled relations between parties in subnational assemblies can spill over into the relations between the same parties at superior levels. These are pieces of the coalition puzzle that are lost when analysis focuses narrowly on the comings and goings of *formateurs* and national party presidents.

Analyzing Organizational Constraints

The internal battle that took place in Belgium's Luxembourg province prompts us to look more systematically and more comparatively at coalitions and intraparty politics. Of interest are a range of factors potentially responsible for variation in the reciprocal relations between territorial deputies and their national party leaders. These factors may be grouped into three categories: party properties, actor properties, and contextual properties. *Party properties* are those attributes most often considered to be determinative in matters of internal decision making and conflict resolution. Chief among these properties are party rules and statutes, centralization, and modes of vertical communication. *Actor properties* are individual-level characteristics or attitudinal predispositions, the balance of which should influence collective choices within party groups and determine organizational deference and dissent. This set of factors includes organizational discontent, levels of participation, and career ambitions. A third and final set of variables, *contextual properties,* links the electoral conditions discussed in chapters 3 and 6 with the organizational pressures under review here.

To analyze organizational constraints, our first goal is to identify the basic parameters of cross-national and cross-party variation. This is accomplished through presentation of survey responses that measure four key indicators: national-subnational coalition congruence, national-subnational motivational disparities, locus of decision making, and influence of national party leadership. The evidence will reveal variation across the three countries, across the parties within each country, and within individual parties. Such variation justifies treating the four concerns as dependent phenomena deserving of explanation. Seeking out empirical relations and meaningful explanations, the chapter proceeds by testing the relative importance of party and actor properties as independent variables. The analysis also raises the possibility that coalition situations in different electoral markets render different probabilities for organizational conflict.

Behavioral and Attitudinal Indicators of Organizational Linkages

NATIONAL-SUBNATIONAL COALITION CONGRUENCE. It might logically be assumed that alliance behavior in the periphery is a direct reflection of party relations at the center. Were this true, we should expect to find parties forming provincial and regional-level governments that match national government-versus-opposition alignments. This would reveal either the periphery's endorsement of decisions made at the center or the center's ability to gain adherence to its strategies among the various party organs in the periphery. As demonstrated in previous chapters, however, the practice of matching subnational and national coalitions where possible is by no means universal. Parties elected to territorial assemblies in Belgium, Germany, and France have chosen power-sharing partnerships that deviate from existing national arrangements even where duplication was a winning option.

How strong an incentive, then, is "matching"? Provincial and regional deputies in each country were asked to characterize the importance of forming subnational governments that duplicate alliances existing among the national parliamentary parties:

> "In forming a new [provincial/regional/Land] government, how important is it for your party to duplicate—i.e., have the same partner(s) as—your national party's alliance strategy wherever possible?"

Several key points arise immediately from the responses (Figure 7.1). First, there is clear variation across parties. Two distinct groupings exist, one in which party members generally believe that matching is of little or no importance and one in which the balance of party members clearly responds that duplication is indeed an important or a very important strategic consideration. Representatives of the German FDP, a quintessential "party of government," profess a far greater flexibility than the French Left Radicals (MRG), whose lot is intimately tied to a national alliance with the Socialist Party (PSF). This finding corroborates the comments of one FDP official who admitted that "coalition decisions, both before and after elections, are for us not really a matter of preferences, but of electoral strategy."[6] Second, as a country-level generalization, the data suggest that French parties see greater value in global alliance strategies than do their German and Belgian counterparts. This finding may be explained in part as a manifestation of the institutional osmosis afforded French politicians by the

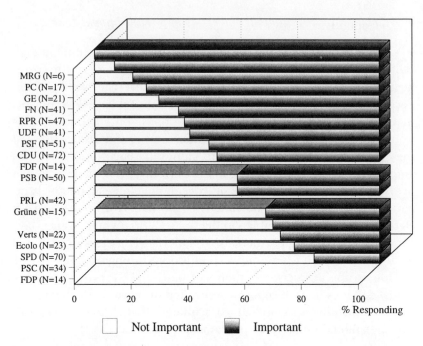

Figure 7.1 Importance of Duplicating National Coalition, by Party

cumul des mandats practice. Third, excepting the French MRG, there are conflicting opinions within in each party concerning the importance of coalition *gleichshaltung* or *égalité*. From these data, it would be difficult, therefore, to accept the generalization that forming exact replicas of national party partnerships is the governing principle of coalition formation in the periphery.

LOCUS OF COALITION DECISION. Where do parties determine coalition strategy for provincial and regional government, at the subnational level or at the level of the national party leadership? This is an important question and one whose answer should provide initial clues as to the variability between national control and local autonomy in matters of strategic choice. If the notion of unified, oligarchic parties holds, we should expect strong national-level determination of subnational coalition strategies across countries and across parties. If, however, the reverse is true and parties in territorial assemblies consistently determine their own coalition strategies, then this should suggest either weaker national-level control or greater decentralized decision making, and perhaps less rather than more deferential behavior.

All respondents were asked to identify the locus of decision making:

"Are the coalition strategies of your [provincial/regional/Land] party, particularly its tactics during and after elections, determined more by [provincial/regional/Land] party members or more by national party leaders?"

German Landtag deputies provide the clearest response, with an overwhelming 94% naming Land-level party figures as the key decision makers in their coalition politics (Figure 7.2). Alternatively, 56% of the provincial councilors in Belgium responded that national-level party leaders determine coalition tactics during and after elections to provincial assemblies. This finding is especially pronounced for the PRL, a "presidentocracy" according to one party veteran and three-term assemblyman in Hainaut province: "The real decisions are made by only a few people at the national level. These decisions do not always faithfully reflect the wishes and desires of provincial party members. Eighty percent of the power is in the hands of the president, and the rest is in the hands of the petite bureau. There is some party democracy, but it is democracy 'descendant.'"[7] Responses from francophone deputies to the Brussels Regional Council (not included in Figure 7.2) were likewise split, with slightly more than half (53.3%) reporting decisions being made by national party officials. And well over half (60.0%) of French respondents indicated that regional level *élus* and party leaders—not the party bureaus in Paris—ultimately determine regional alliance behavior.

Country specialists should find the German results predictable; yet questions about Belgium and France emerge. Why have there been so many "deviant" provincial coalitions in Belgium if national party leaders are themselves calling the shots? Here may be a clue that the assumption that national party leaders always oppose the formation of incongruent coalitions is itself suspect. What, moreover, should we make of the strategic autonomy boasted by many of the respondents in France, a country where national strategies have traditionally determined local tactics? Do national leaders allow party factions in their regional strongholds this indulgence to keep them within the party fold and to avoid internal party disputes?

NATIONAL PARTY INTERVENTION. Measuring the ultimate locus of decision making is not, of course, the same as measuring influence or pressure. Are we to conclude from the German data, for instance,

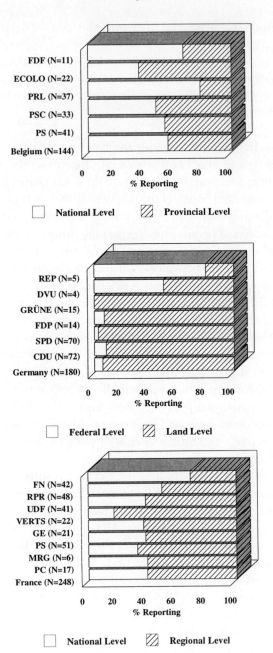

Figure 7.2 Locus of Party Coalition Decision

that coalition strategies in the Länder are strictly the domain of independent, unitary state parties making decisions without pressure from Bonn? Having identified the actual locus of coalition decisions, it is equally important to measure the extent of national party influence and intervention in subnational coalition bargaining. To measure national party influence in the coalition process, the questionnaire asked:

> "How would you characterize the influence of your party's national leadership in the government formation process in the [conseil provincial/conseil régional/Landtag] and in your party group's decisions to form a coalition with another party or parties?"

The majority of respondents in all three countries answered that their national party leadership holds "strong influence" over the party's coalition decisions in subnational assemblies (Figure 7.3). Thus, while German Landtag deputies indicated a clear belief that they ultimately determine their own fate, they nevertheless acknowledged here a substantial degree of involvement and influence coming from Bonn. This provides new empirical support for Culver's (1966) early assessment that "once negotiations on the formation of *Land* governments get under way, considerable pressure is exerted on the local parties by their national counterparts to influence the party composition of the ministries" (306). Responses from the Greens should be highlighted, as they represent an interesting exception to the overall German pattern. Similarly in France, where regional councilors claimed a considerable degree of credit for crafting their own coalition strategies, there is wide recognition here of strong national party influence in the power game. As in Germany, the pattern in France is broken by an ecologist party, the Verts, the majority of whose respondents perceive weak or no influence from national leaders in their regional coalition decisions. Indeed, one of the Verts' regional council vice presidents in Nord-Pas de Calais illustrated the lack of involvement by Antoine Waechter, the party's de facto leader, by saying, "He did not learn of our coalition victory until one day after the fact, when he heard about it on the radio!"[8]

The Belgian data largely mirror the findings of the earlier "locus of decision" questionnaire item, indicating a significant degree of national influence but also the greatest within-party variance regarding the strength of such influence. They also complement responses to another survey question that asked representatives the extent to which their party organization at the national level had advised the

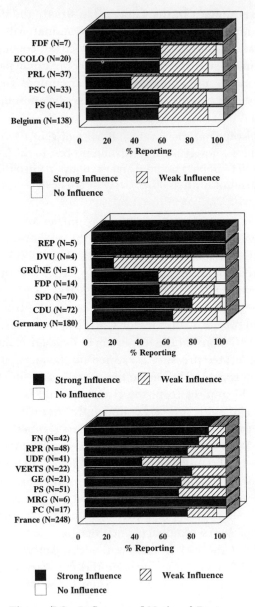

Figure 7.3 Influence of National Party Leadership in Provincial and Regional Coalition Bargaining

subnational party, when composing its most recent election manifesto, "to follow the intentions and policies of the national party." Of the Belgian councilors answering this question, 82% indicated some degree of national involvement in the election manifesto; of the German Landtag deputies, 65%; and of the French regional councilors, 62%. Together, these data further enhance the picture of regional and provincial coalition building as a process involving not only interparty exchanges but also intraparty exchanges.

MOTIVATIONAL DISPARITY. Do disparities exist between subnational parliamentarians and their national party leadership regarding the motivations for government participation? If the chief concerns and preference orderings of party members are the same across subnational and national levels, organizational constraints on coalition decision making are likely to be averted. However, if the objectives of party groups at different levels vary, then the probability of intraparty conflict over strategy increases. Survey questions allow a partial test for mixed motives in the coalition process.

As the respondent pool is made up largely of persons holding office exclusively at the subnational level, measuring national motivations per se is not possible with this survey instrument. Instead, the object here is to gauge motivations at the subnational level and to determine if representatives at this level themselves believe that they are pursuing government office for the same reasons as or for different reasons than their colleagues in national parliament. Here "perception" is an important intermediate variable between objective facts and the reactions of political actors. Regardless of actual intentions, if a regional deputy or provincial councilor *perceives* that his or her national party's motivations for seeking office and for formulating coalition strategy are fundamentally different from those that motivate the regional party group, then the councilor is more likely to find unattractive any pressure to adopt central party policy in the subnational setting.

Assembly members in all three countries were asked:

"From the list below, please rank the importance given by your [provincial/regional/Land] party group to the following considerations when forming a governing coalition with another party or parties:
   a. The need to be part of the majority in the council
   b. Maintaining party and ideological identity
   c. Agreement on a specific policy issue
   d. The electoral advantages of an alliance
   e. Following instructions from national party leaders"

This question was followed immediately by a similar item that asked respondents to characterize the motives of the national parliamentary party and its extraparliamentary leadership in strategic coalition situations:

"To your knowledge, how important are the following considerations for your *national* party when it forms a coalition with one or more parties in the [Chambre des Représentants/Assemblée Nationale/Bundestag]?
a. The need to be part of the parliamentary majority
b. Maintaining party and ideological identity
c. Agreement on a specific policy issue
d. The electoral advantages of an alliance
e. Instructions from [provincial/regional/Land] party leaders"

Table 7.1 provides the results, broken down by party from among those parties that have actually participated at one time or another in governing coalitions at both the national and subnational levels. The percentage of respondents reporting identical preference orderings for both subnational and national levels is presented, as are the most important and least important criteria (scaled according to the mean response for each item).

Only in the German CDU, just one of the 12 parties included in the table, did respondents signify clear agreement that their party's strategic behavior at the subnational level is motivated by precisely the same preference ordering (for all five criteria) as that which compels behavior at the national level. In nine parties (Belgian PS, PSC, PRL, FDF; German CDU, SPD; French PC, PS, UDF), respondents identified cross-party agreement on specific policy issues as their party's primary consideration in forming provincial or regional governments. In two of these nine (French PS and UDF), respondents answered that the party's national elite are more concerned with vote seeking than with the policy affinities of potential partners in government, and respondents from the Belgian PSC indicated that their national parliamentary party is more concerned with its place in the majority (i.e., its "governing vocation") than with the policy or ideological compatibility of its prospective partners.

In one case (German FDP), respondents identified the need to be part of the governing majority as their party's overriding concern at both regional and national levels. Responses also indicate that for some parties (French MRG; also Belgian PRL and French PCF, where

Table 7.1

Motivational Concerns in Subnational and National Government Formation, as Ranked by Subnational Assembly Members

Party	% Reporting Identical Preference Orderings	Most Important (MI) and Least Important (LI) Criteria for Party in Subnational Assembly	Most Important (MI) and Least Important (LI) Criteria for Party in National Parliament
		Belgium	
Socialist Party (PS)	44.0	MI: Policy agreement	MI Policy agreement
		LI: Top-down instructions	LI: Bottom-up instructions
Christian-Social Party (PSC)	35.3	MI: Policy agreement	MI: Majority status
		LI: Ideological identity	LI: Ideological identity
Liberal Party (PRL)	46.5	MI: Policy agreement	MI: Policy agreement
		LI: Electoral advantages	LI: Bottom-up instructions
Francophone Democratic Front (FDF)	64.3	MI: Policy agreement	MI: Policy agreement
		LI: Top-down instructions	LI: Majority status
		Germany	
Christian Democratic Union (CDU)	70.8	MI: Policy agreement	MI: Policy agreement
		LI: Top-down instructions	LI: Bottom-up instructions
Social Democratic Party (SPD)	68.6	MI: Policy agreement	MI: Policy agreement
		LI: Top-down instructions	LI: Electoral advantages
Free Democratic Party (FDP)	42.9	MI: Majority status	MI: Majority status
		LI: Electoral advantages	LI: Bottom-up instructions
		France	
Communist Party (PCF)	23.5	MI: Policy agreement	MI: Ideological identity
		LI: Majority status	LI: Majority status
Left Radical Movement (MRG)	33.3	MI: Top-down instructions	MI: Ideological identity
		LI: Electoral advantages	LI: Majority status
Socialist Party (PS)	52.9	MI: Policy agreement	MI: Electoral advantages
		LI: Top-down instructions	LI: Bottom-up instructions
Union for French Democracy (UDF)	46.3	MI: Policy agreement	MI: Electoral advantages
		LI: Top-down instructions	LI: Bottom-up instructions
Rally for the Republic (RPR)	43.8	MI: Ideological identity	MI: Electoral advantages
		LI: Top-down instructions	LI: Bottom-up instructions

"instructions" ranked second), the need to follow instructions and to stay in line with national strategy is an important factor in developing regional strategy. It should not go unmentioned that of the 12 parties included in the table, responses from representatives of the French Communist Party (PCF) and the French Left Radicals (MRG) indicate not only the greatest role for strategic deference but also the greatest subnational/national discrepancies in preference orderings. This finding perhaps taps into some of the tension experienced by the Limousin Communists in their decision not to toe the national party line in 1992, an exemplary case detailed in the previous chapter.

Given these data, it appears that motives can be mixed across layers of the same party, or at least that members of subnational party groups believe them to be so mixed. This is a powerful finding in that it suggests that groups within parties are not uniformly motivated by office seeking, vote seeking, or ideology advocacy. Together, the data from these survey questions indicate that unlike parties in the oversimplified models of unitary and oligarchic parties, political parties in territorial parliaments may be neither independent bargaining entities nor simple executers of decisions made at superior organizational levels. Instead, evidence suggests that decisions of party coalition strategy are made at multiple organizational levels, that national party influence in matters of strategic decision making varies, and that motivations differ across organizational and institutional layers. There is, in short, sufficient "noise" within the data to suggest that government formation at the regional or provincial level is not a simple or clear-cut process for parties. Variance suggests that strategic decision making involves intraparty exchange relationships—that is, politics within parties.

Explaining Organizational Influences on Coalition Formation

National party involvement and influence in coalition decision making at subnational levels vary, but why, and with what consequences? A knee-jerk analytical response would be that formally centralized parties invariably control subnational strategy, while formally decentralized parties invariably allow local autonomy in strategic decision making. Yet even the most centralized of parties, the French Communist Party, suffers internal conflict over alliance strategy and bears witness to the coalitional deviance of maverick party groups in the periphery (Mazey

1986; Perrineau 1986; Schain 1991; Weber 1990). On the other side, even the most fervent advocates of "basis democracy," such as ecologist parties, are subject to the oligarchic tendencies of their leaders and national governing bodies. The well-documented turmoils of the German Greens in their debates over participation in state government are easy examples (Frankland 1989; Kitschelt 1988, 1989b), as is the more obscure case of an Agalev politician's expulsion by the party organization for negotiating a local coalition after 10:00 p.m., too late according to party rules (Deschouwer 1989)! Formal organizational centralization is probably a necessary but insufficient explanation of party coalition behavior in the regional or provincial arena.

It might also be a logical first assumption that in a federal system, such as Germany, state parties are structurally free to pursue strategies independent of their respective national party organizations. Given the tendency "to view state elections as stages in the bitter contest for national power" (Pridham 1973, 461) and the important federal-level ramifications of coalition decisions in the Länder, however, key *Bundesprominenz* do actively intervene in coalition negotiations. Moreover, parties in the federal system may be organizationally federalized yet functionally "autocratic," as the German Free Democrats are frequently described (Laver and Schofield 1990). Assuming, alternatively, that more unitary political systems inevitably favor tightly controlled parties with top-down decision-making regimes is not satisfactory, either. Excluding the PCF and the Gaullists, French parties have not developed tight bureaucratic organizations (Knapp and Le Galès 1993). The point here is that simple reference to formal statutes and structures neglects what can be very telling organizational struggles over strategy.

A more useful explanation should include measures of organizational centralization and authority structures but must also take into account the attributes and aspirations of subnational politicians and the electoral context in which they find themselves. In asking whether and how organizational oligarchy acts as a determinant of strategic choice in subnational legislatures, we must learn when national party leaders are drawn into local coalition bargaining, what impact that intervention has on bargaining outcomes, and what broader consequences external interference might have for local democracy. One approach is to posit that the electoral conditions addressed in chapter 6 define the organizational hazards of postelection coalition bargaining. Party-level considerations, namely, the openness of internal decision-making regimes, should, in turn, influence the ways in which deputies in subnational parliaments react individually and collectively to organizational risk. Finally, individual-level factors, such as levels of participation and career ambitions, should mitigate the tendency of subnational parliamentarians to risk conflict by breaking from "the party line" in pursuit of local goals. These variables, largely underspecified or neglected outright in previous coalition studies, can further inform our understanding of the political struggles that occur when parties have to decide upon strategies in multiple institutional arenas.

Linking Electoral and Organizational Constraints

The competitiveness and uncertainty of electoral environments should structure the incentives for national party leaders to intervene in the coalitional affairs of their subnational colleagues. Given that central party officials are more likely to be concerned with coalition outcomes where the power and standing of the party are most at stake, national party involvement in local coalition bargaining is likely to be greatest under conditions of electoral instability. When government formation becomes a two-table bargaining process, as parties negotiate horizontally with potential partners in the subnational assembly while also negotiating vertically with party superiors, then the likelihood of intraparty conflict should likewise increase. All else being equal, the potential for intraparty conflict is greatest in high-volatility, localized electoral environments. Under such conditions, the national party has a clear vested interest in intervening, but at the same time subnational parliamentarians recognize that they cannot succeed electorally by getting a free ride from their respective national parties. In localized electoral markets, voters judge regional and provincial parties on their own merits, making it more difficult for those parties to automatically toe the party line without regard for local conditions. Therefore, if coalition preferences differ between national and subnational party organs, then the probability of conflict is high. In sum, coalition situations in different electoral arenas render different probabilities for organizational oligarchy and conflict.

Attitudes and behavior under conditions of electoral uncertainty should differ perceptibly from those under conditions of greater electoral stability. Static considerations such as party centralization should give way to actor properties and contextual properties as more meaningful explanatory factors. When the choice of coalition strategy in a competitive—that is, volatile and localized—environment induces national-subnational disagreement, politicians will respond to organizational demands in different ways depending in part on their "organizational radicalism." In the absence of both electoral constraints and pressure from national elites, debate over the power of party layers is inconsequential. Politicians can pursue unrestricted the coalitions that maximize their basic preferences. Under the weight of both electoral and organizational constraints, however, organizational "radicals" are more likely than "loyalists" to pursue their own strategy and to risk sanction rather than defer to the strategy of their superiors. Tests of these propositions are possible using the data available from survey responses as well as from both primary and secondary accounts of coalition politics at the subnational level.

Hypothesis: Volatility and Nationalization
Increase Incentives for National Party Leaders
to Participate in Decisions
of Subnational Government Formation

All else being equal, national party intervention and influence in local coalition bargaining will be greatest where electoral security is most uncertain (i.e., high volatility) and where elections more often take on the guise of mininational contests (i.e., nationalization). Bivariate correlations between reported levels of national party influence in the bargaining process and both the volatility and localization of respondents' electoral systems are included in Table 7.2. The expected direction and magnitude of the relationship between external influence and volatility is met in 13 of the 16 parties. This finding reinforces our understanding that party leaders calculate the costs and benefits of decentralized decision making according to situation. Under conditions of high volatility, "the troops must obey the orders of their generals; internal decision-making costs are comparative disadvantages in the game" (Heidar 1984, 3). The anticipated inverse relationship between national party influence and localization is also met in 12 of the 16 parties. Under these conditions, party leaders have less information about the local electorate and its preferences: "Thus the national politicians must, as a rule, proceed in co-operation with the provincial colleagues rather than attempt to assert the prerogatives of the central party organisations and the pre-eminence of what they discern as decisive party interests seen from the national level" (Johnson 1983, 160).

Table 7.2

Reported Influence of National Party in Subnational Coalition Choice, by Patterns of Electoral Competition (Pearson r values)

Influence Reported by Party Representatives	Volatility	Localization	N
		Belgium	
PS	0.53*	−0.55*	41
PSC	0.13	−0.29	33
PRL	0.36	−0.52*	37
ECOLO	0.20	−0.11	20
		Germany	
CDU	−0.19*	−0.11*	72
SPD	−0.10*	−0.15*	70
FDP	0.48*	0.44	14
Grüne	0.37	−0.37	15
		France	
PCF	0.34*	−0.13	17
MRG	0.87**	−0.87**	6
PS	−0.30*	−0.32*	51
Verts	0.26	0.18	22
Génération Ecologie	0.28	0.37*	21
UDF	0.13*	−0.21*	41
RPR	0.11*	−0.10*	48
FN	0.19	0.12*	42

*$p < 0.15$. **$p < 0.10$.

Note: Volatility and Localization are of respondent's regional or provincial electoral market, as measured over previous two elections.

That this occurs in practice is confirmed by Gérard Deprez, president of the Belgian PSC: "In some provinces it is very difficult to interfere with the coalitions. There it's a very specific situation, and relations between persons at the local level are essential to make a coalition. As president of the party I do not have enough information . . . enough sensitivity . . . to the relations between the persons . . . to the local problems they have to solve and the capacity they have to work together. In some cases people at the provincial level refuse to receive instructions from the national level. They just refuse. 'That's our job,' they say. 'You have no power, and we decide what we have to do,' and

Table 7.3

Consequences of National Party Intervention

	Bargaining Success (%)	Vertical Conflict (%)	Deference (%)
Intercept	71.72 (1.518)	29.14 (1.723)	8.16 (1.451)
National presence at bargaining table	−31.365 (1.859)	20.675 (2.110)	16.38 (1.778)
R^2	0.322	0.261	0.124
Signif F	0.001	0.001	0.001
N	601	601	601

Note: Standard error in parentheses.

Bargaining Success = % of original demands met; Vertical Conflict = incidence as % of all observed government formations; Deference = % of time local positions conceded.

they refuse."[9] Deprez's remarks complement our statistical findings and supply important evidence of the linkages between coalition bargaining, electoral competition, and organizational control. In doing so, they ultimately support the broader theoretical contention that systemic conditions and patterns of party competition, and not just some putative "inexorable law of oligarchy that governs all voluntary associations" (Kitschelt 1989a, 400), can help explain cross-sectional and intertemporal variation in party strategy.

If electoral uncertainty prompts external intervention in coalition bargaining, then what consequences does such intervention ultimately have on bargaining outcomes? Table 7.3 provides evidence that the effects are profound. Using only the presence or absence of one or more national party officials (parliamentary deputies and/or extra-parliamentary figures) at the subnational bargaining table as a dichotomous independent variable, OLS regressions were run on three dependent variables. The data first indicate that where subnational parliamentarians reported a national presence at the most recent post-election coalition negotiations, the regional or provincial party's success at securing its original bargaining demands vis-à-vis the other parties in the assembly is cut almost in half. National party intervention appears, therefore, to have deleterious consequences for horizontal bargaining. The data also confirm our suspicion that by sending emissaries out into the periphery to help negotiate new governments, national parties risk instigating internal divisions over policy and strategy. Indeed, the reported incidence of vertical conflict over coalition strategy almost doubles when there is a national agent at the bargaining table. Finally, the survey data suggest that a national presence markedly increases the tendency of subnational party groups to concede local policy priorities in favor of national strategic priorities. National party intervention thus induces deference, but by reducing the importance of local issues, two-table bargaining in government formation calls local democracy into question. Clearly, recognizing that parties deviate from the image of "unitary actors" can significantly improve our understanding of the coalition process and its outcomes.

Hypothesis: Volatility and Localization
Increase the Potential for National-subnational
Conflict over Coalition Strategy

Survey data have empirically established the existence of national-subnational conflict over coalition strategy. As presented in Table 7.3, however, there is no indication about the variation across parties in conflict or what we might call "strategic factionalism." Figure 7.4 compares measures of strategic factionalism for parties whose subnational branches compete amidst varying levels of electoral volatility and localization. Strategic factionalism is an indexed variable, constructed from a combination of scores on four survey measures: (1) ideological distance between subnational and national parties, (2) indifference to matching national coalition strategy, (3) aversion to following national instructions, and (4) resistance to party leadership.[10] Higher values on these measures indicate independent identity for the subnational party group and its greater propensity to pursue independent courses of action. The mean index value for each party has then been plotted against the summed value of mean volatility and mean localization for each party in the provinces, regions, and Länder included in the survey sample.[11]

This process provides some support for the notion that electoral constraints induce organizational pressures and reinforce strategic factionalism. Trend lines indicate that, in both Belgium and France, deference, or the likelihood that party subgroups will, "despite their more polarized opinions, submit to the authorities of the party leadership and subscribe to the proposals put forward by it" (Pierre 1986,

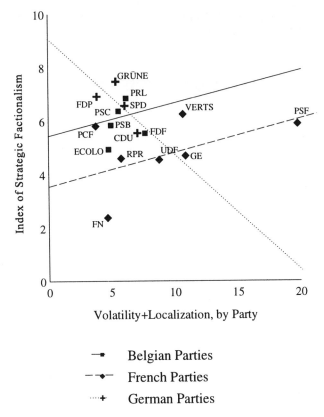

Figure 7.4 Vertical Strategic Factionalism, by Volatility and Localization of Party Vote

472), is a characteristic of those parties whose competitive positions are comparatively stable and linked to the fortunes of the national party. Where party fortunes at the subnational level are erratic and decoupled from national trends, there is likewise some indication that electoral exigencies create incentives to pursue independent courses of action. This dynamic, however, appears to add little to the understanding of intraparty relations among the German parties. There are, moreover, some unexpected findings for individual parties. That Ecolo scores the lowest of all Belgian parties in terms of strategic factionalism is surprising, as is the comparatively high factionalism reported by the French PCF, a party traditionally held together by democratic centralism. On the whole, there is reason to believe that environment conditions organizational approaches to coalitions, but it is also clear at this point that a richer interpretation requires that party-level and individual-level considerations be addressed as well.

Toeing the Party Line

If decisions of government participation and power sharing at provincial or regional levels can instigate organizational conflict, then it becomes important to understand the likelihood that party representatives in the periphery will behave independently of pressure from their national leadership. Do open lines of vertical communication and informal channels of access reinforce a consensual approach to party strategy in the periphery (Brearey 1989)? Do the ideological orientations and participation levels of the middle-level elites who pursue provincial and regional office, particularly their fundamentalism and activism, exacerbate or diminish intraparty conflict (Kitschelt 1989a; Orbell and Fougere 1973; Pierre 1986)? Are, finally, career aspirations within the party and the tendency to view subnational office as a stepping-stone to national elective office real constraints on local strategic autonomy (Laver 1989)? Like the conditions discussed above and in the previous chapter, these factors are generally left untested in studies of strategic party behavior in territorial parliaments.

Hypothesis: Organizational Radicalism Reinforces Strategic Factionalism

Chapter 3 posited that political struggles over party strategy in the periphery are likely to depend as much on the goal-related tendencies of intraparty groups as on more static organizational rules and structures. In this vein, provincial and regional party groups can be seen as mixtures of "loyalists" and "radicals," each subset with its own views of party conflict and consensus, each with its own set of values, and each with different beliefs about the legitimacy of compromise in exchange for government status. Organizational radicalism, it has been suggested, should reinforce the extent to which strategic decisions deviate from the wishes of national party leaders and from the models set by parties in national parliament. In short, organizational radicalism should reinforce strategic factionalism.

Using survey data, a composite index measuring organizational radicalism was constructed and employed to test this proposition. The index of organizational radicalism incorporates measures of four variables: (1) ideological self-placement on a Left-Right scale, (2) self-placement on a pragmatism/fundamentalism scale, (3) respect for party authority, and (4) fidelity to individual party leaders.[12] Party scores on this composite measure are presented in Table 7.4.

These data clearly display the kind of internal party heterogeneity anticipated and outlined in chapter 3. With the lone exception of the French Front National, all parties scoring high on the radicalism measure are leftists or ecologists. The empirical question is whether the attitude-related and belief-related radicalism associated with these parties translates into more divisive approaches (i.e., vertical strategic factionalism) to party strategy. Of the seven parties having previously scored high on the factionalism measure (Belgian PSC, PRL; German FDP, Greens; French PCF, PS, Verts), just three score high on the radicalism measure (Greens, PCF, Verts). This suggests that while attitude-related factionalism over coalition strategy in the periphery is greatest on the ideological Left and along the postmaterialism axis, it also characterizes catch-all parties at the center (PSC), parties on the ideological Right (PRL), and parties that are internally polarized along ideological lines (FDP).

Hypothesis: Informal Party Organization Increases Subnational Autonomy and Deviance

The two remaining concerns of this chapter link, first, the "internal workings of parties to their choice of strategy in a competitive environment" (Kitschelt 1989a, 403), and, second, the patterns of political participation within subnational party groups to their strategic independence. Decentralized party organization, it has been suggested elsewhere, reinforces strategic factionalism (Panebianco 1988). However, given that "the degree of correspondence between a party's statutory norms and its actual power structure" is not always perfect (Maor 1992, 6), a simple categorization of centralized/decentralized parties may mask significant variation. After all, the "formal structures of parties no more than the constitutional arrangements of states will give us the final story on influence and power in the system" (Heidar 1984, 8). While structures cannot be ignored, it may be more meaningful to view organization as a "communication system" (Sjoblom 1968) connecting subnational officeholders and national party leaders. As Brearey (1989) found in her study of local coalitions in North Rhine–

Table 7.4
Summary Index of Organizational Radicalism (%)

	Belgium					Germany				France						
	PSB	PSC	PRL	Eco	FDF	CDU	SPD	FDP	GRN	PCF	PSF	VRT	GE	UDF	RPR	FN
Most radical orientation (9–13)	30	24	24	70	20	6	39	17	62	100	35	57	7	3	17	52
Intermediate orientations (6–8)	30	14	20	10	40	31	15	8	22	0	32	14	21	47	44	39
Most moderate and loyal orientation (0–5)	40	63	56	20	40	63	46	75	16	0	33	29	72	50	39	9
Average value	6.5	5.5	5.5	9.1	6.0	4.9	5.7	4.0	9.3	10.8	6.4	8.5	4.1	5.1	5.5	7.7
N	36	21	26	17	6	71	70	14	12	7	36	23	16	36	33	26

Westphalia, councilors who enjoyed "easy, regular, and informal access" to party officials at the federal level (e.g., as personal acquaintances) as opposed to "formal access" (e.g., as delegates) achieved superior levels of local autonomy in decisions pertaining to coalition strategy. We can therefore hypothesize that informal party organization increases subnational autonomy and deviance.

An important qualifier must be attached: participation in the organs of party decision making outside the region or province is inversely related to organizational risk taking. If those regional or provincial representatives who enjoy informal access to national party leaders also hold elective office at the national level (as in France) or regularly participate in executive leadership committees at the national level, then we may expect to find greater "pressure on the councillors to conform to party line and conventions" (Brearey 1989, 295). In the same vein, where subnational representatives aspire to higher elective office or positions within the party hierarchy, organizational constraints on risk taking in coalition formation are likely to be high. These situational variables—overlapping membership, level of participation, candidate status—all have to be considered as possible organizational determinants of strategic choice. Table 7.5 presents bivariate correlation coefficients for survey measures of vertical authority structure and levels of participation, revealing significant associations between these factors and deferential behavior.

VERTICAL AUTHORITY STRUCTURE. Do open lines of vertical communication and informal channels of access reinforce a consensual approach to party strategy in the periphery? Members of territorial subgroups in tightly organized political parties are likely to be at a structural disadvantage when it comes to pursuing their own strategic preferences. They are apt to be the group least likely to have their views considered by party superiors, least likely to win internal party disagreements, and most likely to submit to party leadership under threat of sanction or promise of support. Therefore, the measures of organizational centralization presented in Table 7.5 are based on representatives' assessments of national-subnational relations within the party and on the capacity of the national party to punish maverick party behavior in the periphery.

On a five-point scale, politicians could indicate whether communication between subnational and national party tiers is regular and informal, regular and formal, limited and informal, limited and formal,

Table 7.5

Strategic Deference and Influence, by Authority Dynamics and Levels of Participation (Pearson r Values)

	Deference to Coalition Choices of National Leadership	Importance Attached to Duplicating National Coalition	Leadership Receptivity to Respondent's Coalition Preferences
Vertical authority structure			
Informality of communication	−0.16***	−0.21****	0.10
Openness of access	0.15****	0.07	−0.27****
Subnational success in intraparty conflict	0.05	0.07	0.32****
Capacity to punish subnational deviance	0.22****	0.20****	−0.23****
Level of participation			
Localists (N = 159)	−0.08*	−0.09*	−0.19***
"Meso"ists (N = 359)	−0.13***	−0.14*	0.12**
Party leaders (N = 42)	0.39****	0.24***	0.22***
Candidates (N = 160)	0.10**	0.10**	0.06

*$p < 0.10$. **$p < 0.05$. ***$p < 0.01$. ****$p < 0.001$.

or nonexistent. Subnational representatives who perceive communication to be "limited and formal" are likely to be those belonging to more centralized organizations, where formalized mechanisms of vertical communication translate into reduced scope for subnational influence. Those indicating vertical communication to be either "regular and informal" or "nonexistent" are indicating that relations, when they occur, are less rigid and more personal, and that when they apparently do not occur, their absence is indicative of greater local autonomy. A corresponding question challenged respondents to indicate the openness of their group leaders' access to the party's national leadership. "No access" or "limited access" indicates a closed vertical party system, whereas "open access" or "very open access" signifies the opposite. In apparent confirmation of Brearey's earlier findings, the results suggest that the informality of vertical communication and the openness of access to central party leaders are inversely related to deferential attitudes vis-à-vis the party leadership and to the importance ascribed to duplicating national models in subnational assemblies. Moreover, they both are positively associated with respondents' beliefs that their own views and preferences regarding coalition strategy are actually considered by the party leadership.

Two additional measures of vertical authority structure are provided in Table 7.5. "Subnational success in intraparty conflict" reports respondent observation of the frequency of provincial or regional party group success in resolving disputes with the party leadership (100%, >50%, 50%, <50, 0%). Assuming that subnational success is inversely related to central leadership power, this variable has been tested for association with indicators of strategic deference and leadership receptivity to individual coalition preferences. The strong finding that emerges is that with a track record of success in internal party disputes, subnational party groups gain—or at least perceive that they gain—added stature in the formulation of coalition strategy by national party leaders ($r = 0.32$). The final measure of vertical authority structure, "capacity to punish subnational deviance," presents some of the clearest relationships of all the authority variables. Where provincial councilors, regional councilors, and Landtag deputies believe that the leading figures and bodies of the party at the national level can punish them for dissident behavior, deference follows, and the importance of duplicating national party strategy increases. At the same time, the capacity to punish also translates into much weaker "collective" strategic decision making. This finding goes far in explaining discrepancies in earlier measures: for example, why a party such as the French Front National scored high on radicalism but low on factionalism. It may also shed some light on why French parties, almost all of which have active "discipline committees" that warn, censure, and expel maverick members, scored surprisingly low on measures of factionalism.

LEVELS OF PARTICIPATION. The second half of Table 7.5 examines patterns of party participation and attitudes toward party authority. The expectation here is that participation, when low or when restricted to local party sections, is likely to reinforce the pressures of vote maximizing, local public opinion, and local concerns over and above those of submitting to the authority of the party leadership. Localism and "mesoism," like the systemic electoral localization discussed in earlier chapters, should therefore reduce the larger organizational constraints on forming strategy at the subnational level. Respondents have been coded as either "localists," "mesoists," or "party leaders." Localists have indicated greater participation in communal and municipal party sections than in provincial, regional, or national party organs. "Mesoists" have likewise indicated greater participation in party affairs at the middle or supralocal (i.e., provincial, regional, or Land) level than at both the local and national levels. Party leaders are those subnational representatives participating regularly in the national governing bodies (i.e., bureaus, permanent committees) of their respective parties. To gauge the risk-inhibiting pressures of national office seeking (e.g., selection processes, financial support, campaign backing), respondents were also coded as "candidates" if they answered affirmatively to a direct question regarding their future intentions to stand for election to a seat in national parliament.

If these data do tell a story, then it clearly is that situation within a party influences the degree to which members accept a top-down approach to coalition strategy in the periphery. While party leaders and those active at the party's highest tiers strongly support a "leader-follower" approach to authoritative decision making, localists and mesoists are more apt to disagree with such a conception of deference and imitation. The inverse association between localism and leadership receptivity to coalition preferences should be noted here, as it contrasts with the positive coefficients recorded for mesoists and party leaders. Although somewhat weaker than anticipated, the correlations between future candidacy for national elective office and measures of strategic dependence are positive and statistically significant. All told, there is definite empirical evidence pointing to situational party variables as important considerations in the coalition game.

Discussion

This chapter opened by raising the issue of whether and how organizational considerations condition coalition behavior in the subnational parliamentary institutions to which parties aspire to gain power. This issue, it was proposed, is an important research concern for both practical and theoretical reasons. As a matter of practical politics, it is of real interest to know whether individuals and groups chosen by the electorate to determine the allocation of power and the direction of public policy in their respective provinces, regions, or states are functionally independent of party bosses and party strategies at the center. The extent to which party groups in the periphery pursue strategies— of which coalition building and power sharing are crucial elements— independent of their national parties is an indication of the democratization of decision making within political parties. The extent to which local preferences override national circumstances and pressures also reflects directly on the health of representative democracy at subnational levels of governance. These are important concerns, even in the "mature" democracies of Belgium, France, and Germany.

At the same time, the analysis has addressed important theoretical issues, using the coalition process as a lens with which to examine assumptions about organizational oligarchy, parties as "unitary actors," and electoral sources of party conflict. Such issues have long been staples in works by political scientists in the tradition of Duverger, Michels, and Downs. They have also long been oversimplified by theorists attempting to understand party behavior in coalition situations such as government formation, leading to an unproductive polarization of ambitious game theorists on one side and empiricists of the "European politics tradition" on the other. Certainly, little effort has heretofore been devoted to testing many of these assumptions against the evidence offered by coalition politics in subnational institutions. Hence, it has been a major goal of this chapter to gauge the existence and magnitude of a range of possible relationships linking strategic behavior with systemic, party, and individual variables.

Evidence presented in this chapter contributes to both these sets of practical and theoretical concerns. Across three countries with varying state structures, it is clear that subnational power is valuable enough to merit the active pursuit and intervention of party players external to the immediate bargaining environment. Yet party behavior in the periphery can deviate substantially from politics and cross-party co-operation as it is practiced in the capital. This is manifested most overtly in coalitions that fail to match national partisan alignments, as well as in those that experiment with alternative coalition formulas. Party attitudes and approaches to coalition situations and collective action problems can likewise bear little resemblance to party strategy at superior levels. Motivational disparities and ideological discrepan-cies such as those measured empirically in the previous sections pro-vide tangible evidence that parties are not single-minded bargaining entities with a single set of preferences regarding the range of potential coalitions. Furthermore, where local preferences and national strate-gies collide, it is apparent from these data that party leaders cannot feel entirely comfortable in expecting deference from the lower ech-elons of their organizations.

The picture painted by the data is ultimately one in which patterns of electoral competition, ideological extremism, organizational mili-tancy, authority structures, and activism all intervene to condition what otherwise rational actors should be expected to do in collective bar-gaining situations. In other words, there is far more to bargaining and strategy than the legislative "weights" of the parties elected to subna-tional parliaments. Systemic conditions, namely volatility and localiza-tion, appear to increase both the electoral stakes and the organizational risks of coalition strategy. Party conditions, primarily the openness of vertical communication and access, appear to increase the likelihood that subnational groups will enjoy strategic autonomy in their own arena. Individual considerations, such as career aspirations and high levels of participation in party bodies above the provincial or regional level, appear to increase the incentives for representatives to trade elec-toral risks for organizational unity. Recognizing these relationships allows a more informed and a more theoretically meaningful under-standing of an important political process and of complex political be-havior in an overlooked institutional setting.

———

Part Four

Application and Conclusions

Chapter Eight

Coalition "Proving Grounds": A Functional Role for Subnational Parliaments in Multiparty Systems

In his classic study, *Coalitions in Parliamentary Government,* Dodd (1976) proposes that "provincial or state parliaments could provide an experimental setting in which party coalitions could be attempted between long-term adversaries, with the intermediate provincial experience making national-level coalitions more possible than they would be without the provincial experience" (217). Given this proposition that subnational parliaments "could" serve a functional purpose as proving grounds for future national coalition arrangements, the literatures on coalition behavior and multiparty government have nevertheless failed to systematically explore whether they really do.

This chapter investigates Dodd's suggestion of subnational-national coalition linkage, and in doing so it evaluates subnational institutions as suppliers of the information that national party leaders need when they sit down at the bargaining table to negotiate a new government. In demonstrating the (in)compatibility of parties, their (in)efficacy in governing, and the electoral (un)popularity of a partnership, coalitions in regional and provincial parliaments should be valuable sources of feedback. To establish this linkage empirically, three questions are posed: Do subnational coalitions alter the number of coalitions available to parties in national government? Do subnational politicians themselves perceive any direct or indirect influence on national coalition patterns, and if so, are they motivated by the prospect of such influence when they negotiate the party composition of their own executives? Finally, do national party leaders actually make use of the knowledge gained through coalition experiences in the periphery when weighing alternative coalition strategies in the national arena?

Conceptualizing the Feedback Role

The recent rise of ecologist or "Left-libertarian" parties and the resurgence of regionalist, populist, and extreme right-wing nationalist parties have resulted in the introduction of new parties into the representative assemblies of most European countries. This has been most pronounced at local and regional levels, where parties such as the Front National in France, Die Grünen in Germany, and Ecolo and the Vlaams Blok in Belgium have gained entry and consequently complicated the once predictable coalition calculus. The theoretical and empirical literatures on parliamentary politics and coalition government generally neglect the wider implications and subnational-national linkages inherent in these developments. This deficiency could be redressed if two parallel research trends would only merge. First, there is nascent interest among scholars of multiparty government in the coalition politics of subnational assemblies. Second, there is increasing recognition that national government formation and coalition building are not one-shot events but instead parts of an iterative bargaining process. The problem is that these two research lines have yet to intersect. The possibility that subnational coalitions offer both experience and information to parties in the national bargaining arena is underexplored.

The periodic formation of coalitions in subnational institutions is the most overt manifestation of coalition behavior outside of national parliaments. These are events that may be full of national connotations, and they should be included in a dynamic explanation of coalition formation. Detailed in chapter 3, the essential tenets of such a dynamic model are depicted in figure 8.1. Here coalition choices are driven by the rational pursuit of certain preferred goods (e.g., spoils of office) but are constrained by pressures external to a pure utility calculation. These constraints include the necessity of adapting to the immediate electoral environment (chapter 6) and to the preferences of party superiors (chapter 7). Government formation and party alliances

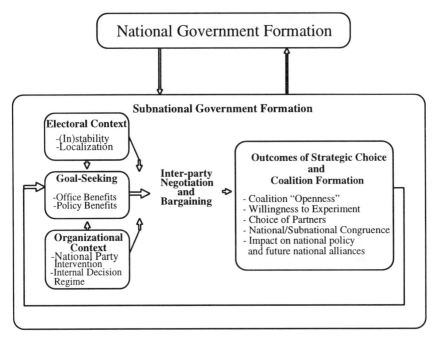

Figure 8.1   Linking National and Subnational Government Formation

are interdependent across levels of the political system. Visualizing the determinants of coalition choice in this fashion adds spatial and temporal dimensions to our understanding of an important political process. Coalition politics in subnational assemblies may take place within the larger context of national coalitions, transforming government formation from a discrete event into a dynamic process "nested" within the national coalition game. Coalitions at one level of government can, moreover, have an impact on coalitions at other levels, with a feedback loop connecting past, current, and future iterations of coalition bargaining.

The model essentially posits a process of "coalitional learning." A baseline for thinking about coalitional learning first envisions a set of relatively exclusive coalitional strategies (i.e., alternative combinations of governing parties) that dominate the parliamentary game until environmental shifts and policy problems emerge that require new coalitional strategies (i.e., new combinations of parties) in order for the government to govern effectively as a policy-making entity. As long as the environment remains relatively constant, coalition actors engage in iterative maneuvers within the existing set of coalitional strategies that define the game, leaving the permissible combinations within the game unchanged. However, when governing crises or electoral upheavals emerge, the national parliament must learn which new party combinations are politically viable and effective as governing solutions. One way to learn is to assess coalitional experiments at the regional or provincial level. When subnational assemblies have created viable and effective coalitions among new parties, that experience becomes strong evidence that such coalitions may work for the national parliament. When a national parliament faces a governing crisis and sees new coalitions at subnational levels that appear viable and capable of addressing the crisis, then the national parliament may embrace a coalitional strategy or set of strategies that previously seemed impossible to consider—thereby transforming the strategic structure of the coalitional game within the national parliament. We can justifiably call this a process of coalitional learning (figure 8.2).

Inherent in such a process are two key dimensions: influence and experimentation. Regarding influence, we are concerned with whether and how much subnational coalition activity affects the behavior of parties at superior levels of government. Regarding experimentation, we recognize that coalition change itself implies different and often untried forms of multiparty power sharing. To test for influence, it is necessary to establish a temporal connection and direction of coalition change using historical events data. To discern if influence is conscious, real, and not merely apparent, it is necessary to reconstruct decision-making processes and experiences through survey and interview data. Beyond this, it is necessary to determine whether politicians at subnational levels consciously experiment with novel coalition models for the express purposes of gauging voter response, testing cross-party loyalty, or determining the within-party consequences of a new governing partnership. Experimentation presupposes a certain amount of openness in the coalition system. If subnational assemblies are to be considered as experimental laboratories for national coalitions, then such experimentation must assume willingness on the part of subnational parliamentarians and party leaders to form alliances with unconventional partners. Survey and interview data prove useful in testing for how "open" councilors are to the entire range of coalitions available following an election.

To explore each of these possibilities empirically, the following propositions are offered: First, bottom-up strategic influence and learning exists when coalition innovations—that is, new power-sharing

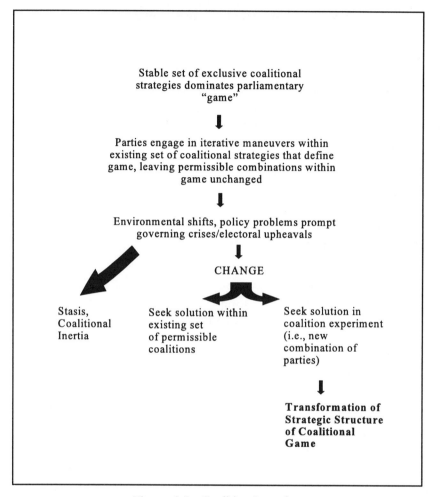

Figure 8.2 Coalition Learning

arrangements—first appear at the subnational level and are subsequently introduced at the national level following a brief "lag" period. Second, the functional utility of subnational parliaments as coalition proving grounds is enhanced when regional and provincial councilors (a) perceive a "spillover" or "trickle-up" influence and (b) are motivated to pursue alternative coalitions by the prospect of such influence. Third, the "feedback" or test value of subnational coalition experience increases with the active intervention of national party leaders in the local bargaining process.

Evidence: Direction of Temporal Change

It is possible to compare, country by country, the major changes in national coalition arrangements against coalition developments in subnational government. The temporal dimension of change—whether a new coalition model is adopted first at the national or subnational level, and if once inaugurated at one level is duplicated elsewhere—is a necessary initial indicator of national-subnational coalition linkages.

Belgium

In Belgium, there have been four important innovations, or "firsts," in government coalitions since 1961.[1]

FIRST "TRIPARTITE" COALITION. In the face of mounting challenges from new parties' pressing demands for regional devolution, the Socialist, Christian Social, and Liberal parties formed their first grand coalition since a string of all-party governments in the immediate postwar period. The institutional setting was Brabant's provincial assembly following general elections in November 1971. Twelve months after this model's inauguration at provincial level, a tripartite coalition linking the same parties took shape in national government under Socialist Prime Minister Leburton.

FIRST COALITION TO INCLUDE A "COMMUNITY" OR FEDERALIST PARTY. The earliest power-sharing arrangement based on territorial rather than socioeconomic cleavages formed in Luxembourg province following the March 1974 general election. Instead of responding to the crisis of an electoral breakthrough by a regionalist party by closing ranks against it (the strategy followed in Brabant three years earlier), in Luxembourg province Socialists and Liberals allied with the francophone Rassemblement Wallon (RW). Three months later, the RW negotiated its way into national government. The RW's elevation to government status, first at the provincial level and then at the national level, signified a recognition by Belgium's traditional parties that they could not hope to recoup mounting electoral losses without addressing the grassroots demands for territorial and cultural integrity championed by the RW.

FIRST POWER-SHARING COALITION IN THE FLEMISH HALF OF BEL-
GIUM TO EXCLUDE THE CHRISTIAN PEOPLE'S PARTY (CVP). Flemish
Socialists, Liberals, and the Volksunie ousted the CVP from government for the first time in 161 years by coalescing in Limburg's provincial assembly after the November 1991 general election. Fifteen days
later, the Belgian monarch for the first time since 1958 charged a "formateur" with the task of forming a non-Catholic national government.
Although his mission ultimately proved unsuccessful, the attempt was
rife with political symbolism and exemplified the country's search for
new alternatives to an increasingly inert leadership.

FIRST "ASYMMETRICAL" COALITION. The first coalition government chosen by a bilingual assembly to include one but not both halves
of a traditional political "family" arose in Brabant province following
the November 1991 election. In Brabant, the Flemish CVP joined a
governing coalition with the Socialists and Liberals, but without its
Walloon counterpart, the PSC. No such asymmetrical coalition subsequently formed in national government, although the respective
memberships of the CVP and PSC split dramatically in their desire to
join the new government.[2] Four years later, the Flemish Christian
Democrats in the Brussels Regional Council repeated this act of fratricide by joining an asymmetrical government without their francophone counterparts.

Of the four cases of major coalition change in Belgium, therefore,
all clearly originated at provincial level. As a consequence of these
provincial-level coalition innovations, two were ultimately adopted in
national government after a short lag period, one was duplicated in
regional government, and a fourth profoundly altered the calculus of
national party bargaining.

Germany

There have been six important instances of coalition innovation and
change since 1960 in Germany, each with possible federal-state linkages.

FIRST "GRAND" COALITION. The Christian Union and Social Democrat parties adopted a "grand" coalition model for the first time in
federal government in 1966, prompted by the outgoing FDP's disagreement with the CDU over economic policy. Harbingers of the

grand coalition, however, had been set repeatedly in the state parliaments, especially in the immediate postwar period: Bavaria (1945–54), Bremen (1951–59), Hamburg (1945–46), Hessen (1945–51), Lower Saxony (1946–51, 1957–59), North Rhine–Westphalia (1946–50), Rhineland-Palatinate (1946–47, 1947–51), and Schleswig-Holstein (1946–47). More contemporary with the Bonn change was the shift from SPD-FDP to CDU-SPD in Lower Saxony in 1965, as well as the CDU-SPD coalition arrangements in Berlin (1955–63) and in Saarland (1956–61). Subsequent to the change in Bonn, only one Land government (Baden-Württemberg 1966–72) adopted the grand coalition formula.

FIRST SOCIAL-LIBERAL (SPD-FDP) COALITION. After two full decades of Christian Democratic presence in the young democracy's federal government and amidst growing fears of a "CDU-staat," the first SPD-FDP federal government assumed power in 1969. Social Democrat–Free Democrat governments in the Länder clearly predated Bonn's new left-leaning alliance: the SPD and FDP had already been coalition partners in 7 of the 11 Länder since 1946. Additionally, in the immediate prelude to the Bonn change, SPD-FDP coalitions constituted the governments of Hamburg, Hessen, North Rhine–Westphalia, and West Berlin. In the aftermath of the Bonn change, the social-liberal coalition reproduced itself in Hamburg, Hessen, and North Rhine–Westphalia, but of these there were no actual alternations of coalition partners.

WENDE. The 1982 SPD-FDP to CDU/CSU–FDP coalition change in Bonn represents an alternation but not an innovation in the German coalition system. The FDP had already betrayed the Social Democrats in Saarland (1977–84) and Lower Saxony (1977–78), and the FDP's willingness to play junior partner to the Christian Democrats rather than the SPD in Hessen in 1982 heralded impending change at the federal level. No major coalition alternations occurred in the Länder following the Bonn change, and only five years later did the FDP stray to the SPD (e.g., in Hamburg in 1987).

FIRST "RED-GREEN" COALITION. In Hessen, the SPD chose coalition with Die Grünen over minority government in November 1985. The radical new model spawned similar arrangements in other Länder, usurping the FDP's traditional role as *the* coalition partner and introducing "new politics" policy issues into state government. However, heading into the 1994 Bundestag elections, Social Democrats and Greens failed to reach any formal cooperative agreement to share federal power if the opportunity arose, as in the event it did not.

FIRST "TRAFFIC LIGHT" COALITION. The earliest government to include the SPD (red), FDP (yellow), and Die Grünen (green) parties formed in the eastern state of Brandenburg in 1990 and in Bremen in 1991. This unlikely new type of coalition, as yet untried at the federal level, nevertheless sets the precedent for such a creative configuration in national-level politics. The SPD-FDP-Grüne coalitions thus further expand the set of coalition alternatives in a system that was, before the emergence of the Greens in the late 1970s, relatively closed.

FIRST ATTEMPTED "BLACK-GREEN" COALITION. Negotiations to form an unprecedented CDU-Grüne coalition took place in Baden-Württemberg following the 1992 state election. The coalition ultimately failed to form; however, the Baden-Württemberg attempt introduces the "eco-libertarian" model as still another new alternative in the universe of coalition possibilities.

It is clear from these six cases that no coalition change in German federal government has occurred without precedent in Land government. No combination of parties has governed in Bonn without previous power-sharing experience at regional level. The historical sequencing of coalition change in Germany is a necessary first indicator of a bottom-up process of coalition learning and diffusion.

France

Principal alliance shifts and coalition innovations in France since the first election of autonomous regional assemblies in 1986 are limited to three particular developments.

FIRST COLLABORATION WITH FRONT NATIONAL. Aside from a city-level coalition with the Gaullist RPR in Dreux in 1983, the first power-sharing coalitions between the extremist Front National and the orthodox center Right emerged following regional council elections in 1986. In such key regions as Aquitaine, Languedoc-Roussillon, Haute-Normandie, and Picardie, moderate conservatives made pacts with the FN to secure power and to allocate important executive posts. Despite this extensive network of regional collaboration, the UDF and RPR, upon gaining the majority in the Assemblée Nationale, rejected formal cooperation with the Front National's 35 deputies. By 1988, nonetheless, the UDF and RPR were making second-ballot deals with the FN to save national parliamentary seats and coopting key FN policy themes, such as immigration reform, in an effort to reunite the right-wing electorate.

SOCIALIST-COMMUNIST RUPTURE. The Socialist Party's (PS) coalition "ouverture" in 1988 to the Center marked a clear shift away from the old "Union of the Left" socialist-communist axis. Stopping short of a formal alliance with the centrist parties in parliament, Michel Rocard wooed several centrist and right-wing figures into his government, including Jean-Pierre Soisson (ex–UDF-PR), Jean-Marie Rausch (CDS), Olivier Stirn (ex–UDF-Rad), and Lionel Stoléru (ex–UDF-PR). By 1990, the non-Socialist members of the "majorité présidentielle" had formed the France Unie (FU) movement, a "party" with which the PS did not sign a global accord but with which the Socialists attempted regional coalitions in Lorraine and Bourgogne in 1992.[3] The price for the national-level shift, however, could be seen in the widespread refusal by PCF councilors to support PS presidential candidates in the regions.

FIRST "ROSE-VERTE" COALITION. Socialists and ecologists for the first time agreed to share power following the 1992 regional council election in Nord-Pas de Calais. Just days later, a national spokesman for the PS declared, "An alliance with the ecologists is today indispensable. Not only would this permit us to maybe win the legislative elections, but it would represent a first phase of enlarging the political space."[4] Another leading party official stated that "it is now the socialists, the communists, and the Verts who must emerge as a new majority."[5] By February 1993, former PS Prime Minister Michel Rocard had launched his campaign for a political "big bang" on the Left to constitute a vast new movement including socialists, centrists, ecologists, and reform communists that would be based on the Nord-Pas de Calais model.

In France, therefore, two of the three primary coalition innovations since the mid-1980s have involved mainstream parties attempting alternative regional-level coalition models with ecologists and national-

ists. In both cases, developments at regional level generated a political
dynamic that influenced national-level cooperation.

Summary

Table 8.1 summarizes the nature and direction of major coalition
innovations in the three countries. In these innovations and in their
consequences is initial evidence of the primary locus of coalition experimentation and of apparent bottom-up coalition learning. On the
surface at least, national coalitions do seem to be reacting to developments at subnational levels, and by setting precedents for alternative
types of cooperation, parties appear to have enlarged the number of
permissible coalition options in national parliament available to them.
Is there some systematic reason that may indicate why "learning" a new
coalition might be easier first at the subnational level than at the national level, as well as vice versa? One possibility is that coalitional
learning is easiest first at the subnational level when policy problems
are driven primarily by domestic regional-economic concerns, whereas
coalitional learning is more viable first at the national level when policy
problems are driven primarily by constitutional or international concerns. Thus, in Belgium, the one clear example of a national-level
coalition innovation coming first is that prompted by the issue of constitutional reform of the state's structures. Similarly, the example of
the breakdown of the "Union of the Left" in France comes in 1988
amid the general breakup of communist dominance in the Soviet
Union and throughout Europe. By contrast, the remaining examples
of subnational influence revolve more around domestic and regional
issues and events rather than shifting international developments or
those dealing with the core identity of the nation-state.

It might also be tempting to assume that because a country has multiple subnational units but only one national parliament, the probability of a new coalition's emergence at the subnational level is simply
by definition higher, assuming a random distribution of outcomes.
This might then be consistent with an argument that coalition building
is a discrete event and that any connection between national and subnational levels is spurious. This assumption, more likely, is a moot
point since the important concern is ultimately not with estimating the
likelihood of where new coalitions will emerge but with if and how a
coalition strategy that previously seemed impossible to consider can,
once adopted somewhere in the system, transform the coalition game

Table 8.1

Origins and Directions of Coalition Change

Coalition Innovation	Site	Consequence	Time Lag	Direction of Influence
		Belgium		
First "tripartite" coalition	Brabant Province, 1971	Tripartite national government formed	12 months	←
First coalition with "Community" Party	Luxembourg Province, 1974	Community Party (RW) enters national government	3 months	←
First coalition with regional-nationalist parties	National Government, 1977	Federalist parties join Brabant provincial coalition	12 months	→
First non-Catholic (non-CVP) government in Flanders	Limburg Province, 1991	First formateur since 1958 with mission to form national government without Catholic parties	2 weeks	←
First "asymmetrical" coalition	Brabant Province, 1991	Split between CVP and PSC over joining new national government Asymmetrical coalition established in Brussels Region	5 months 4 years	← ←

232

	Germany			
"Grand" coalition	Lower Saxony, 1965; Berlin, 1955; Saarland, 1955; and most immediate postwar Land governments	CDU/CSU–SPD grand federal coalition from 1966 to 1969	Years	←
Social-Liberal government	7 of 11 Länder from 1946 to 1969	SPD-FDP government from 1969 to 1982	Years	←
First "red-green" coalition	Hessen, 1985	SPD-Green government in Lower Saxony, 1990	Years	↔
First "traffic light" coalition	Brandenburg, 1990	SPD-FDP-Green coalition in Bremen, 1991	11 months	↔
	France			
First coalitions with National Front	Dreux, 1983; multiple regions, 1986	2nd-ballot deals in 1988 national election	Years	←
Socialist collaboration with center (France Unie)	National government, Rocard cabinet, 1988	Alliances with France Unie in Lorraine and Bourgogne in 1992	Years	→
First "rose-verte" coalition	Nord-Pas de Calais, 1992	PS announces "big bang" strategy to reorient Left	10 months	←

throughout the system. Moreover, it may be dubious to assume a priori a random distribution of coalition outcomes, given Laver's theoretical contentions that "local coalitions are negotiated in the context of a *particular* coalition government at national level," that subnational politicians "attempt as a first recourse to form an equivalent local coalition," and thus that there may be "very heavy constraints that national politics can conceivably impose upon local coalitional behaviour" (Laver 1989, 24–27).

Councilors' Perceptions of Strategic Influence

Prima facie evidence that coalition precedents are set in subnational assemblies with a subsequent impact on national alliances is a powerful and necessary first indicator of linkage. It is not sufficient, however, and we must look deeper to determine if such linkages are conscious or merely coincidental. Do subnational politicians themselves perceive any direct or indirect influence on national coalition patterns? Are subnational politicians *motivated* by the expectation that the coalitions they choose may affect coalition decisions at the national level? How *open* (a precondition for experimentation) are subnational legislators to alliances with "alternative" partners? Do national politicians actually seek out evidence from coalitional experiments at the subnational level? These are crucial questions that are explored with survey data and with interview probing.

Recognizing Interdependence

Councilors responding to the survey questionnaire were asked the following two complementary questions:

"Can successful coalitional cooperation in your [subnational government] lead to a coalition between the same parties in the [national government]?"

"Can successful coalition cooperation in [national government] lead to a coalition between the same parties in your [subnational government]?"

Both questions sought only to measure local legislators' perceptions of (a) bottom-up and (b) top-down coalition influence. If government formations are discrete events, as conventional coalition theories often assume, then we should anticipate the null hypothesis—namely, that respondents perceive no real connection between coalitions in separate institutional arenas.[6] Alternatively, if either distinct bottom-up or top-down coalition influence does exist, then response patterns should reveal clear discrepancies in one direction or another.

The story as told by elected councilors (table 8.2) is that alliances formed in territorial assemblies can serve a functional purpose by influencing future coalition arrangements at the national level. Even though federalism emerges here as a potentially important variable, this pattern is consistent across structurally different countries. While it is not especially surprising that the null hypothesis of no perceived linkage does not hold at the individual level, the magnitude of perceived bottom-up influence is striking, particularly in France and Belgium, with their strong traditions of elite control and centralization. Such evidence suggests that the temporal sequence of coalition innovation in the three countries, as discussed in the previous section, is more than coincidental. Actors in the system perceive not only that national coalitions assume the position of the status quo in local coalition bargaining but also that exchanges in the Länder are antecedents of coalition innovation at the federal level in Germany. Provincial and regional experiments in Belgium likewise herald national coalition changes. Regional coalitions as testing grounds ("bancs d'essai") in France have yet to produce the major changes in national government of the magnitude found in the other two countries; nevertheless, their consequences in terms of cabinet shake-ups, electoral deal making, and policy shifts are seen as real by individuals immersed in the process.

Numerous factors may account for differences in attitudes about the relationship between subnational and national coalition politics: the structure of party organization (level of central control), party ideology (extreme or moderate), a party's past history of government participation, past electoral history, fractionalization of the party system, incentives in the electoral law, and the visibility and importance of subnational governments, to name a few. The informational value of subnational parliaments as coalition "proving grounds" should, for example, increase with the active intervention of national party leaders and other prominent national political figures in the local bargaining process. This "nationalization" of local coalition bargaining strips the postelection government formation of its purely parochial character, heightens the stakes, and subjects the strength of national interparty relations to well-publicized tests. In such cases, learning is enhanced,

Table 8.2

Perceptions of Coalition Influence across Institutional Tiers

	Bottom-Up		Top-Down		Primary Direction of Change		
	% Reporting Weak or No Vertical Influence	% Reporting Some or Strong Vertical Influence	% Reporting Weak or No Vertical Influence	% Reporting Some or Strong Vertical Influence	% Indicating Top-Down	% Indicating Bottom-Up	% Indicating Bi-Directional
Germany	6.5	93.5	9.5	90.5	20.5	12.6	66.9
Belgium	41.3	58.7	31.8	68.2	16.2	23.7	60.1
France	50.8	49.2	22.6	77.4	5.9	10.3	83.8
N	222	358	119	460	69	75	405
N as % of survey sample	38.3%	61.7%	20.6%	79.4%	12.5%	13.7%	73.8%

and subnational coalition experiences become more accurate providers of the information required by parties in the national bargaining arena—for example, the compatibility of parties, their loyalty to one another, and the coalition's electoral popularity. When such intervention manifests itself as control, however, restrictions on local experimentation inhibit coalitional learning. Similarly, barriers to effective organizational communication across subnational-national levels (characteristic especially of extremist parties led by strong, charismatic leaders) can reduce the capacity for bottom-up influence.

These propositions are largely supported by consistent patterns in the survey data (table 8.3). Despite the deleterious consequences for local issue priorities and success in horizontal bargaining as revealed in chapter 7, national party intervention in regional or provincial coalition negotiations appears to have an additional but more constructive side effect of increasing bottom-up influence on party strategy. Similarly, where party discipline is relaxed and channels of communication linking parties' peripheries to their respective cores are open and informal, the evidence shows higher levels of reported vertical influence. Finally, influence is greatest in parties located at the political center and weakest on the extreme Right. Given the natural advantage that centrist parties enjoy in being able to look in two directions for potential partners, this reported receptivity to influence from the periphery makes logical sense.

Together, these data on vertical influence make it clear that a meaningful understanding of strategy and cooperation among national parliamentary parties should not neglect models attempted in the periphery. In so doing, they indicate a functional role for meso-level politicians, most of whom do recognize an interdependence of coalitions across different levels of government. Here, then, is tangible evidence supporting the theoretical assertion that "coalition behavior in one situation both affects and is affected by behavior in other situations" (Hinckley 1981, 81). The survey data do not, however, adequately gauge the extent to which subnational legislators are themselves motivated to action by the expectation that their coalition choices in the subnational arena can influence coalition choices in the national arena. This was a matter for systematic probing in elite interviews.

Motivation

Responding to questions in face-to-face interviews, politicians tell stories of previous experiences negotiating new governing alliances in

Table 8.3
Perceptions of Coalition Learning,
by Party and Individual Variables

	Bottom-Up	
	% Reporting "Weak" or "No" Vertical Influence	% Reporting "Some" or "Strong" Vertical Influence
Party Variables		
Intervention by National Party		
Extensive	22.7	77.3
Limited or none	45.6	54.4
Level of Central Control		
Local dissidence allowed	17.8	82.2
Local dissidence punished	32.9	67.1
Vertical Communication		
Free and open	20.6	79.4
Limited or none	40.8	59.2
Party Ideology		
Left	19.8	80.2
Center	13.3	86.7
Right	31.0	69.0
Extreme*	47.1	52.9
Left-libertarian (e.g., Green)	26.5	73.5

Party variables: $\chi^2 = 2.563$, $df = 1$, sig. $= 0.103$
Level of central control: $\chi^2 = 2.933$, $df = 1$, sig. $= 0.087$
Vertical communication: $\chi^2 = 4.534$, $df = 1$, sig. $= 0.049$
Party ideology: $\chi^2 = 6.790$, $df = 4$, sig. $= 0.049$
*Includes FN (France and Belgium), DVU, REPs, CPNT.

regional and provincial parliaments that inform theoretical expectations about the motivation and direction of "flow." Particularly relevant are councilors' replies to the following question:

> "How important is it for you and your party group to influence national coalition strategy through the coalition decisions you make in [regional/Land/provincial] parliaments?"

The interview subjects, selected according to past participation in coalition negotiations, were asked whether bottom-up influence had been a "primary motivating influence," an "important factor," "something considered, but only secondarily" during negotiations, or an element that "did not enter into the decision-making process."

All 22 German Landtag deputies interviewed, representing five parties and with more than half holding some leadership position within their respective parliamentary groups, answered that federal-level implications are an "important factor" considered in forming a Land government, although none answered that causing a change in the Bonn coalition had been the "primary motivating influence" behind the formation of a Land coalition. Christian Democrats and Social Democrats in Baden-Württemberg and Berlin, for example, were pressed on the extent to which influencing the creation of a new "Große Koalition" in federal government had motivated the formation of CDU-SPD governments in the two Länder. Members of both parties generally echoed the thoughts of a senior CDU member of Berlin's governing executive: "A great coalition following federal elections is only possible if it is necessary. If voters suggest no other alternative, then a great coalition is acceptable. That is what happened here in Berlin. *Yes, our coalition sends a signal to Bonn as we knew it would.* But I do not anticipate a great coalition unless there is no other choice."[7] For a former SPD *Fraktionvorsitzender* and 16-year veteran of the Berlin parliament: "I would always fight a grand coalition if there is a sensible alternative to it. . . . It can only be justified to have a grand coalition if you have dramatic problems that call for something like a 'national union.' If you think of jobs, housing, reunification, and moving the seat of government from Bonn to Berlin, then right now I think that we are at the stage that everyone agrees that there are big problems. In the SPD we had two choices: a minority cabinet with outside support from the PDS, or a grand coalition with the CDU. Mathematics forced the two big parties together, but in doing this *we knew at the time that the eyes of those who desire a new national union government would be on us.*"[8]

For the CDU *fraktion* leader in Baden-Württemberg's Landtag, the federal-level implications of forming a CDU-SPD government in Stuttgart had been deliberated after the 1992 state election: "The majority in the CDU desired the SPD because the issues demanded a large majority. This, you may say, is also true in Bonn with the issues of asylum seekers and rebuilding the eastern Lands. *And some here in our party wanted to make the comparison.* To duplicate the grand coalition is possible, sure, in Bonn. It is not a wish of mine. If election results dictate that it must be done, it would be done. It is a question of necessity more than anything else."[9] The SPD's parliamentary leader in Baden-

Württemberg concurred that electoral necessity usually overrides choice and motivation: "There was no realistic alternative to a CDU-SPD government in 1992." However, the SPD placed strategic value on the opportunity once it had been presented: "Being in opposition at the federal level, *it is important for the SPD to show the ability to form coalitions with many parties. Perhaps this is a motivation for us.* We can show that CDU-SPD government works effectively. We have already solved a lot of problems in our state: we have the biggest program to build houses in all states in Germany; the increase of deficit spending is stopped; we combat the Neo-Nazis; we will hire much more policemen and teachers. We give our party at federal level all this information."[10] These well-placed participants in Germany's state-level coalition process all point to the messages that Landtag coalitions send to federal government, and all admit that the anticipated consequences of these messages entered the parties' precoalition calculations.

In recounting the motivations for entering into provincial and regional-level coalitions, almost half of the 44 Belgian politicians questioned responded that influencing national coalitions had for them been an "important factor." The only representatives to respond that causing a change in national government had been the "primary motivating influence" behind subnational coalition strategy were members of the francophone ecologist party, Ecolo, despite the fact that the party has never participated in anything but a handful of municipal coalitions. The Ecolos stated that gaining a place in an intermediate-level government would be a step toward real participation in national government. For one party leader in Luxembourg province, "It is our ultimate wish to be able to influence political decisions at the national level. We are getting there slowly. You see this in [Prime Minister] Dehaene asking for Ecolo's support to pass the federalization reforms. In this province we do not want to stay in the opposition for a long time because it is not very pleasant. If we want our ideas to be concrete, we must go into the majority. We want this because we know it will bring us closer to greater influence in Wallonia and in Belgium."[11] A step up the institutional ladder at the Brussels-Capital Regional Council, Ecolo's leader predicted, "We expect to be in the next majority in the regional council. Brussels will likely be the first council in which Ecolo will be in the majority. In the future the same coalition all over Wallonia should be expected, and that coalition should determine the national parliament."[12]

For assembly members from other Belgian parties, the expectation that subnational coalitions can influence national coalitions does not rank as a primary motivating factor. It is worth comparing the responses of two Liberal Party (PRL) provincial councilors, the first of whom lamented: "In Hainaut, Socialists can choose their allies, and they usually just choose the weakest party or the party they can best manipulate. We tried to put together a non-PS majority with three parties. We wanted to do that for Hainaut, not because we thought we could change politics in the nation. If it had worked and we had eliminated the Socialists in their strongest province, then of course there would have been some people thinking about how this might change things in Brussels."[13] A second PRL councilor suggests that pure office-seeking motivations outweigh hopes of influencing national coalition configurations: "Liberals and Socialists have been in the provincial majority since 1981, but Liberals and Socialists have not been together, alone, in national government once during that time. That should tell you something. It is important for us to be in the deputation in Liège; after that, then we worry about national government."[14] While only the Ecolo councilors admit to deriving primary motivation from the prospect of influencing national alliances in the pursuit of subnational coalition strategies, most suggest that national-level implications of a subnational coalition do become apparent subsequent to its formation.

All 31 French interviewees, including regional council executives and party leaders, responded that the national-level implications of a regional coalition had at least been "considered" during the majority formation process. Only the interviewees from the extreme-right Front National, however, went further to express a belief that these implications had for them been the "primary motivating influence." Most of the subjects suggested that the expectation of influencing national party alliances had been "considered, but only secondarily" in pursuing a particular coalition strategy. Characteristic of most regional councilors are the comments of one Socialist in Picardie: "The state of relations between the parties across France can be very much the same state of relations in this region. That means that certain things are not possible here because they are not possible elsewhere in France. *It also means that if something new happens here it may then be possible somewhere else in the country.* Everyone knows this, but it is not the only thing we think about. Our goal is to put together a majority that can work together. We make a strategy so that we can pass a budget, not because we want to make a coalition with this party or that in Paris."[15]

If the ecologists in Belgium are those who place the most concern on influencing national patterns through subnational coalition building, in France it is the right-wing nationalists. According to one leading FN party figure in Nord-Pas de Calais, "It is at the top of our priorities that the Front National be in regional government. We now have members in all regional councils, more than 230 in all. The party has been represented in the executives of many regions. These are the facts. You cannot deny them. We expect that our success in the regions will help us succeed later as a party of government. Part of our strategy in the regions is to help the Right save itself from itself, but *our larger strategy is to prepare for national government.*"[16]

Among most mainstream parties in France, there is strong sentiment in the regions that coalition decisions can set a "tone" for future party relations at the national level and that some prominent figures are motivated by this prospect. While agreeing that these linkages are growing stronger, some regional councilors nevertheless reject for the moment the conclusion that France's regions have yet become the coalition "proving grounds" that the Länder appear to be in Germany. A typical response is that of a Languedoc-Roussillon regional councilor and local Socialist Party secretary: "In the South of France political discussions rest much more on the quality of human relations between elected representatives than on national political engagements."[17] Others, such as a regional councilor in Alsace and party spokesperson for Les Verts, argue that the French national electoral system ("scrutin majoritaire") simply keeps regional coalitions from being "pertinent" at the national level. The variety of responses from French politicians suggests a wider range of motivational concerns and a greater uncertainty about the strategic import of the new regional assemblies than is to be found among members of the well-established subnational institutions in Germany and Belgium.

Together, these assessments from key actors in each of the three countries provide evidence that politicians in subnational assemblies are to a large degree aware of the possible national-level implications of their decisions and that some even perceive these implications to be important motivational considerations in the decision-making process. But there is not sufficient evidence to suggest that the overriding concern in government formation and coalition bargaining is the expectation of changing national coalition patterns. This appears to be for many a secondary concern, but still one to be worried over once the dust has cleared from the more immediate and proximate issue of forming the subnational majority.

The View from Above

National politicians corroborate the stories told by their colleagues in regional and provincial assemblies about the presence and direction of coalitional influence and learning. Like most subnational representatives, party leaders in the capital agree that an existing national parliamentary alliance generally defines the initial negotiating positions of parties in local coalition bargaining. More important, strategists in national party headquarters admit to carefully studying the policy capacities and popular approval of subnational coalition governments. Such scrutiny informs the party leadership as to whether it can afford to continue the coalition realignment and whether the new coalition pattern at the subnational level might be regarded as a model for activities at the national level.

Indicative are comments from national-level representatives of three center parties, each of which normally occupies a position in national government:

Federal Party Spokesman, German FDP: We never had the situation from the Länder where there was pressure on us to join this or that coalition. This is of course different than the question of whether we can learn from successes and failures of experience in the Länder. This we do. We must to survive.[18]

Secretary General, French UDF-CDS: When one is a small party in the center—small in numbers—but indispensable to all governmental coalitions, one is forcibly solicited by persons on the Left and persons on the Right. The ecologists in the regions have tried to charm us. Because of their offers there, we decided to see them here in Paris, to receive them, and to listen to them. So far we have only told them, "You are very nice, but no thank you." We have been tempted by alliance with the Right—for example, with the Front National in Alsace. We are extremely opposed to the Front National, and we are faced with a political reality that we profoundly regret. But the introduction of the extreme Right in the regions at least allows us to test a new manner of alliance and to see if the duties of governing might tame the party of Le Pen.[19]

Senator, Belgian CVP: It is a realistic possibility now in Belgium to govern without the CVP. Being the party of government for so many years has made us weaker and weaker, because people are always looking for a scapegoat. You can compare it to a domestic situation: If you have some brothers fighting, the father takes the oldest one

aside and punishes him even though the oldest may have been trying
to find a solution. The oldest should have known better—that's his
responsibility. Because the CVP is being punished election after election, we have to search more creatively for new coalition partners.
We look seriously at our relations with other parties in the regions,
the communes, and the provinces. Unfortunately, past experience
has taught us that the Volksunie cannot be trusted and that it has
no future, that the ecologists have many slogans but no concrete solutions for implementation, and that the Vlaams Blok is too parochial and egoistic in its approach to policy.[20]

Each of these parties faces a crisis. The FDP flirts with disaster each
time it misses or comes near to missing the 5% threshold for entering
parliament at federal and state levels. The Christian Democrats and
the UDF in France watch the FN on the extreme Right scale to levels
of 15% in electoral support. The CVP in Belgium bears the brunt of
anti-incumbency sentiment. In each case, knowledgeable actors at the
national level report that they look to subnational experience for at
least some of the information they need to devise strategy. This fact
goes far toward supporting Dodd's proposition and our expectations
about coalitional learning.

Experimentation

Players in the coalition game report important national-subnational
linkages and the existence of learning across time and parliamentary
levels in all three countries. Learning entails experimentation. In turn,
experimentation presupposes a certain amount of *openness* in the coalition system. Openness is a "learning condition." If subnational assemblies are to be considered laboratories for national coalitions, then
such experimentation must assume the willingness of subnational
councilors and party leaders to form alliances with nontraditional partners. Unconventional coalitions, perhaps concocted by national elites,
may however be resisted from the grass roots and by the very persons
whose task it will be to govern with the nontraditional parties. Lower-
or middle-level politicians "who may have little chance of holding major office may distrust those who tell them, often from the back seat
of a chauffeur-driven Mercedes, that policy compromises are necessary so that the party can get into office" (Laver and Schofield 1990,

57). How "open"[21] politicians in subnational parliaments are to the entire range of coalitions following an election is therefore an important
empirical question. While formal theoretical expectations hold that the
set of all mathematically possible combinations of political parties constitutes the actual universe of coalition possibilities, such expectations
should be tested and not merely assumed.

Survey data allow a limited test of the "openness" hypothesis. The
questionnaire presented respondents with a list of the parties competing for seats in each respective territorial parliament. Respondents
were then asked: "Which party or parties from the following list could
you *never* envision forming a coalition?" A binary code (0, 1) was assigned to a respondent's reply for each party listed, (0) if the respondent indicated that he or she could never collaborate with the party
and (1) if the respondent indicated otherwise. Summing the total and
averaging by the total number of parties listed provides a general indicator of the respondent's openness to the range of parties in the coalition system. If a respondent checked no parties, then the openness
measure would equal 1. Alternatively, if a respondent checked all the
parties listed, the openness measure would equal 0.[22]

The a priori expectation of traditional theory is one of perfect openness. Hence, we can hypothesize that the closer the mean score for a
given unit is to 1.0 the greater the openness, the more facilitative the
conditions for coalition experimentation and the more appropriate
the assumption of "allgemeine Koalitionsfähigkeit." Table 8.4 provides the mean openness values by country and party.[23] In no single
case is openness absolute. Of the three countries, Belgium's subnational legislators suggest the greatest openness (0.76), while the mean
response of German state parliamentarians is lowest (0.62). Variance
across parties is greatest in France, with coalition openness ranging
from 0.87 (France Unie) to 0.37 (FN).

Which are the offending parties that lead respondents to restrict
the set of permissible coalitions? In most contemporary liberal democracies, the "new politics" ecologist parties and the "old politics"
nationalist parties are those attempting to use territorial parliaments
as forums for legitimation and as stepping-stones for their national
ambitions. In the absence of a major breakthrough election that would
give one of these parties an absolute majority, however, each must
search for at least one coalition partner willing to engage in political
experimentation. How open, though, are the mainstream parties in
each country to governing coalitions with the Green parties as well as

Table 8.4

Openness to All Possible Coalition Partners (respondent means)

Belgium (N = 145)		Germany (N = 182)		France (N = 254)	
Francophone Democratic Front (FDF)	0.83	German People's Union (DVU)	0.66	France Unie (FU)	0.87
Socialists (PS)	0.82	Christian Democratic Union (CDU)	0.64	Radical Leftists (MRG)	0.80
Ecologists (ECOLO)	0.80			Socialists (PS)	0.77
Christian Socials (PSC)	0.75	Free Democrats (FDP)	0.62	Ecologists (GE)	0.77
Liberals (PRL)	0.69	Republicans (REP)	0.60	French Democratic Union (UDF)	0.73
		Social Democrats (SPD)	0.60	Rally for the Republic (RPR)	0.69
		Greens (Grünen)	0.56	Ecologists (Verts)	0.64
				Communists (PC)	0.39
				National Front (FN)	0.37
Mean	0.76		0.62		0.65

Note: Complete openness = 1.0; complete closure = 0.0.

with the emergent parties on the far right? Official pronouncements from national party elites aside, it is clearly worth examining the attitudes of subnational officeholders.

Figure 8.3 provides an indication of the willingness of traditional parties not to exclude ecologist parties from their set of potential coalition partners. For all but the French Front National, representatives of the major parties in each country refuse to rule out the possibility of coalition with the ecologists. This is true even of the German CDU, although no such "black-green" coalition has ever formed successfully at the Land level. French regional councilors, faced with two Green alternatives (Verts and Génération Ecologie), appear more open to partnership with Brice Lalonde's GE, the less "fundamentalist" of the two parties. One notable exception to the French pattern is the Communist Party, whose respondents suggest a much stronger preference for Antoine Waechter's Verts.

The right-hand side of figure 8.3 details the coalition openness reported by respondents from the respective ecologist parties in Belgium, Germany, and France. Although most Greens ("ni gauche, ni droite") reject placement of their parties on a single-dimension Left-Right ideological scale, these councilors suggest much greater openness toward left-of-center socialist and social democratic parties than toward right-of-center conservative parties. Belgian Ecolos suggest overwhelming acceptance of coalition with both the PS and the PSC, but their enthusiasm is more muted for the Liberal PRL. The German Greens register strong approval of the SPD as possible and actual partners, and many refuse to discard the Christian Democrats or even the Liberals as potential coalition allies. Of the French Greens, it is worth noting the complete closure with regard to the FN, the hesitancy with respect to the PCF, and the almost equivalent openness to coalitions with very different political forces: the PS and the UDF.

Coalition openness with regard to ecologist parties stands in stark contrast to the reported openness of subnational councilors toward possible power-sharing arrangements with parties of the far right. Figure 8.4 indicates widespread aversion among traditional parties to the idea of participating in coalition with right-wing nationalist parties. In Belgium, the Front National had by 1991 gained entry into the Hainaut and Namur provincial councils, the Council of the French Community, and the national parliament. A clear majority of respondents from the mainstream Walloon parties do, however, rule out a future coalition that might include the FN, but in the three "traditional" par-

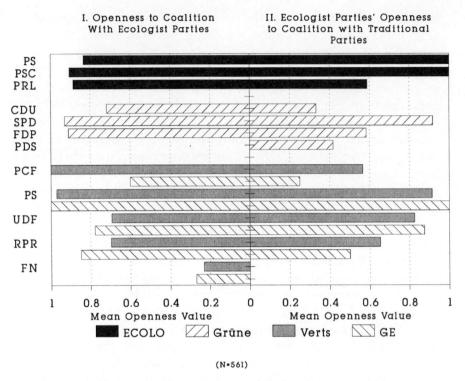

I. Openness to Coalition
With Ecologist Parties

II. Ecologist Parties' Openness
to Coalition with Traditional
Parties

PS
PSC
PRL

CDU
SPD
FDP
PDS

PCF

PS

UDF

RPR

FN

1   0.8   0.6   0.4   0.2   0   0.2   0.4   0.6   0.8   1

Mean Openness Value   Mean Openness Value

■ ECOLO   ⧄ Grüne   ▨ Verts   ⧅ GE

(N=561)

Figure 8.3 Coalition Experimentation with Green Parties

ties even this attitude is not absolute. Apparently much stronger is the
resolve of the French Left and the French ecologists to avoid collaboration with Le Pen's FN. In Germany, whispers about sympathies
within the CDU toward the Republikaner party and the Deutsche
Volksunion appear to be not without at least some substance. For example, of the 19 CDU respondents from Baden-Württemberg, where
the Republicans gained 15 seats in the 1992 Landtag election, 9 refused to reject the possibility of working with the far-right party.

Evidence also shows that far-right parties, although generally labeled untouchables by mainstream parties, are themselves quite open
to coalitions with "the establishment." This openness, however, is confined to coalitions with parties of the Right or center Right. Thus, coalitions with socialists, communists, and ecologists are both unlikely
and off limits. It is worth pointing out here how well responses from
regional representatives of the French Front National graphically

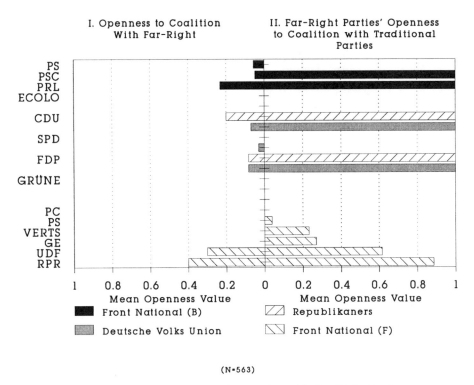

I. Openness to Coalition
With Far-Right

II. Far-Right Parties' Openness
to Coalition with Traditional
Parties

PS	
PSC	
PRL	
ECOLO	
CDU	
SPD	
FDP	
GRÜNE	
PC	
PS	
VERTS	
GE	
UDF	
RPR	

1   0.8   0.6   0.4   0.2   0   0.2   0.4   0.6   0.8   1

Mean Openness Value   Mean Openness Value

■ Front National (B)   ▨ Republikaners

▨ Deutsche Volks Union   ◩ Front National (F)

(N=563)

Figure 8.4 Coalition Experimentation with Far-Right Parties

match expectations about coalition preferences based upon ideological proximity and minimum "distance": openness toward the right-wing RPR reduces almost evenly as one moves leftward across the ideological spectrum to the PCF.[24]

It is apparent from these data that the universe of politically possible coalitions—while perhaps not as large as the universe of mathematically possible coalitions—is still significantly larger than what might be deduced from the set of coalitions that have in fact already formed. There is no absolute "openness" in any of the three countries nor among any of the parties. This formal assumption falls apart upon inspection of attitudes and behavior at the micro-level. However, there is enough evidence to argue that at subnational levels we should continue to assume that all mathematically possible combinations of parties constitute the universe of possible governing coalitions. This is not to say that all coalitions are equal in the eyes of those who must participate in them. The point is that given the right conditions, almost no coalition can be ruled out at the subnational level. Hence, the possibility of experimentation is real.

"Perfect Information": Cases of Experimentation

The example discussed in chapter 7 of Luxembourg province and the deleterious effects that its rupture of the PSC-PRL "pacte de huit ans" had on Belgian government in 1987 is but one case of party policy at one governmental tier having an impact on relations at another. There are numerous others, most of which have been ignored in the comparative literature. The following three cases address instances of subnational political engineering and their potential as proving grounds for new coalitional strategies. In these cases, parties pursue new and unique forms of political cooperation for a variety of reasons: electoral necessity, displeasure with previous partners, instructions from party leaders, issue-based affinity, unity in the face of challenge from extremists, and signal sending to national counterparts. Whatever the root motivation, experimentation involves risks and compromises. Exploring how parties weigh the costs and benefits of experimentation and determine strategy should tell us something about political motivations at the subnational level, should highlight the influential role of contextual conditions on government formation, and should indicate the opportunities to use subnational institutions as laboratories for creative policy making and as a learning process for political cooperation.

Case I. Experimenting with "Asymmetry": Brabant Province and the Five-Party Coalition of 1991

Observers of Belgian politics traditionally regarded the problems of Brabant province as being like those of the entire country, but in miniature. Before its scission in 1995, the province of 2.2 million inhabitants straddled the country's linguistic dividing line to include bilingual Brussels within its borders. Here the Dutch-speaking and French-speaking communities meet and compete. Here issues of economic development, jobs creation, education, culture, and health care have demanded Brabantine solutions, not Flemish or Walloon ones. Before the 1995 division of the province into Walloon Brabant and Flemish Brabant, Brabant's provincial council had been the only subnational assembly in Belgium to include political parties from both linguistic regions. Predictably, this enlarged the universe of coalition possibilities available following elections, although the singular characteristic of provincial governments in Brabant since the early 1970s has been one of "tripartism" among the six parties of the Socialist, Catholic, and Liberal families. The "pentapartite" coalition of 1991, however, challenged this pattern.

In Belgian terms, the provincial coalition established in November 1991 can be regarded as historic, though again in miniature. Throughout the country, voters registered their displeasure with mainstream politics by turning their backs on traditional parties at the polls, allowing ecologists and right-wing extremists to record significant gains. In Brabant, elections to the provincial assembly largely followed national patterns, with four of the six majority parties (PS, SP, CVP, PRL) losing seats in the 90-member council (table 8.5). The remaining two parties of provincial government, the PSC and PVV, maintained their 1987 levels of representation. Still, as the previous majority had been an oversized coalition boasting 71 of the 90 seats, the losses in 1991 had only reduced a potential traditional tripartite majority to a healthy 63. As the results were tallied on election night, Francis De Hondt, reelected to the provincial council on the PSC list, analyzed: "The current majority has lost eight seats, but it is still a comfortable majority. All other possibilities seem to me to be quite improbable."[25] Similarly, Jan Anthoons, a CVP member of the outgoing provincial executive, predicted: "A majority of only two [party families] is impossible in view of the results. Therefore we will very probably continue with the same partners."[26]

What neither De Hondt nor Anthoons anticipated were the events that would occur the week following the election. In what the Brussels daily *Le Soir* proclaimed to be "un accord historique" that would "inaugure l'asymétrie,"[27] five parties—PS, SP, PRL, PVV, CVP—formally agreed to share provincial power and to divide the Brabant executive. Noticeably absent from this arrangement were the francophone Christian Socials (PSC), a party that had been part of the provincial majority without interruption for the previous 30 years. For the first time ever in Belgium, one linguistic wing of a party family had entered a governing coalition without its partner: in this case, the Flemish CVP had accepted a coalition without the French-speaking PSC.

Reactions to the coalition decision ranged from dismay to resignation. Jean Courtin, president of the PSC federation in Brabant, la-

Table 8.5
Brabant Provincial Assembly, November 1991

Party	Seats		Votes (%)		Executive Portfolios	
Francophone Socialist Party (PS)	10	(−5)	10.29	(−4.22)	1	(=)
Flemish Socialist Party (SP)	9	(−1)	9.36	(−1.47)	1	(=)
Christian Social Party (PSC)	6	(=)	6.90	(−0.07)		(−1)
Christian People's Party (CVP)	13	(−1)	13.02	(−2.34)	1	(=)
Liberal Reform Party (PRL)	15	(−1)	14.10	(−2.06)	2	(+1)
Flemish Liberal Party (PVV)	10	(=)	10.49	(+0.06)	1	(=)
Francophone Democratic Front (FDF)	7	(=)	7.06	(+0.34)		
Flemish People's Union (VU)	5	(−2)	5.43	(−1.55)		
Ecolo	7	(+3)	7.71	(+3.49)		
Agalev	4	(+2)	4.72	(+1.26)		
Vlaams Blok	4	(+4)	6.24	(+4.55)		
Total	90		95.32		6	

mented, "I am outraged by the attitude of the CVP. In fact I am astonished at the attitude of the CVP that it did not defend its small francophone brother." Jean-Paul Dumon, spokesman for the PSC group in the provincial council, declared that he was "surprised and scandalized" by the coalition outcome. The PSC's national office judged "scandalous" the attitude of the PRL, which "pleads for a place in a tripartite national government," as well as that of the PS, which "would like to govern with the PSC at all levels of power."[28] In responding, the CVP said only that "we did not really have a choice; it was either us in the coalition, or the alternative: Volksunie or the FDF."[29]

At issue, at least on the surface, had been personality conflicts over the PSC's proposal to designate one André Antoine as député permanent for the new legislative period, an initiative at which both Socialists and Liberals balked. More important were fresh political memories. Still smarting from the PSC's abandonment after the demise of the PSC-PRL "pacte de huit ans" in 1987, the national PRL leadership saw in the Brabant coalition situation an opportunity to inflict retribution: "We feel that in 1987 we were betrayed by the Christian Socials with the so-called pacte de huit ans. Three years later we betrayed the PSC. At that time the president of the party was Louis Michel, and in 1991 he said, 'We want to make coalitions with everybody in the provinces but the PSC.' It was some kind of revenge."[30]

The Brabant CVP's willingness to enter government without the

PSC is a clue that office seeking may outweigh any intrafamily loyalty or unity. This adds important insight to what is a familiar topic of speculation in Belgium, namely, whether familial party unity has eroded to such an extent that a Flemish or Walloon party might enter a national coalition cabinet without its counterpart. Dewachter and Clijsters have written that "the former linguistic wings operate as autonomous parties, maintaining only loose ties on the national level, but strong enough to prevent the other wing from joining a coalition without its linguistic counterpart" (1982, 198). In their own review, Laver and Schofield conclude that "most authors, while noting that members of the same family have thus far always acted in concert over coalition formation, do not rule out the possibility of independent action" (1990, 221). The CVP's behavior in Brabant in 1991 thus sets an interesting precedent. To be sure, the stakes in Brabant province are not commensurate with those of national government formation. Nevertheless, the taboo of an "asymmetrical" coalition has been broken.

The context in which the Brabant "experiment" developed gives some indication as to its higher-level implications. Provincial politics in Brabant are characterized by both electoral stability and nationalized election results. In 1991, for example, the net seat change per party on the provincial council was only 1.8%, and the net vote change per party was a mere 1.7%. These minor changes closely mirrored party change in national legislative elections, with the net difference between changes in provincial and national vote shares between 1987 and 1991 being just 0.79%. Clearly, the electoral risks for the CVP in committing what amounted to political fratricide were low in Brabant province. Moreover, despite sharing the same party headquarters building with the PSC in Brussels, the top CVP leadership endorsed the scission. For the provincial CVP, then, the organizational risks of venturing into an asymmetrical alliance were also low.

Our theoretical assumptions would thus lead us to anticipate that the Brabant coalition is of relatively high experimental value. No clear electoral constraints pressured the provincial politicians to try the five-party formula. The effort to evict the PSC had been purposive on the part of both the PRL and the PS, and it could not have been accomplished without the knowledge and complicity of the CVP. No overriding organizational constraints compelled the CVP councilors to reject coalition participation without the PSC. Although both are members of one supposed political "family," it is now clear that the CVP and the PSC can have very different preferences about coalition participation. In this respect, it is worth comparing how party votes in March 1992 on whether to join the eventual Dehaene national government diverged: 94.5% of the PSC voted in favor of the proposed government, but only 61.8% of the 3,000-strong CVP Party congress voted in favor. It is also evident that the loyalty of the two parties to one another as indispensable coalition partners cannot simply be assumed.

It is worth noting that among all Belgian provincial councilors responding to the survey employed in this study, those from Brabant province indicated the greatest acceptance of the proposition that subnational coalitions can lead to national coalitions. As a group, they also score highest on the measure of coalition openness. Learning conditions in Brabant are facilitative. This is not to say that an asymmetrical coalition of the type formed in 1991 can or will be reproduced in national government. The risks of forming such a coalition, as well as the impediments, are much greater in national government, especially now in the federal state. Reactions from voters in future elections will, however, suggest to the participating parties whether the new coalition model should continue, as will the instructions of national elites. Significantly, the postscript to Brabant's coalition experiment finds the CVP joining another asymmetrical government after elections in 1995 to the Brussels regional parliament. Clearly, actors can assess coalitional experiments and thereby learn new strategies previously seen as impossible and thus beyond the realm of strategic foresight.

Case II. A Rose-Verte *Experiment in France: The 1992 "Little Bang" in Nord-Pas de Calais*

Like Brabant in Belgium, Nord-Pas de Calais in France is a region traditionally characterized by a comparatively high degree of electoral stability and by voting patterns that generally follow national trends. Thus the red-green or "rose-verte" coalition that emerged following the 1992 regional election deserves investigation. What are the factors that led to the formation of this novel coalition, and what experimental value can be assigned to it? Answers to these questions suggest that as with Brabant in Belgium, the ability to view Nord-Pas de Calais as French politics in miniature places a high value on the region as a proving ground for future cooperation.

Nord-Pas de Calais is one of the great prizes in French regional politics, especially for the Left. The third-most populous region in France, this northern region—the "maison de Léon Blum"—is also one of the two strongest in the country for both the socialists and the communists (the other being Limousin). This strength is especially evident in the department of Nord, where the socialists have monopolized power since the early 1930s. At the first regional elections in 1986, cooperation between the PS and the PCF "survived the collapse of the left wing alliance at the national level" (Mazey 1986, 299), allowing Noël Joseph (PS) to capture the top executive post in the second round with 58 of 113 votes. In 1992 the PS, PCF, and UPF (RPR-UDF) all lost seats in the regional council, although for the PS and PCF the losses were less severe than the national average. The big winners in 1992 were the ecologists and the Front National. A renewal of the 1986 majority would yield only 42 seats, a weak relative majority at best if no stronger coalition could emerge.

In the postelection government formation process, Michel Delebarre, PS regional leader and national government minister, promised to put together a "majorité de progrès."[31] His challenge on the Right came from Jacques Legendre, National Secretary of the RPR, supported by the 27 members of the UDF-RPR alliance, and from Carl Lang, General Secretary of the FN, with 15 councilors. Thus, a hypothetical PS/PCF bloc with 42 votes stood evenly matched against a hypothetical right-wing bloc, also with 42 potential votes. The ecologists (Verts with 8 seats, GE with 6), the CPNT contingent (2 seats), and the group of independent followers of Jean-Louis Borloo, mayor of Valenciennes (13 seats), all waited in the wings ready to play the role of arbiter.

Meeting in Lille on March 30, the Nord-Pas de Calais regional councilors fought their battle for control of executive power. In the first round of voting for regional president, seven candidates representing each of the parties in the assembly—with the two Green parties forming one group—gained only the votes of their respective groups, thus forcing a second round (table 8.6). After some hours of negotiations and bargaining, the second round proceeded without the candidacy of Carl Lang (FN), whose supporters then divided their votes between Legendre (RPR, 39 votes) and the independent Borloo (22 votes). Delebarre, failing to win the support of either the obstinate communists or the upstart ecologists, mustered only the same 27 PS and MRG votes. With no majority evident, a "majorité de coalition" would have to emerge in the decisive third round.

During protracted negotiations leading to the third round, the PS implored the communists to abandon their "opposition de gauche"

Table 8.6

Nord-Pas de Calais Regional Council, March 1992

Party	Seats		1st Round		2nd Round		3rd Round	
Socialist Party (PS)	25	(−11)	Delebarre (PS)	27	Delebarre	27	Delebarre	27
Communist Party (PCF)	15	(−4)	Renar (PCF)	15	Renar	15	Renar	15
National Front (FN)	15	(+3)	Lang (FN)	15				
Union for French Democracy (UDF)	14	(=)						
Rally for the Republic (RPR)	13	(−8)	Legendre (RPR)	27	Legendre	39	Legendre	42
"Borloo 59-62" (Independent)	13	(+13)	Borloo (Ind.)	13	Borloo	22		
Verts	8	(+8)	Blandin (Verts)	14	Blandin	8	Blandin	52
Génération Ecologie (GE)	6	(+6)						
Left Radicals (MRG)	2	(−1)						
Anti-Ecologists (CPNT)	2	(+2)	Frémaux (CPNT)	2	Frémaux	2	Frémaux	2
Total	113		No majority		No majority		Relative majority	

strategy and rally "without illusion" to Delebarre's candidacy in order to "block the Right and the extreme Right." Sensing the opportunity to topple the Left in its own backyard, the conservatives changed tactics, as Jacques Legendre announced he would retire his candidacy in favor of Jean-Louis Borloo so that a "new regional majority of change" could emerge. Borloo, now with 46 votes, including 6 from GE, held a potential relative majority over Delebarre's still uncertain 42 votes. To have any hope of retaining Nord-Pas de Calais for the Left, Delebarre would need the 8 remaining votes of the Verts, barring the possible acceptance by Borloo of FN votes. Finding themselves in a extremely strong bargaining position, however, the Verts would not retire their nominee. At half past midnight, Michel Delebarre, the Minister of State and mayor of Dunkerque, conceded his candidacy and agreed to coalition terms with the eight-member group of Verts.[32]

At three o'clock in the morning, Marie-Christine Blandin, a 38-year-old professor of natural sciences and member of Greenpeace, gained 52 votes (from the PS, PCF, Verts, and GE) and the presidency of Nord-Pas de Calais. The first red-green coalition in the French regions had formed successfully, if not intentionally. Subsequent to the election of the regional president, the region's executive posts were divided among the Verts (three vice presidencies) and the PS (seven vice presidencies). The PCF, which had distanced itself from Delebarre throughout the government formation process under orders from the party's central committee, did not join the regional executive, nor did Génération Ecologie, which had supported the Borloo cause in the second round. Blandin's Verts, therefore, could reap the rewards of a major bargaining breakthrough, while Delebarre's PS avoided losing entirely the party's historical bastion and in fact maintained a significant presence in the regional government itself.

Delebarre's own analysis is that the coalition was inevitable: "Mathematically, we were beaten. If the Right took power, it would have rolled over us for two years and then it would be the end of the Left in Nord for 20 years."[33] One negotiator for the Verts, however, confirms an important element of *choice* in the coalition decision: "Our strategy was based upon autonomy, therefore refusing classical forms of mixing and coalitions. Therefore, the strategy was for Marie-Christine Blandin to maintain her candidacy at all three rounds, which she did. Monsieur Delebarre chose to step down in favor of the Green candidate, but of course he did not have to. We chose to accept a government with the Socialist Party, but we did not have to. This decision will be an

internal problem for us in that most of the Verts' party members come
from associations which are not especially fond of politics."[34] This
choice made by Socialists and Greens in Lille confirms the openness
reported by survey respondents of both parties to such an arrangement. Despite the element of choice, it is evident that unlike Brabant
in Belgium, the Nord-Pas de Calais coalition is at least partly a mar-
riage of circumstance. Given an alternative distribution of seats in the
council, it is unlikely that Delebarre and the PS would have chosen to
invite Blandin and the other Verts into regional government.

Thus, unlike the Brabant case, the "rose-verte" coalition in Nord-
Pas de Calais took on the dimensions of an experiment only after its
formation. With the fortunes of the PS dwindling on the national level,
the possibility of reconstructing a "majority of progress" beyond the
Nord-Pas de Calais region gained wide currency. Michel Rocard's cru-
sade for a "big bang" on the Left to regroup socialists, ecologists, reform communists, and centrists followed the "little bang" in Nord-Pas
de Calais. Indeed, only days after the news of the coalition in Lille
reached Paris, Laurent Fabius announced: "The Socialist Party needs
to affirm its identity and, at the same time, to be open to others, to see
if we can strike up new alliances."[35] For many at the national level, then,
the success or failure of the regional experience would to some degree
be a test of the parties' ability to overcome mutual suspicions and a
chance for the Verts to overcome their amateur status as a party of
government.

The theoretical expectations advanced earlier in this study indicate
that since Nord-Pas de Calais region is less electorally volatile and more
nationalized (when compared to others in France), the coalition's experimental value should be high. Here the PS in 1992 lost nine seats
and 9.3% of its 1986 regional vote share, but elsewhere the losses were
much higher: 14 seats in Lorraine (−58.3%), 29 seats in Ile-de-France
(−52.4%), 22 seats in Rhône-Alpes (−51.1%). Here the net difference
between changes in regional and national vote shares for all parties
combined between 1986 and 1993 is little more than 3%, while in Alsace it is 5.4%, in Basse-Normandie 4.9%, in Lorraine 4.7%, and in
Rhône-Alpes 4.5%. For the Left in Nord-Pas de Calais, the situation
in 1992 may have been bad, but elsewhere it was quite worse.

Unlike other red-green collaborations and supposed "laboratoires
de l'ouverture"[36] in Lorraine or Bourgogne, where electoral volatility
is much higher and where changes in voting patterns have more
unique regional characteristics, the Nord-Pas de Calais coalition is by

most accounts more durable and more efficient. Relative electoral stability enhances parties' investments in new modes of political cooperation, just as stability reassures investment in any other marketplace.
The "Projet d'Accord" between the Socialist Party and the Verts, ham-
mered out by October 1992, testifies to the two parties' ability to devise
and agree upon detailed common plans in the areas of economic development, environment, transportation, and infrastructure.[37] According to a Verts' spokesman: "In Nord-Pas de Calais the experiment is
one in the politicians' sense of the word. But the experiment is also
that for the first time in France we are trying to implement, to put
forward through the planification, a sustainable development strategy.
And the Socialist Party has agreed to join the Greens on that basis. As
for Rocard's suggestion of melting the Green parties, the socialists, the
social democrats, and the centrists all together, it is of course possible,
but for many there would be a loss in the message if these groups were
to melt at this point."[38]

The red-green mix thus has the opportunity to demonstrate the
effectiveness of an alternative political approach to some basic economic and social issues. Based on what the PS-Verts policy declaration
calls "eco-development, respectful of the human person as well as of
natural resources,"[39] the regional government has since 1992 set out
to combat unemployment in the region's key economic sectors and localities: iron works and industry (Lille-Roubaix-Tourcoing) and port
commerce (Dunkerque, Calais, Boulogne). True to "new politics" doc-
trines, the Verts have also used their new-found government status to
"combat the crisis of representative democracy" and "reinvent regional
government" by increasing citizen participation in a "more transpar-
ent, concertative process of decision making."[40]

In the short term, no heed was taken of the message of successful
partisan collaboration coming out of Lille. Socialists, ecologists, and
communists failed to work out second-ballot deals that may have improved the Left's score as well as that of the ecologists in the disastrous
1993 legislative elections. Nor did Mitterrand or his government introduce a degree of proportionality into the national elections and thus
make them more like those at the regional level. In the wake of the
1992 regional elections, a SOFRES study projected the 1993 legislative
results based on a proportional system: the 138 projected PS deputies,
plus those of the ecologists (Verts, 19; Génération Ecologie, 18) and
those of the PCF (28) would have still been insufficient for a majority
but would have forced the conservative parties to ally with the Front

National to gain a majority.[41] Without the more proportional system, the conservatives secured 485 Assemblée Nationale seats, overwhelming the PS (67) and PCF (25). Despite garnering significant numbers of votes in the first round of the legislative vote, the new regional-level coalition players (FN 12.4%, Verts 4.1%, GE 3.6%) were shut out of parliament. Rules do matter. Clearly, any future reform of the electoral system will increase the experimental value of regional coalitions.

To conclude, it may be said that French regional coalitions, to a much greater degree than those in Belgium or Germany, are minimum winning arrangements, exhibiting overt power aggrandizement and office-seeking behavior of the first order. Greater fractionalization and the possibility of relative majorities contribute to this fact. It is much more difficult, therefore, to argue that a coalition such as that formed in Nord-Pas de Calais had from the outset been premeditated and created as a test model for future use elsewhere, perhaps in national government. More appropriately, innovative regional coalitions in France *become* conscious experiments. This has clearly been the case in Nord-Pas de Calais.

Case III. An Alternative Shade of Coalition: The Unsuccessful "Black-Green" Experiment in Baden-Württemberg

Unlike the coalition experiments illustrated by Nord-Pas de Calais and Brabant, the experiment in the southwestern German state of Baden-Württemberg never actually came to fruition. Although the 1992 Landtag election did result in a CDU-SPD coalition incongruent with party alignments in federal government, the postelection government formation process is more interesting for the novelty of the CDU-Green coalition that was attempted but that ultimately failed to form.

Baden-Württemberg is a traditional Christian Democratic stronghold. There the CDU has enjoyed an uninterrupted presence in government since 1953, alone during the 1972–92 period and before that in coalitions with the SPD (1966–72) and FDP (1964–66), and in various other "all-party" governments. Despite the CDU dominance, elections in Baden-Württemberg have historically proven more volatile than those in most other Länder (Müller-Rommel 1989), with the average interelection changes in vote shares for the CDU, SPD, FDP, and Greens approaching 4%. Additionally, interelection changes in party vote shares are generally more localized, with the average difference vote shares are generally more localized, with the average difference between changes in state and federal party vote shares between 1960 and 1992 exceeding the national mean.

The April 1992 election in Baden-Württemberg reinforced this pattern of volatility (table 8.7). The CDU lost 8% and the SPD 3% of their respective 1988 vote shares, while the FDP only lost 0.6% and the Greens gained almost 2%. The real jolt came from the far right, where the Republicans broke into the state parliament with 15 seats and 11% of the vote. The 1992 election thus deprived the CDU of its absolute majority and handed the SPD its worst score since 1968. Several post-election coalition possibilities presented themselves to party leaders in Stuttgart. Needing 74 seats to form a winning majority, some combination would have to emerge from among the CDU, SPD, FDP, Greens, and Republicans. A CDU-FDP coalition would fall just short of a majority, and a "traffic light" SPD-FDP-Green government would also prove insufficient. The winning combinations appeared to include an oversized CDU-SPD government, which would leave the parliament with a feeble opposition of only 36 members (of which only 21 had clear democratic credentials); an unprecedented CDU-Green or "black-green" coalition; an unprecedented conservative–far-right (CDU-Republican) alliance; or an equally unique "coalition of minorities" that would form only to eject the CDU from its bastion.

The government formation process, which lingered for several weeks, commenced with an offer by Rölf Schlierer's Republicans to support a CDU-FDP minority government. The Christian Democrats rejected the proposal, according to Schlierer, because "the CDU has internal problems and they are too scared to have to depend in the future on the votes of the Republican Party. For us it would have been a natural combination. The Republican Party is a conservative party, a normal right-wing party that is successful because the CDU cannot keep a right wing. We are not a nationalist or extremist party like the DVU. . . . It could have been possible for us to support a CDU-FDP government."[42] This possibility brushed aside, negotiations turned to the possibility of a CDU-Green coalition government. Such an alliance had occurred occasionally at the municipal level but had never been attempted in earnest at Land level.

The Greens had campaigned on a theme of placing the CDU into opposition and of forming another of the increasingly familiar SPD-Green Land governments. Unable to pursue this preferred course of action, the Greens chose to enter into negotiations with the CDU, well

Table 8.7
Baden-Württemberg Landtag, April 1992

Party	Seats		Votes (%)	
Christian Democrats (CDU)	64	(−2)	39.6	(−9.4)
Social Democrats (SPD)	46	(+4)	29.4	(−2.6)
Republikaner (REP)	15	(+15)	10.9	(+9.9)
Greens (Grüne)	13	(+3)	9.5	(+1.6)
Free Democrats (FDP)	8	(+1)	5.9	(=)
Total	146		95.3	

aware of the "dangers this posed because at least half of Green voters do not understand this and would criticize and probably not vote Green in future times."[43] Armed with a list of demands that a preelection Green Party congress had adopted as conditions for participation in government with the SPD, the Green delegation, headed by Fritz Kuhn, challenged CDU leader Erwin Teufel to accept the same demands and to share a "new vision" of Baden-Württemberg. According to Kuhn: "Our parliamentary experience here has shown it to be easier to speak on a personal level with the CDU than with the Social Democrats. It's a psychological phenomenon, because many Social Democrats in Germany see the Greens as their illegitimate children. So for the Greens the talk with the CDU was serious. My vision of the coalition was to make a new ecological policy for industry and the economy of Baden-Württemberg, especially to transform the old industries like the automobile industry."[44]

The right wing of the CDU, led by Finance Minister Gerhard Mayer-Vorfelder, fought the possibility of a CDU-Green coalition from the very beginning. Mayer-Vorfelder issued Teufel a public warning that there might be a split in the party ranks if he went too far in negotiating with the Greens. Others in the party were more sympathetic to the idea, recognizing it as a "really interesting experiment" that could give the CDU a "political blood transfusion." "There was a federal interest in negotiating with the Greens not so much for the purpose of forming a coalition but for the purpose of having done it. This is mainly because the federal CDU is in a strategically weak position. The CDU can form coalitions with the SPD, but might not be able to form coalitions in the future with the Liberals because both together may not be a majority. The CDU cannot as of now form a coalition with the Greens, or with the FDP and the Greens, because there is no past political basis for doing so. So, it was part of the strategic interest to sound out if it might become an additional coalition possibility for the future to integrate the Greens into the coalition system."[45]

Ultimately, those in the CDU sharing Kuhn's "new vision" proved to be too weak. A part of the CDU had believed that the Greens with their strong contingent of eco-libertarians ("Ökolibertären") would offer a cheaper price for coalition than the Social Democrats, but the Greens made clear from the beginning that their price would not be cheap and would in fact be higher than that of the SPD: "There was part of the CDU that expected the Greens to be a more handy partner, but they found out this was not to be the case. The Social Democrats did not defend demands that the Greens made and that the SPD also made during the election campaign, but they dropped them in their talks just to get into government."[46]

Claiming that a majority with the Greens would have been "too small and too difficult to maintain for four years,"[47] the CDU ultimately opted for coalition with the SPD. In retrospect, many in the Baden-Württemberg Landtag believe that the Christian Democrats failed to commit to the black-green adventure because they were simply caught off guard by the possibility: "In the first round of negotiations it was clear that the CDU was not really prepared to consider our demands. Not more than one or two people in the CDU delegation had even read our program by that point. Minister President Teufel had ordered up copies of the program only two days in advance. So, they had never figured on this possibility beforehand."[48] Persons in both parties thus believe that if the opportunity arose again in the future, the CDU would be better prepared and would "know better what they were embarking upon."[49]

The CDU's lack of preparation is one explanation for the failure of the CDU-Green experiment. Organizational pressures and risks may also account for the hesitation. The CDU's parliamentary leader admits that "Kohl's strategy was to keep the SPD out of coalition in Baden-Württemberg. Some other coalition would have increased his power against the SPD. But he was not excited about the black-green coalition." This in addition to warnings from Teufel's own right wing in Baden-Württemberg could have figured largely in the decision. Teufel, generally characterized as "faithful to the Chancellor and with only regional horizons,"[50] was not inclined to risk an organizational crisis for an uncertain future with the Greens. Several Landtag deputies speculated, however, that Lothar Späth, Teufel's predecessor as minister-president and rival to Helmut Kohl, would have been more likely to have ventured into the black-green arrangement because of, not in spite of, the organizational pressures from Bonn. This suggestion is interesting, for it provides an alternative understanding of the role played by career ambitions to that outlined in chapters 3 and 7.

It is important also to recognize the electoral context and constraints at play in this case. Our theoretical expectation that in localized, high-volatility arenas, coalitions that minimize policy distance between parties are most likely to form is in this case met. Although wide in its own right, the gap between CDU and SPD is perceptibly narrower than between CDU and Greens, despite protestations from the latter that they are neither "Left" nor "Right." Volatility and localization clearly increased the perception among decision makers that the coalition chosen following the April 1992 election would directly affect their future electoral fortunes. The electoral shock provided by the Republicans raised the stakes even higher. If high stakes reinforce short-term strategies, then Baden-Württemberg is a classic example: "The funny thing about a grand coalition is that it joins forces in order to fight each other as soon as possible. As you know, you do not want to continue it after the next election. That is a real strange situation. You work with these people, and when we want to introduce a bill we have a rule that we always discuss it with the CDU first. And really these are friendly people and I try to be friendly to them. And we know full well that at the next campaign we are going to go out and hit each other over the head."[51]

There was, for the CDU especially, not enough electoral stability to justify the serious risk that a radical coalition of the kind a black-green government would bring. Therefore, it seems reasonable to suggest that given the openness of certain elements in the CDU and Green camps to formal cooperation, if the situation had arisen under different conditions and especially without the uncertainty injected by the Republican breakthrough, the chances for a different outcome would have been greater.

Can any experimental value be attached to the short-lived CDU-Green test in Baden-Württemberg? Because the coalition did not actually form, it is difficult to compare the experimental value of a Baden-Württemberg with that of a Nord-Pas de Calais or a Brabant. Our theoretical expectation, nonetheless, is that if the coalition had indeed formed, its value as a laboratory for future coalitions would have been comparatively low. The continuous presence of electoral constraints and localized electoral patterns would decrease the long-term incentives for cooperation. In contrast, the value of a black-green experiment in North Rhine–Westphalia, for example, would be much higher given that state's tradition of low electoral volatility and nationalized electoral patterns. In the parlance of game theory, a CDU-Green coalition in a low-volatility, nationalized arena like North Rhine–Westphalia would require fewer "iterations" than in a high-volatility, localized arena in Baden-Württemberg before the coalition could be ready for consideration in federal government. Nevertheless, a black-green Landtag government, once considered unimaginable, is now legitimately within the set of potential coalition alternatives.

Summary

The overarching goals of this chapter have been to address, first, whether coalitions formed in subnational parliaments alter the number of coalition options available to parties in national government; second, whether negotiators at subnational levels are themselves motivated in their local strategic choices by the prospect of influencing party relations beyond the locality; third, whether the transmission of knowledge gained through coalition experience at subnational levels has an impact on party leaders at the national level and conditions their behavior in the "supergame" of national government formation; and fourth, whether the conditions under which an experimental coalition develops influence its value as a model for future coalitions elsewhere in the system. Given the evidence presented, it seems a justifiable conclusion to suggest affirmative, though qualified, answers to all four questions.

In the three countries examined, national-level coalition behavior does react to developments in the subnational coalition system, and on most occasions coalition innovation in national government occurs only after a cooperative arrangement has been tested in subnational government. This linkage is substantial enough to warrant dismissal of the formal theoretical assumption that coalition formation is a discrete event; party leaders negotiating coalition arrangements, it would seem, suffer from neither amnesia nor myopia. Councilors at subnational levels themselves appear to be quite conscious of the influence that their coalition decisions have on party relations at superior levels of government, and for some the expectation of this influence is a motivating factor. Additionally, provincial and regional representatives appear to be generally open to the universe of coalition partners available to them; hence, the presence of a crucial precondition for experimentation. Openness is not absolute, however, and for some, the prospect of cooperating with certain parties is uninviting and thus a potential source of contention. There is, moreover, evidence to suggest that coalition experience in the periphery does supply part of the informational feedback needed by party leaders forming governing alliances in the national arena.

Coalition innovation occurs in a variety of contexts. This has been demonstrated by the cases of government formation in Brabant, Nord-Pas de Calais, and Baden-Württemberg. The electoral environment in which a coalition emerges can condition its value as an experimental model. Of the three case examples, it may be suggested that the Brabant "asymmetrical" coalition is most significant for its particular system because a relative absence of electoral constraints allowed the coalition to form primarily as a choice of the actors involved. Conversely, electoral and organizational constraints raised the costs of a black-green coalition in Baden-Württemberg to a prohibitive level. Nevertheless, all coalition innovations at subnational levels, in success and in failure, can provide some of the "perfect information" and "feedback" needed by party leaders forming coalitions in the national arena. It is necessary as a future step to pursue survey and interview analysis of national-level decision makers to better gauge the nature of this intent.

By expanding the study of government formation to include subnational assemblies, we have emphasized that authoritative decisions about coalition strategy can flow upward as well as downward. Parties and their leaders are influenced by past experiences as well as by the prospect of future iterations of the bargaining process. In this respect, cooperative arrangements at one level of government are affected by, and may themselves affect, those forming at another level of government. Beyond labeling regional elections as simply "barometers" of support for the national government, therefore, more serious consideration should be given to the impact that postelection coalition change in the periphery has on party relations at the center.

Chapter Nine

Dividing Power in the Periphery: Some Comparative Conclusions

This book has been presented with three purposes in mind. First, the study has attempted to depict a fundamental political process as it occurs in an underresearched set of institutions in three European democracies. In doing so, it has focused on the building of power-sharing coalitions as an outward and well-defined manifestation of political motivation, governing intent, and democratic representation. Second, the research has endeavored to collect and assemble attitudes and observations from middle-level politicians, elected representatives whose obligations, experiences, and ambitions are largely overlooked by comparativists. Their stories are frequently left untold by researchers more concerned with the "cleaner" and more celebrated process of national government formation. Third and finally, the analysis has sought to identify and isolate theoretically meaningful relationships between electoral risk, organizational pressure, and strategic choice. Exposing the process of collective decision making in mixed-motive situations reveals the limited utility of some existing theoretical constructs, but more importantly it suggests how individuals and groups endowed with political responsibility weigh the costs and benefits of alternative strategies according to the environments in which they must act. This concluding chapter summarizes the main findings of the study and ties this particular line of research back into the comparative politics literature.

267

A Deeper Understanding of Coalition Politics in Belgium, Germany, and France

At its most basic level, this book contributes to a deeper and richer understanding of coalition politics as practiced in Belgium, Germany, and France. In systems that obstruct the monopolization of political resources by any one party, the necessity for competitors and adversaries to cooperate so that they may each share a portion of those resources is a fact of political life. Where elections fail to award one party with an absolute majority of seats in a representative assembly, negotiation, bargaining, and compromise ensue. Political parties become intermediaries between voters and governmental authority, immediately faced with the tasks of interpreting the electorate's verdict and of establishing a workable and durable partnership that will hopefully have some success at formulating, legislating, and implementing public policy—all with an eye toward reelection. Despite differences in their institutional structures and in their electoral and party systems, Belgium, Germany, and France have each created political systems that encourage the formation of coalitions. While coalition building as it regards national parliamentary institutions has long been a source of curiosity for political scientists familiar with European democracies, much less is known about how the same necessity for majority formation plays out in regional or local institutions of representative government.

Evidence presented throughout the preceding chapters conclusively demonstrates that the struggles for government status at subnational levels are profoundly important to both parties and voters. Outcomes of these struggles can, moreover, result in a variety of governments of varying political complexion, each illustrating the relative capacity of competitors to cooperate, each indicating the relative openness of the political system to rule by a diversity of parties, and each exhibiting the relative responsiveness of parties to electoral verdicts. Parties competing in the Belgian provinces and regions, the French regions, and the German Länder have created coalition dynamics that in some ways are distinct from those generated by the same constellation of parties competing for national government status. Nonideological cooperation, participation of ecologists and extremists, minority government, and all-party government are subnational phenomena that cannot always be predicted by simple reference to partisan alignments in Bonn, Paris, or Brussels. Even where possible, subnational branches of national political parties do not invariably follow the lead of their colleagues at superior levels of the polity. This is most evident in the propensity of parties in all three countries to form partnerships incongruent with those in national parliament.

While coalition systems at the subnational level manifest their own distinctive elements, it is possible to answer in the affirmative the questions of whether government formation and alliance behavior in the periphery "enter the strategic considerations of national party leaders," whether they "complicate the coalition environment across the country," and whether in fact they may also "act as some determinant of actual coalition behavior" in the capital (Pridham 1984, 240). National elites do make conscious attempts to communicate instructions and influence strategy in the subnational institutions to which their respective parties gain entry. Directly elected representatives charged with serving their regional or provincial constituencies are therefore subject to pressures, constraints, and inducements from leaders of the voluntary organizations to which they belong. Although officials involved in national-level politics often possess the inclination to demand loyalty and obedience from their putatively subordinate followers, evidence presented in this study suggests that neither deference nor the ability to compel behavior from the top down can be assumed. Authoritative decisions about coalition strategy can flow upward as well as downward, and the success of party strategy at the subnational level can even function to supply some of the information necessary to national party leaders faced with gauging the reliability of certain parties as potential cabinet partners.

Restricting the findings to single countries highlights important features of individual political systems. If we are concerned only with, say, Germany, then the discussion of subnational coalition politics must recognize the very strong pressures on parties to form governments that match at the federal and state levels. This has been, after all, the stated preference of powerful leaders such as Adenauer, Brandt, Schmidt, and to a certain extent Kohl as well. A country-sensitive analysis must also acknowledge the small number of parties competing in the German system and thus the comparatively decisive elections that occur there. That Land elections frequently occur at the midpoint in the life of a Bundestag legislative period, and thus can take on the character of a plebiscite on the federal government of the day, must also be taken as an important aspect of the German system. Equally critical to the understanding of the German case are the baseline motivations of the pivotal Free Democratic Party, namely, government participation at all costs. An analysis of recent trends in state-level coalition politics must, finally, recognize the emergence of the Greens, the PDS, the Republikaners, and the DVU as complicating what had previously been a relatively stable and closed coalition system. Simple reference to Germany's federal status certainly accounts for some of the importance attached to outcomes at the state level as well as some of the de jure independence that state parties are supposed to enjoy, but it risks overlooking the de facto antagonisms that develop when Land parties have to respond to both local electoral imperatives and the intervention of federal authorities who have their own vested interests in the outcomes of strategic choice.

If we are to restrict the findings to the singular case of Belgium, then a host of country-specific factors likewise has to be emphasized. That Belgium is a culturally artificial country with different political, social, and economic cleavages dividing peoples and parties across a north-south line—complicated by Brussels as a francophone enclave within Dutch-speaking Flanders—cannot be ignored. Since all the major parties competing for political power have since the 1960s had their own semiindependent Flemish and Walloon branches, the number of coalition possibilities is much greater than in a country such as Germany. It must also be remembered that with provincial elections traditionally taking place on the same day as national parliamentary elections, the importance of purely provincial concerns tends to be more diminished than in a system in which elections for territorial and national parliaments occur on separate occasions. To fall back—as some might wish to do—on conventional assumptions about Belgium as a consociational democracy and as a traditionally unitary state with napoleonic structures would, however, neglect the political battles fought in the country's oldest representative assemblies, overlook the adversarial relations between political elites in the periphery, disregard the leverage that local party groups can have over their superiors, and ignore the bottom-up system change that has transpired in what was supposed to be a top-down country. The importance of such battles only increases with Belgium's federalization, with the new regional parliaments as battlegrounds.

If, finally, the analysis were to address only the French case, then key aspects particular to that country would have to be remembered. Chief among these considerations is the immaturity of the French regional government system itself. That directly elected regional institutions have existed only since 1986, though increasing the necessity and possibilities of original research, nevertheless cuts down on the ability to generalize about behavior at this level. An analysis of French regional coalition behavior must likewise recognize the large number of parties competing for regional power (an average of eight per region), the wider variety of alliances available, and the strong presence of national personalities (through the holding of multiple elective mandates). That France has a mixed presidential-parliamentary system at the national level as well as a two-ballot electoral mechanism (thus reducing the representation of smaller parties) of course inhibits the degree to which regional coalition dynamics may be reproduced in Paris. Still, to simply assume that these factors automatically relegate regional political patterns to marginal importance naively ignores the impact that developments in the regions have on national cabinet stability, party image, legitimation of previously excluded political forces, and alternative policy approaches.

Explanations of events in these countries individually have to take all of these factors into consideration. Doing so also contributes rich descriptive images of the peculiarities of political structures, processes, and historical developments at the subnational level. Such a contribution was the primary concern of chapter 5. Since this study has been concerned with elevating the analysis of subnational coalition politics to a broader level of generalization, effort has also been devoted to identifying how politicians and parties at the meso level in all three countries respond to different opportunities and constraints offered by coalition situations. In this way, it has been possible to recognize that different subnational branches of the same political party can respond to collective action problems—such as government formation—with different strategies. The competitive positions of parties vary across the respective regions of all three countries, as does the very competitiveness of the regional political "markets" themselves. Moreover, the extent to which peripheral electoral systems have either succumbed to or evaded the process of political nationalization, in which elections and parties' fortunes depend on the general political climate and politics at the national level, is an important variable common to all three countries. These two factors, it has been demonstrated, intervene to influence, condition, and constrain the choices parties make.

Recognizing that coalitions are built, to borrow the phrase, in a "constrained real world" (Laver and Schofield 1990) informs our understanding of why coalitions in the Belgian province of Namur have been far more unstable and unpredictable than in a much more politically inert West Flanders. Awareness of electoral context and risk clarifies discrepancies between party behavior in Hamburg, where short-term adversarial strategies and short-lived governments have been the rule, and party behavior in Lower Saxony, where comparative stability has reinforced the durability of cooperative arrangements such as the current red-green experiment. Acknowledging the variable competitiveness of French regional environments, and not just the legislative weights of the parties elected to the councils, adds to an understanding of why the PCF-PS "Union of the Left" met with such different fortunes in regions such as Limousin, Nord-Pas de Calais, and Provence-Alpes–Côte d'Azur. Recognizing electoral risk and the organizational pressures exacerbated by such risk thus allows us to better comprehend the issues of accountability and intraparty conflict normally avoided in studies of government formation.

Views from Below: Telling Some Untold Stories

One of the strengths of the analysis has been the collection and assembly of heretofore unavailable comparative survey data regarding the coalition experiences of representatives elected to subnational assemblies. There is something inherently appealing in learning about the democratic process, its ideals and its realities, from individuals acting outside the more familiar boundaries of national politics. The insights provided by actors at subnational levels supply important clues about strategic choice as it occurs in their milieu. Patterns in the survey data pointed to the surprisingly weak influence of local public opinion in matters of strategic choice, revealed varying levels of national intervention in the government formation process, suggested motivational disparities between subnational-level and national-level decision makers, and indicated the general openness of individuals and groups to coalition experimentation. Controlling for the effects of electoral environment produced legitimate evidence to suggest that the coalition game does mean different things to different players, and elicits different reactions from them, depending upon where the game itself is being played.

Interview data, which have been used to help corroborate patterns discerned in the survey data, have allowed some substantively interesting political stories to be told that otherwise would be left out of accounts of multiparty government in the three countries. The cases of Limburg and Brabant served to show how parties use the coalition process to overturn long-established models of political cooperation and to send messages to wider audiences that alternatives to the status quo exist. The cases of Luxembourg and Limousin clearly illustrated how subnational party groups, even those that represent tightly controlled organizations, can challenge the direct authority and advice of national party leaders in order to pursue strategies that optimize more "local" benefits. The case of Baden-Württemberg, and to a similar extent that of Berlin, demonstrated difficulties that parties have in accepting coalition—indeed "grand" coalition—with their chief rival. The Baden-Württemberg case also shows how even in the failure to establish a formal coalition, parties attempting to experiment with untried alliances can enlarge the universe of political possibilities and thus set the stage for future iterations of the government formation process. Devoting some attention to these cases puts "politics" back into the discussion of coalition formation.

Alone, attitudinal data cannot be relied upon to automatically predict behavior. Nor can the professed observations and subjective impressions of political actors be used exclusively to produce a precise image of motivation, power, and influence in the decision-making process. Together, and along with historical evidence from more than 260 cases of subnational government formation, the data collected for this study do, however, provide a comprehensive accounting of outcomes and beliefs—the totality of which allows us to confidently link our existing understanding of multiparty coalition government with the reality of party behavior in the subnational institutions of Belgium, France, and Germany.

Theoretical Advances and Prospects for Future Research

This work has also sought to contribute to the literature linking organizational and systemic aspects of strategic party behavior. This literature contends that many assumptions fundamental to most existing coalition theories seriously neglect contextual constraints and attitudinal considerations that may intervene to influence coalition choices and the pursuit of political self-interest. Deploying the assumptions of a "conditional model of coalition behavior," it has been possible to examine the relationship between electoral subsystems and strategic choice within party organizations.

The account of strategic choice offered by this study is not consistent with the generalizations made by conventional coalition theories that anticipate discrete outcomes determined by unified and unconstrained parties. Instead, from an expanded examination of government formation that includes intermediate-level subnational assemblies, it is evident that parties rarely act as unitary actors, monolithically pursuing office benefits according to an agreed-upon set of preferences and by command of an oligarchic chain of command. Moreover, it is clear that government formation is a dynamic process and not a static, discrete event. Party groups and their leaders are, borrowing from Strom, "neither amnesiac nor myopic" (1990b, 569). Cooperative arrangements at one level of government may be affected by, and may themselves affect, those forming at a different level of government. Similarly, past iterations of the government formation process as well as the anticipation of future iterations condition what rational actors might do otherwise than might be expected if the contest were "single shot." The latter point is important not just for coalition studies but for theory building in political science more generally. Its importance lies in the impetus that it gives us to look beyond preexisting preference orderings and iterative strategies and to envision a real world, illustrated nicely by parliamentary coalition building, in which political actors may truly have to let go of preexisting expectations and experiment with new governing strategies.

To build upon these advances, future research into multiparty subnational government must continue to attract the attention of mainstream coalition theorists and comparativists. The still largely untapped reservoir of empirical evidence offered by party behavior in territorial parliaments can be used to further refine our notions of parties as oligarchies or stratarchies, unitary actors or coalitions of factions. Beyond the labeling of regional-level elections as simply "barometers" of support for the national government, more serious consideration should be given to the relative localization/nationalization of subnational electoral systems and to the impact of alliance change in the periphery on partisan relations at the center. These kinds of issues should, of course, continue to receive scholarly attention within the particular contexts of the Belgian, German, and French systems.

In Belgium, the provinces are likely to continue to be minibattlegrounds for political parties; however, future studies will have the ability to examine how parties cope with the task of jointly composing governments in the new regional parliaments. It will also be necessary in the future to watch closely the kinds of coalition patterns developing in the five new Länder of eastern Germany. Will the eastern parties duplicate, where possible, the Bonn (or by that time, Berlin) alliances? The so-called traffic light coalition in Brandenburg is evidence that they may not. Finally, it will be important to follow the maturation of the regionalization process in France, as it may increase the authority and thus the stakes of regional power. Of special interest will be the fortunes of the two parties on opposite sides of the political spectrum in France that have each gained a share of regional power and responsibility. The Verts, on the one hand, and the Front National, on the other, have each skillfully manipulated their pivotal position as arbiters of power. To what extent they are able to transform their regional experiments into greater payoffs—legitimacy, acceptability as coalition partners, stepping stones to national power—should concern observers of that country.

Perhaps most important, the broader comparative politics literature, especially the part that deals with politics in liberal democracies, must use the government formation process as a lens through which to assess the "democraticness" of decentralization. If "decentralization is one of the elements of political institution-building through which acceptance of the political order can be improved" (Kaase and Gibowski 1988, 8), then comparativists must not restrict their analyses of regional institutions to measures of economic development and administrative efficiency. These are no doubt important concerns, but so too are basic issues of representation, accountability, transparency, citizen participation, and political cooperation. In this regard, future research must come to some assessment of the effectiveness of Green models of regional governance, since they most closely embrace the ideals that reformers have long touted as the merits of decentralization. Similarly, future research should work to expand the number of cases compared; recent events suggest Spain and Italy as particularly fruitful areas for empirical exploration. Ultimately, for all parliamentary democracies, the study of multiparty, subnational government should be linked with the broader issue of effective and durable government. Nations that create conditions that aid coalitional learning in response to new environmental conditions may improve the capacity for durable, resilient, and effective government across time.

In contributing to our understanding of how the power game is played at subnational levels, this book has taken what previously may have seemed an insignificant political process and shown it for what it is: a valuable link in the democratic system. This has been done in something of a pioneering spirit, intentionally working to open an area of inquiry to comparative empirical study. Hopefully, it has provided compelling illustrations that such study could prove rewarding.

Appendix One

The Survey Questionnaire

Cover Letter

Dear _____, [MdL, Conseiller]

We are conducting a survey sponsored by the Department of Political Science at Emory University (Atlanta, USA). Our purpose is to learn more about the nature of coalition politics as practiced by political parties in the German Landtage, French Conseils Régionaux, and Belgian Conseils Provinciaux and Conseils Régionaux. We are especially concerned that we should understand how individual Deputies like yourself feel about cooperating and sharing power with the members of other political parties.

Attached please find a copy of our questionnaire. The questions concern you, your Land [regional, provincial] party, and particularly your parliamentary group's strategies in forming new governing majorities following elections. Also included are questions about the impact of national party politics on Land [regional, provincial] party politics, as well as the impact of Land [regional, provincial] policies on national strategies.

We hope that you will take the time to complete the questionnaire and return it to us in the enclosed self-addressed stamped envelope. The information you provide will contribute to an important study and be of significant interest and value to observers in both Europe and America.

Your responses will, of course, be completely confidential. Your name will not be revealed or associated with your responses in any way.

We appreciate your willingness to help us in our research effort. We believe that you will find the questionnaire both interesting and provocative, and we look forward to receiving your reply.

Thank you for your cooperation!

Sincerely yours,

William M. Downs
Department of Political Science
Emory University
Atlanta, Georgia 30322
USA

QUESTIONNAIRE (Sample)

1:1 Are the coalition strategies of your state party group, particularly its tactics during and after elections, determined more by state party members or more by national party leaders?

☐ State Politicians   ☐ National Party Leaders

1:2 In forming a new Land government, how important is it for your party to duplicate--i.e., have the same partner(s)--your federal party's alliance strategy wherever possible?

( ) a. Very Important   ( ) c. Not Very Important ( ) e. Uncertain
( ) b. Important   ( ) d. Not at all Important

1:3-4 Do you agree with the following statements? (Please circle your responses.)

	Strongly Disagree (1)	Disagree (2)	Agree (3)	Strongly Agree (4)	No Opinion (0)
1:3 "Successful coalitional cooperation in the Länderparlamenten can promote an interest in cooperation between the same parties at the federal level."	1	2	3	4	0
1:4 "Successful coalitional cooperation in the Bundestag can promote an interest in cooperation between the same parties at the Land level."	1	2	3	4	0

1:5 Within most political parties tensions exist between "pragmatists" and "ideologues." Pragmatists seek government participation, even if the party's goals have to be modified in compromises with alliance partners. Ideologues seek government participation, but not if the party's goals have to be modified in compromises with alliance partners. Where would you place yourself, closer to the pragmatists or the ideologues?
( ) a. Clearly among the pragmatists
( ) b. Among the pragmatists
( ) c. Closer to the pragmatists
( ) d. Between the pragmatists and the ideologues
( ) e. Closer to the ideologues
( ) f. Among the ideologues
( ) g. Clearly among the ideologues

1:6 Are there any parties with whose members you would not even consider working with in a coalition? (Please check from list below.)

( ) a.CDU	( ) c.SPD	( ) e.Die Grünen	( ) g.DSU	( ) i.ÖDP	( ) k. NPD
( ) b.CSU	( ) d.FDP	( ) f.PDS	( ) h.REP	( ) j.DKP	

1:7 If you have answered "yes" to question 1:6, please specify why you could not cooperate with the members of such other party groups.

For reasons of:
( ) a. Ideological Differences
( ) b. My party follows a policy of parliamentary opposition
( ) c. Previous disappointing experience of cooperation with party
( ) d. Advice or Directions from state party leaders
( ) e. Advice or Directions from party group at federal level

2:1 Please indicate to what extent you believe your personal views are considered by your party leaders prior to the party's decision to share power with another party.

( ) a. My views are always considered in matters of coalition strategy
( ) b. My views are frequently considered in matters of coalition strategy
( ) c. My views are sometimes considered in matters of coalition strategy
( ) d. My views are rarely considered in matters of coalition strategy
( ) e. My views are never considered in matters of coalition strategy

2:2 How frequent is cooperation among the parties in the Landtag in the following situations?

	Rare	Occasional	Frequent
a. Election of Ministerpräsident	1	2	3
b. Selection of Cabinet Members	1	2	3
c. Approval of Budget	1	2	3
d. Passage of Legislation	1	2	3

2:3 What types of coalitional activity occur in the Landtag? (Check all relevant responses.)
( ) a. Written agreements between party groups
( ) b. Verbal agreements between party groups
( ) c. Frequent voting support in plenary sessions
( ) d. Frequent voting support in committee meetings
( ) e. Agreements between party groups not to hinder one another
( ) f. Agreements between party groups to disadvantage other group(s)

2:4 In the process leading to the formation of a new coalition you and your party are likely influenced by many considerations in your approach to negotiations. From the list below, please circle the number that best represents your party's concerns.

	Not at All Influential	Somewhat Influential	Very Influential
a. The need for a majority in Landtag	1	2	3
b. The need for a majority on primary committees	1	2	3
c. The securing of committee chairs for your fraktion	1	2	3
d. Obtaining concessions on policy	1	2	3
e. The ideology of other parties	1	2	3
f. The climate of local public opinion	1	2	3
g. The climate of national public opinion	1	2	3
h. Federal party policy on coalitions	1	2	3

2:5 Thinking about all of the new Land governments you have seen negotiated, in what percentage of those cases would you say there has been some conflict between the Land party and the Bund party over partners, policies, or concessions? _____

2:6 Please rank from 1-3 the importance given by <u>state</u> party to the following considerations when negotiating a coalition with another party or parties.

	Not Important	Somewhat Important	Very Important
a. Agreement on a specific policy issue	1	2	3
b. Need to be part of majority in council	1	2	3
c. Maintaining party and ideological identity	1	2	3
d. Electoral advantages of an alliance	1	2	3
e. Instructions from federal party	1	2	3

2:7 To your knowledge, how important are the following considerations for your <u>federal</u> party when it negotiates a coalition with another party or parties at the federal level.

	Not Important	Somewhat Important	Very Important
a. Agreement on a specific policy issue	1	2	3
b. Need to be in parliamentary majority	1	2	3
c. Maintaining party and ideological identity	1	2	3
d. Electoral advantages of an alliance	1	2	3
e. Instructions from state parties	1	2	3

2:8 Will voters at the next election hold you and your party accountable for a coalition you may have sought with another party or parties to influence the distribution of government posts or to promote a policy?

☐ Yes ☐ No

3:1-5 Do you agree with the following statements? (Please circle your responses.)

	Strongly Disagree (1)	Disagree (2)	Agree (3)	Strongly Agree (4)	No Opinion (0)
3:1 "The national party has a legitimate right, considering its position, to expect that its suggestions will be carried out at all levels of government."	1	2	3	4	0
3:2 "State party members respect the national party's competence and good judgment about things with which it is more experienced than they."	1	2	3	4	0
3:3 "State party members admire national party leaders for their personal qualities, and want to act in ways that merit the respect and admiration of their national leaders."	1	2	3	4	0

3:4 "The national party can
give special help and
benefits to those who
cooperate with it."   1   2   3   4   0

3:5 "The national party can
apply pressure or penalize
those who do not cooperate
with it."   1   2   3   4   0

3:6 How would you characterize the influence of your party's national leadership in the government formation process in the Landtag and in your party group's decisions to form a coalition with another party or parties?

      ( ) a. Very Influential   ( ) c. Not Very Influential ( ) e. Uncertain
      ( ) b. Influential   ( ) d. Not at all Influential

3:7 Does your federal party organization advise you, when composing the state manifesto, to follow the intentions and policies of the federal party?

    ☐ Yes, in everything   ☐ Yes, in some respects ☐ No

3:8 In politics, one often talks about "Left" and "Right". Where would you place your state party, ideologically, in relation to your federal party? (Please place an "L" on the scale for your state party and a "B" on the scale for your federal party.)

      Far   Left   Center Center Center Right Far
      Left   Left   Right   Right

3:9 After the most recent election, were any members of the national parliament or of the national party leadership physically present during any part of the negotiations to form a new regional government?

    ☐ Yes   ☐ No

▸PLEASE ANSWER QUESTIONS 4:1-4:2 ONLY IF YOUR PARTY IS PRESENTLY PART OF THE GOVERNING COALITION. IF YOUR PARTY IS NOT CURRENTLY A PART OF THE STATE GOVERNMENT, PLEASE GO TO QUESTION 5:1.

4:1 In order that a governing coalition could be formed following the most recent Landtagswahl, please indicate whether your party made or obtained concessions with respect to another party or parties in the following policy areas.

	CONCESSIONS MADE			CONCESSIONS GAINED		
	MAJOR	MINOR	NONE	MAJOR	MINOR	NONE
Finance	1	2	3	4	5	6
Education	1	2	3	4	5	6
Transport	1	2	3	4	5	6
Health	1	2	3	4	5	6
Environment	1	2	3	4	5	6
Labor	1	2	3	4	5	6
Agriculture	1	2	3	4	5	6
Justice	1	2	3	4	5	6

4:2 Which of the following aspects of coalitions do you think contributes most to your state party's electoral appeal? (Please circle your responses.)

	Least Important	Somewhat Important	Most Important
a. Publicity gained from being in the government	1	2	3
b. Psychological boost gained by being part of the government	1	2	3
c. Opportunity to distribute patronage	1	2	3
d. Opportunity to implement a program	1	2	3

5:1 Would you say that elections in your Land are determined more by national issues and personalities, more by Land issues and personalities, or more by issues of local public administration? (Please only check one.)

( ) a. More by national themes, personalities, and parties
( ) b. More by Land themes, personalities, and parties
( ) c. More by administrative concerns and not party politics

5:2 How would you characterize the intensity of the most recent Landtag election campaign compared with others around the country?

( ) a. More competitive   ( ) b. Less Competitive   ( ) c. Equal in Intensity

5:3 Given the current electoral system in your Land, is it more politically prudent for you as an incumbent official to assure your position vis-a-vis the electors in your Wahlkreis or the party leaders who will determine your place on the election list?

( ) a. Electors in my Wahlkreis
( ) b. Party leaders who will determine my place on an election list

6:1 What in your view is the actual influence of the following individuals or groups in determining the course of Landtag policy? (Please circle your responses.)

	Little or No Influence	Some Influence	Quite a Bit of Influence	Great Deal of Influence	Very Great Deal of Influence
a. Individual Deputies	1	2	3	4	5
b. Präsidium	1	2	3	4	5
c. Council of Elders	1	2	3	4	5
d. Parliamentary Committees	1	2	3	4	5
e. Minister-präsident	1	2	3	4	5
f. Staatsminister	1	2	3	4	5
g. Parliamentary Parties	1	2	3	4	5
h. Landesverbände	1	2	3	4	5
i. Kreisverbände	1	2	3	4	5
j. Bezirksverbände	1	2	3	4	5
k. Bundesvorstand	1	2	3	4	5
l. Bundesgeschäftsstelle	1	2	3	4	5

6:2 Following the most recent election, what percentage of your party's original demands as a price for membership in a coalition were ultimately met? _____

6:3 Please check the response that best describes your personal access to the members of the Bundestag.
( ) a. Easy and regular formal access to members of Bundestag
( ) b. Easy and regular informal access to members of Bundestag
( ) c. Limited, formal access
( ) d. Limited, informal access
( ) e. No access

6:4 Please check the response that best describes communication between your state party and the party organization at the federal level.
( ) a. Regular but formal communication
( ) b. Regular and informal communication
( ) c. Limited and formal communication
( ) d. Limited and informal communication
( ) e. Nonexistent

6:5 In your opinion, which of the following best describes the access of your state party group to the chief officers of the party at the federal level? (Please check one.)

( ) a. Very Open ( ) c. Limited
( ) b. Open   ( ) d. No access

7:1 In resolving disagreements with your federal party organization, how often does your state party group emerge successful?

( ) a. Always   ( ) d. Less than half of the time
( ) b. More than half of the time ( ) e. Never
( ) c. Half of the time

7:2 Where would you place yourself on the following scale? (Please put an "X" at the appropriate point.)

```
  |----+----+----+----+----+----|
 Far  Left  Center Center Center Right  Far
 Left        Left         Right        Right
```

7:3 Do you participate in or attend the meetings of the following bodies? (Please check the appropriate boxes.)

	Never	From Time to Time	Regularly	Most of the Time	Always
a. Bundesvorstand	1	2	3	4	5
b. Bundesausschuss	1	2	3	4	5
c. Landesverbände	1	2	3	4	5
d. Kreisverbände	1	2	3	4	5
e. Bezirksverbände	1	2	3	4	5

7:4 How active do you consider yourself to be in affairs of your party at the local, state, and federal levels?

Local Level	State Level	Federal Level
( ) a. Very Active	( ) a. Very Active	( ) a. Very Active
( ) b. Fairly Active	( ) b. Fairly Active	( ) b. Fairly Active
( ) c. Rarely Active	( ) c. Rarely Active	( ) c. Rarely Active
( ) d. Not Active	( ) d. Not Active	( ) d. Not Active

7:5 Do you plan to stand for election to the Landtag at the next election?

       ☐ Yes   ☐ No

7:6 Would you consider standing for election to the Bundestag?

       ☐ Yes   ☐ No

Thank you for your cooperation!

Appendix Two

Survey Responses by Country, Subnational Assembly, and Party

Country, Subnational Assemblies	Parties							Totals	
Belgium	PS	PSC	FDF	PRL	FN	AGIR	ECOLO	*N*	%
Brabant Conseil Provincial	8/10	4/6	7/7	5/15	—	—	4/7	28/45	62.2
Hainaut Conseil Provincial	13/42	8/20	—	7/14	1/1	—	4/13	33/90	36.7
Liège Conseil Provincial	12/36	12/18	—	7/19	—	0/1	6/12	37/86	43.0
Luxembourg Conseil Provincial	5/13	6/18	—	7/15	—	—	3/4	21/50	42.0
Namus Conseil Provincial	3/26	3/17	—	11/14	—	—	3/3	20/60	33.3
Brussels-Capital Conseil Régional	9/18	4/9	7/15	6/15	1/2	—	3/8	30/67	44.8
Totals *N*	50/145	34/88	14/22	43/92	2/3	0/1	23/47	169/398	
%	34.5	38.6	63.6	46.7	66.7	00.0	48.9		42.5

Germany	SPD	CDU	FDP	REP	DVU	Grüne	*N*	%
Baden-Württemberg Landtag	16/46	19/64	3/8	5/15	—	4/13	49/146	33.6
Bremen Bürgerschaft	11/41	13/32	4/10	—	4/5	4/11	28/99	28.3
Hesse Landtag	17/45	18/47	3/8	—	—	4/12	42/112	37.5
Lower Saxony Landtag	26/71	22/67	4/9	—	—	3/8	61/155	39.4
Totals *N*	70/203	72/210	14/35	5/15	4/5	15/44	180/512	
%	34.5	34.3	40.0	33.3	80.0	34.1		35.2

France	PC	MRG	PS	FU	UDF	RPR	CPNT	FN	Verts	GE	*N*	%
Alsace Conseil Régional	—	—	2/6	—	4/11	3/8	—	6/9	4/6	2/3	21/43	48.8
Aquitaine Conseil Régional	3/6	—	4/20	—	7/15	4/14	—	4/8	1/2	3/7	26/72	36.1
Bourgogne Conseil Régional	2/3	—	6/9	2/3	3/11	5/12	0/1	4/8	1/5	2/2	25/54	46.3
Languedoc-Roussillon Conseil Régional	2/8	—	4/14	—	2/11	3/11	1/1	5/13	2/3	2/4	21/65	32.3
Lorraine Conseil Régional	1/3	—	3/10	2/6	5/11	7/21	—	4/10	2/5	1/6	25/72	34.7
Midi-Pyrénées Conseil Régional	2/5	3/5	8/23	—	4/16	5/18	2/9	4/6	2/5	2/2	32/89	36.0
Picardie Conseil Régional	2/6	—	4/9	—	4/11	6/11	1/3	3/8	2/5	3/4	25/57	43.8
Pays de la Loire Conseil Régional	1/3	3/4	6/16	3/6	7/20	6/20	—	5/8	5/6	4/6	40/89	44.9
Provence-Alpes Côte d'Azur Conseil Régional	4/10	—	14/30	—	5/24	9/17	—	7/34	3/3	2/3	44/121	36.4
Totals *N*	17/44	6/9	51/137	7/15	41/130	48/132	4/14	42/104	22/40	21/37	259/662	
%	38.6	66.7	37.2	46.7	31.5	36.4	28.6	40.4	55.0	56.8		39.1

NOTES

Chapter One

1. After the 1992 French regional council elections, Les Verts (Greens) outmaneuvered the Socialists to gain control of the Nord–Pas de Calais region.

2. The Parti Social-Chrétien (PSC) "won" Luxembourg's five provincial elections between 1981 and 1994, yet lost provincial power to an alliance of Socialists (PS) and Liberals (PRL).

3. The Republikaner Party caused an electoral "earthquake" in Baden-Württemberg at the 1992 Landtag election when it gained 15 seats and became the third-largest party in the parliament, surpassing both the Greens and the Free Democrats.

Chapter Two

1. Quotations are from interviews with provincial councilors conducted on 12 June 1993 in Brugge and 10 July 1993 in Namur.

2. Bogdanor's (1983) introduction to *Coalition Government in Western Europe* provides a useful summary of these different types of coalitions.

3. For an excellent discussion of "coalition avoidance," see Strom and Leipart (1993, 870–87).

4. Controversy over Fourons played a large role in bringing down the Esykens CVP/PSC-PSB government in 1972 and more recently the Martens CVP/PSC-PRL/PVV coalition in 1987. The issue stems from a 1962 drawing of linguistic borders, a move that transferred six villages of the Fourons district from the French-speaking province of Liège to the Flemish province of Limburg. A summary of this complex issue is provided in "Les Fourons: Alsace-Lorraine des Wallons," *Le Monde* (13–14 June 1993).

5. The unlikelihood of a SP-PVV-VU coalition was suggested by the CVP spokesman in Limburg in a 12 November 1992 interview with the author. However, the specter of such an outcome was raised by the CVP itself during

the last days of the campaign when it asked voters: "L'électeur ne compte-t-il plus? Une alliance monstreuse contre le CVP?" (*Le Soir,* 26 November 1991).

6. "Le CVP dans l'opposition," *La Libre Belgique,* 30 November 1991.

7. "Overeenkomst SP-PVV-VU met betrekking op het bestuur van Provincie Limburg" (Document obtained by the author).

8. For more on the choice of a center-left "losers coalition" and its apparent rejection of the electorate's verdict, see Fitzmaurice (1992).

9. Interview with CVP senator (Brussels, 8 December 1992).

Chapter Three

1. On "nested" behavior, see Tsebelis (1990).

2. Figure 3.6 builds upon the graphical framework suggested by Kitschelt (1989b, 253).

Chapter Four

1. Three questionnaires were produced in order to make sense in the particular lexicons of the German, Belgian, and French political systems. Naturally, the questionnaires sent to Belgium and France were written in French, and those sent to Germany were composed in German. Translations of the questionnaires from English to French and from English to German were facilitated by independent language experts as well as political scientists familiar with the precise terminology of the individual political systems. A cover letter explained to potential respondents the questionnaire's emphasis on government formation and alliance politics. Anonymity and confidentiality were assured to all respondents, although ultimately a large number voluntarily identified themselves. A pilot questionnaire was first administered to a small sample of subnational representatives from one party in each of the three country cases. Questionnaires were sent in May 1992 to preselected individuals in the German CDU, the Belgian Parti Socialiste, and the French Parti Socialiste with the request that they be completed and with an added solicitation to comment further on specific questions where necessary. A sufficient number of returns bearing both substantive and stylistic remarks served the process of refining the survey instrument, helping to eliminate several inappropriate questions as well as those that seemed to add little information and could have diluted response rates. Such an initial test also helped minimize the possibility of introducing systematic errors that could bias the results.

2. For their assistance in this regard, the following persons deserve mention: Jos Vandeputte (Brabant), Leon De Winne (East Flanders), Gisèle Keersebilck (West Flanders), Omer Coenen (Antwerp), Marc Martens (Limburg), André Cornet (Luxembourg), Philippe Hugé (Namur), Charles Simon (Hai-

naut), and Jean Claude Piret (Liège). Additional assistance was provided by Ernest Staes, Consul General of Belgium in Atlanta.

3. Following Pijnenburg (1987), local coalitions are congruent when they match the national majority versus opposition pattern, either directly or in reverse. In a five-party (A, B, C, D, E) national parliament where parties A and C constitute the government, "direct congruency" in a five-party (A', B', C', D', E') regional assembly is the situation in which parties A' and C' share executive power, and parties B', D', and E' do not. Reversed congruency is the situation in which B', D', and E' share regional power and A' and C' do not. "For each cluster of parties, whether it finds itself on the majority or the opposition side is not really important here (direct vs. reversed congruency), as long as there is an identical (i.e. between the same partners) 'alliance' or interparty bond at the national and local level" (Pijnenburg 1987, 58). Coalitions are incongruent when they do not match the national majority–versus–opposition pattern. However, I expand Pijnenburg's operationalization of incongruent coalitions to include those coalitions in which parties that share parliamentary opposition status but that also have explict policies of noncooperation choose to cooperate locally. In this regard, when the mainstream center-right opposition parties in France adopt "hands-off" policies toward opposition National Front legislators in the Assemblée Nationale but then collaborate in regional majorities, such alliance patterns are deemed incongruent because there is no identical alliance or interparty bond at national and subnational levels. This we may deem the "pariah rule."

4. All the provinces chosen for inclusion in the survey population lie in the francophone Walloon half of Belgium except for bilingual Brabant, whose provincial assembly is composed of equal representations from the province's Wallon and Flemish districts. The decision to exclude the Flemish provinces and the Dutch-speaking councilors in Brabant province and in the Brussels-Capital Region was a deliberate choice to control for linguistic divisions within the party "families," a potentially confounding variable.

5. France Unie formed in 1990 to regroup the nonsocialist or "ouverture" members of the "majorité presidentielle," frequently referred to in the French press as "gaullists de gauche."

6. Unfortunately, "the goal of error-free measurement—while laudable—is never attained in any area of scientific investigation" (Carmines and Zeller 1979, 11). Chance or random error is always a possibility. Like any other method, moreover, the survey questionnaire technique is subject to these chances and to the criticism that its results can blur "reality." If, for example, repeated measurements of the same phenomenon do not yield the same results (i.e., if they are not reliable), then results and analysis may both be skewed. Similarly, if some conceptual indicator does not actually measure what the researcher intends, then the results and subsequent analysis may be invalid. Concerns about reliability and validity raise the possibility of nonrandom error;

however, nonrandom error is, to a certain extent, within the power of the researcher to control.

7. Interviews lasted between 30 minutes and three hours in length. In all cases, notes were made during the interview; in others, the interview was tape recorded and subsequently transcribed. Recording the responses, which clearly improves subsequent evaluation, had no perceptible impact on the respondents' candor. Anonymity proved to be a concern for only some of the interviewees, but I generally refrain from attaching names to quotations in the text.

Chapter Five

1. A useful example of this treatment of subnational coalitions as "interferences" can be found in Mabille and Lentzen (1988, 49–50).

2. A comprehensive discussion of Belgium's constitutional development is provided by Alen (1990). See also chapters 3 and 4 on central, regional, and local government in John Fitzmaurice (1983).

3. "L'institution provinciale, organisée par la Loi provinciale du 30 avril 1836, présent bien des analogies avec l'organisation de l'Etat belge" (CRISP 1972, 2).

4. The Permanent Deputation predates the Belgian state itself, with the first reference to such an institution being in 1664. A useful discussion of these origins may be found in *Le Soir,* 12 April 1992.

5. Interview with Ecolo party group leader in Luxembourg Provincial Council (Arlon, 21 October 1992).

6. This is especially true among provincial councilors in the Parti Social-Chrétien. See "PSC: le baroud des provincialistes," *Le Soir,* 19 January 1993.

7. Ibid.

8. Provincial councils' election of members of the Belgian Senate dates from 1893, a practice that ended with the reform of the Senate in 1993.

9. See for example "Conseil Provincial: Le budget 93 est accepté majorité contre opposition; Les Ecolos voient une taxe-santé inégale et les PSC rejettent une fiscalité allant crescendo," *La Meuse—Luxembourg,* 5 November 1992.

10. Interview with Ecolo councilor in Luxembourg Province, (Arlon, 21 October 1992).

11. Province de Luxembourg, *Projet de Budget: Des Recettes et Dépenses Provinciales Pour l'Année 1993,* Arlon, 1992.

12. For every 200,000 inhabitants each province received one senator; for any remaining 125,000 the province obtained an additional senator.

13. "Dépoussiérer la Province," *La Meuse—Liège,* 4 November 1992.

14. "Scission de la province du Brabant: De troublantes questions pour l'avenir de Bruxelles," *Vlan,* 4 April 1993.

15. Interview with Socialist provincial group leader (Hasselt, 19 November 1992).

16. The Communists did not receive a seat or a portfolio in the provincial executive (CRISP, 1972).

17. CRISP (1972, 24).

18. A valuable account of the demise of Vanden Boeynants's government and the Leuven/Louvain controversy is found in Chapter 1 of Lemaître (1982).

19. Namely the town of Fourons/Voeren, trapped as it is between the provinces of Limburg and Liège, and the object of a certain amount of gerrymandering.

20. Lemaître (1982, 7).

21. CRISP (1974, 4).

22. *Le Soir*, 13 November 1971.

23. *Het Volk*, 14 November 1972.

24. *La Libre Belgique*, 26 December 1978.

25. *La Peuple*, 19 December 1978.

26. Article 28 of the Basic Law.

27. Useful overviews of the German federal system can be found in Kloss (1990) and in Johnson (1983).

28. Enough time has not yet elapsed since reunification to allow for meaningful longitudinal comparisons between party behavior in the five eastern Länder and party behavior at the federal level. This analysis thus limits itself in large part to a discussion of the traditional 11 Landtage of the former West Germany.

29. The one-vote system is described in Zinnkann (1991). For a comparison with the federal two-ballot system see *Electoral Law* (1986).

30. A SPD-FDP coalition would have produced a six-seat parliamentary majority.

31. The FDP had already been in coalition with the Saarland CDU since 1977, although this had occurred between elections.

32. A similar "traffic light" coalition emerged the same year in the eastern state of Brandenburg, where the SPD, FDP, and Bündnis 90 agreed to share power.

33. Regional elections in Corsica had already taken place in 1984.

34. *Le Monde*, 16 April 1992.

35. *Le Monde*, 24 March 1992.

36. The two-thirds criterion is not always the deciding factor in national government formation even during periods of constitutional revision. The government formed in 1991, although charged with legislating Belgium's federal status, did not command such a majority. The Catholic-Socialist government had to build legislative coalitions with the ecologists and the Volksunie to secure the necessary two-thirds support in parliament.

37. These are conveniently arranged in Appendix B of Laver and Schofield (1990).

Chapter 6

1. One drawback in the area of temporal comparability exists with France: there have been only two sets of regional elections, and thus there is only one measurement point of volatility. Whereas a significantly broader historical span of comparable evidence is available for Belgium and Germany, it simply does not yet exist for France. This fact is a liability only in that *changes* in net volatility for the French regions are not available for comparison with the other two countries.

2. Most observers agree that the start of the 1960s also marked a consolidation of the party systems in the Federal Republic. This, then, is a sufficient point of departure for the measurement. See Roberts (1989) and Müller-Rommel (1989).

3. Following Pedersen (1983), it is necessary to note that an "average may not be typical for the diachronic pattern, but may, for example, reflect the occurrence of one or a few highly atypical elections" (37). Therefore, it was useful to examine the dispersion of volatility measures around their respective Land, province, and regional means. In the German case, for example, plotting the mean volatility of the Länder for the period from 1961 to 1995 against the standard deviation for each Land reinforces the conclusion that groups of states may be characterized by different levels of electoral uncertainty. Bavaria, Rhineland-Palatinate, Lower Saxony, Schleswig-Holstein, and North Rhine–Westphalia stand out as states with stable and comparatively low levels of electoral volatility. Alternatively, the state party systems in Bremen, Hamburg, Hessen, Baden-Württemberg, and Saarland appear similar in that each has a high mean volatility and a high degree of fluctuation around that mean. Applying the same procedures to the Belgian provinces also yields two apparent clusters. Three of the Walloon provinces (Luxembourg, Liège, and Namur) score high on both the volatility and fluctuation measures, whereas all four of the Flemish provinces and Brabant score comparatively low on both. In Flanders more than in Wallonia, the relative electoral fortunes of parties hardly change from one election to the next. The anomoly is Hainaut, which demonstrates moderate to high average net gains/losses but which is not included in the same cluster as the other southern provinces. This finding is partially explained by a 1965 Hainaut election that was highly atypical in terms of average volatility. Plotting regional volatility averages against their standard deviations for France is not as useful as in the other two countries, given that there is no purpose in trying to identify the effects of "atypical" elections with only two time points available.

4. For the sake of comparability, data from the 1994 provincial election are

excluded. In the 1994 election, unlike the previous 10 elections under consideration, the vote was held separate from national parliamentary elections. Moreover, the division of Brabant Province into two separate provinces makes comparison with earlier elections impossible.

5. The existence of two distinctive subgroups of nationalized (i.e., "federalized") and localized (i.e., "regionalized") state electoral systems in Germany is reinforced by plotting mean localization values against the respective standard deviations. Plotting the localization measure for the Belgian provinces against the standard deviations around their respective means likewise provides supporting evidence to classify Namur and Luxembourg as the more "localized" electoral systems in comparison to the more "nationalized" electoral systems in Liège, Brabant, East Flanders, and West Flanders. For the same reasons outlined in note 3, it would be inappropriate in the French case to attempt a plotting of localization and interelection standard deviations around regional means.

6. One questionnaire item, for example, asked assembly members to compare the importance of local versus national issues and personalities to the outcome of the most recent election in the province or region. The correlation between area means for this item and area scores on the aggregate localization measure was $r = 0.92$ ($p < .10$).

7. As Paterson (1989) reports, talk of grand coalition in Germany at this time was serious, and implementation of such an arrangement in one or more of the Länder was not an unrealistic option. A survey taken before the 1987 federal election found 43% of SPD supporters in favor of a coalition with the Christian Democrats (360).

8. It should be noted that electoral volatility in Hamburg before the 1974 watershed election had been comparatively mild. The average interelection change in party vote shares before 1974 was 2.9%, whereas after 1974 the average volatility per election was 4.6%. This may in part explain the cooperative stance of the SPD in including the FDP in governments where the SPD already had a majority by itself (1961–66, 1970–74).

9. "M. Robert Savy (PS) perpétue l'union de la gauche," *Le Monde*, 30 March 1992.

10. *Le Point*, 30 March 1992.

11. *Le Monde*, 30 March 1992.

Chapter 7

1. *Le Soir*, 16 December 1987.

2. Although absent from the provincial majority since the 1978–81 legislative period, the PSC has consistently been the largest single party in the Luxembourg provincial council.

3. See "Luxembourg PRL-PS: O.K." (*Le Soir*, 16 December 1987); and "Le Pacte est mort au Luxembourg" (*Le Peuple*, 16 December 1987).

4. *Le Soir*, 16 December 1987.

5. Interview with Gérard Deprez, president of the Parti Social-Chrétien (Brussels, 24 February 1993).

6. Interview with International Relations Officer, FDP Bundesgeschäfts-stelle (Bonn, 5 May 1993).

7. Interview with PRL provincial councilor in Hainaut (Mons, 6 November 1992).

8. Interview with Verts regional assembly member and vice president in Nord-Pas de Calais regional government (Lille, 29 April 1993).

9. Deprez interview (Brussels, 24 February 1993).

10. The strategic factionalism index is derived from four variables. The DISTANCE variable captures respondent placement of subnational party on a 10-point Left-Right ideological scale in comparison to placement of national party. DISTANCE is an absolute value. The IMPORT variable measures the importance for the subnational group to replicate the party's coalition strategy at the national level (very important, important, little importance, not at all important). The INSTRUCT variable measures the importance of following the instructions of national party leaders in coalition situations (very important, important, little or no importance). The DEFER variable gauges respondents' agreement with the statement that "the national party has a legitimate right to expect that its instructions will be accepted at all levels of the party" (strongly agree, agree, disagree, strongly disagree).

11. Cumulative measures of volatility and localization are used here. Again, it should be noted that the relative differences of these cumulative measures are corroborated by measures of volatility and localization limited to the two most recent elections.

12. The IDEOLOGY variable measures respondent placement on a Left-Right ideological scale, with values -5 through +5. The PRAGMAT survey item asked respondents to place themselves on a seven-point scale, ranging from "clearly among the pragmatists" to "clearly among the ideologues." The third component of the organizational radicalism composite measure is the RESPECT variable, with respondents indicating the extent to which they respect the judgment and authority of national party leaders (strongly agree, agree, disagree, strongly disagree). The fourth variable, ADMIRE, asked respondents to indicate their level of agreement with the statement: "Subnational party members admire their party's national leaders for their personal qualities and would like to act in a manner that will merit the respect of their leaders" (strongly agree, agree, disagree, strongly disagree).

Chapter 8

1. This discussion omits coalitions formed in municipal councils, although evidence suggests that many coalition experiments originate in local government.

2. For more on this split, see Mabille and Brassinne (1992, 27).

3. The PS did not make a formal alliance with the France Unie movement, largely on the objections of the MRG. See *Le Monde*, 12–13 January 1992.

4. *Liberation*, 18–19 April 1992.

5. Le Monde, 11 April 1992.

6. Despite some advances in this area, the standing indictment against coalition theory remains valid. Not only are spatial influences on coalition building generally neglected, but so too are temporal influences. Laver (1989), for example, indicates that "one of the great weaknesses of coalition theories as they apply to national governments is they do not take a long-term view of party competition" (27).

7. Interview with senior CDU executive in Berlin Senate (Berlin, 29 March 1993). Emphasis added.

8. Interview with Social Democrat Landtag deputy (Berlin, 1 April 1993). Emphasis added.

9. Interview with CDU *Fraktionvorsitzender* in Baden-Württemberg Landtag (Stuttgart, 27 Janaury 1993).

10. Interview with SPD *Fraktionvorsitzender* in Baden-Württemberg Landtag (Stuttgart, 27 January 1993).

11. Interview with Ecolo councilor in Luxembourg provincial assembly (Arlon, 21 October 1992).

12. Interview with Ecolo *chef de group* in Brussels Regional Council (Brussels, 5 November 1992).

13. Interview with PRL councilor in Hainaut provincial assembly (Mons, 6 November 1992).

14. Interview with PRL *chef de group* in Liège provincial assembly (Brussels, 2 December 1992).

15. Interview with PS official in Picardie regional council (Amiens, 7 December 1992). Emphasis added.

16. Interview with FN regional councilor in Nord-Pas de Calais (Lille, 14 June 1993). Emphasis added.

17. Letter to author (1 July 1992).

18. Interview with FDP spokesman (Bonn, 5 May 1993).

19. Interview with CDS secrétaire général (Paris, 21 April 1993).

20. Interview with CVP Senator (Brussels, 8 December 1992).

21. Kitschelt (1989a) considers that the "generalized ability of all parties to coalesce with each other is a sign of the regime's openness" (411).

22. The latter would not be likely to occur, of course, given that respon-

dents should generally not indicate an unwillingness to participate in cooperation with their own party!

23. Belgian respondents were asked to indicate their openness to the following set of parties: PS, SP, PSC, CVP, PRL, PVV, Ecolo, FDF, Volksunie, FN, Agalev, Vlaams Blok. For German respondents the list included: CDU, CSU, SPD, FDP, Grünen, PDS, DVU, Republikaner. French regional councilors responded to the following list of parties: PC, PS, MRG, Verts, GE, UDF-CDS, UDF-Rad., UDF-PR, UDF-PDS, RPR, France Unie, FN.

24. These data are restricted in that they are limited to a very small pool of available respondents. The responses of the Belgian FN are limited to those of one of the party's only two provincial councilors. Those of the German Republicans come from 5 of the 15 Baden-Württemberg parliamentarians, and the DVU's responses are provided by four of the five party members in the Bremen Bürgerschaft. As the French FN has councilors in all of the regions, there is less concern about generalizing from the 42 (40.4%) respondents from the nine regions surveyed.

25. *Le Soir,* 26 November 1991.

26. Ibid.

27. *Le Soir,* 29 November 1991.

28. "Brabant: Le PSC sur la touche," *La Libre Belgique,* 29 November 1991.

29. Jan Anthoons, quoted in *Le Soir,* 29 November 1991.

30. Interview with PRL spokesman in national party headquarters (Brussels, 14 December 1992).

31. *Le Monde,* 29–30 March 1992.

32. Calling the process a "mascarade," Borloo retired his candidacy and announced that his group would not participate in the third round of voting. This done, Legendre felt it his obligation to present his own candidacy once again. Details of the three rounds of presidential voting may be found in *Le Monde,* 30 March–1 April 1992.

33. *Le Monde,* 1 April 1992.

34. Interview with Verts regional councilor and regional vice president (Lille, 29 April 1993).

35. *Le Monde,* 2 April 1992.

36. Jean-Pierre Soisson, quoted in *Le Monde,* 8 April 1992.

37. *Projet d'Accord Entre Le Parti Socialiste et Les Verts: Faire du Nord-Pas de Calais la Première Région de Developpement Durable* (Lille, 9 October 1992).

38. *Projet d'Accord,* 3.

39. *Ibid.,* 4.

40. *Le Soir,* 24 March 1992.

41. Interview with Republican Party *Fraktionvorsitzender* in Baden-Württemberg Landtag (Stuttgart, 27 January 1993).

42. Interview with Green Landtag deputy (Green "A," Stuttgart, 27 January 1993).

43. Interview with Green Party *Fraktionvorsitzender* (Stuttgart, 27 January 1993).

44. Interview with Green Landtag deputy (Green "B," Stuttgart, 27 January 1993).

45. Interview with Green Landtag deputy (Green "B," Stuttgart, 27 January 1993).

46. Interview with CDU *Fraktionvorsitzender* (Stuttgart, 27 January 1993).

47. Interview with Green Landtag deputy (Green "C," Stuttgart, 27 January 1993).

48. Interview with Green Landtag deputy (Green "A," Stuttgart, 27 January 1993).

49. *Le Monde,* 7 April 1992.

50. Interview with SPD Landtag deputy, (Berlin, 1 April 1993).

BIBLIOGRAPHY

Alen, André. 1990. *Belgium: Bipolar and Centrifugal Federalism*. Brussels: Ministry for Foreign Affairs.

Austen-Smith, David, and Jeffrey Banks. 1990. "Stable Governments and the Allocation of Policy Portfolios." *American Political Science Review* 82:891–906.

Axelrod, Robert. 1970. *Conflict of Interest: A Theory of Divergent Goals with Applications to Politics*. Chicago: Markham.

Baron, David. 1993. "Government Formation and Endogenous Parties." *American Political Science Review* 87:34–47.

———. 1991. "A Spatial Bargaining Theory of Government Formation in Parliamentary Systems." *American Political Science Review* 85:137–64.

Batley, Richard, and Gerry Stoker, eds. 1991. *Local Government in Europe: Trends and Developments*. New York: Macmillan.

Bergman, Torbjörn. 1995. *Constitutional Rules and Party Goals in Coalition Formation*. Umeå, Sweden: Umeå University Press.

Bernard, Michel. 1992. *La problématique des finances provinciales*. Brussels: Bulletin du Crédit Communal.

Blondel, Jean, and Ferdinand Müller-Rommel, eds. 1993. *Governing Together: The Extent and Limits of Joint Decision-Making in Western European Cabinets*. New York: Macmillan.

Bogdanor, Vernon. 1983. "Conclusion." In Vernon Bogdanor, ed., *Coalition Government in Western Europe*. London: Heinemann.

Bogdanor, Vernon, ed. 1983. *Coalition Government in Western Europe*. London: Heinemann.

Botella, Joan. 1989. "The Spanish 'New' Regions: Territorial and Political Pluralism." *International Political Science Review* 10:263–71.

Brans, Marleen. 1992. "De Provincieraadsverkiezingen van 24 November 1991." *Res Publica* 34:245–62.

Braunthal, J. 1983. *The West German Social Democrats, 1969–1982*. Boulder, Colo.: Westview.

Brearey, Patricia. 1989. "City Coalitions in West Germany: A Case-Study of Nordrhein-Westfalen." In Colin Mellors and Bert Pijnenburg, eds., *Political Parties and Coalitions in European Local Government*. London: Routledge.

Broughton, David, and Emil Kirchner. 1986. "The FDP and Coalitional Behaviour in the Federal Republic of Germany: Multi-Dimensional Perspectives on the Role of a Pivotal Party." In Geoffrey Pridham, ed., *Coalitional Behaviour in Theory and Practice*. Cambridge, U.K.: Cambridge University Press.

Browne, Eric C. 1973. *Coalition Theories: A Logical and Empirical Critique*. Beverly Hills, Calif.: Sage.

Browne, Eric C., and John Dreijmanis, eds. 1982. *Government Coalitions in Western Democracies*. New York: Longman.

Browne, Eric C., and Mark N. Franklin. 1986. "New Directions in Coalition Research." *Legislative Studies Quarterly* 11:469–83.

Budge, Ian, and V. Herman. 1978. "Coalitional Government Formation: An Empirically Relevant Theory." *British Journal of Political Science* 8:454–77.

Budge, Ian, and Hans Keman. 1990. *Parties and Democracy: Coalition Formation and Government Functioning in Twenty States*. New York: Oxford University Press.

Budge, Ian, and Michael Laver. 1986. "Office Seeking and Policy Pursuit in Coalition Theory." *Legislative Studies Quarterly* 11:485–506.

Bueno De Mesquita, Bruce. 1975. *Strategy, Risk and Personality in Coalition Politics: The Case of India*. Cambridge, U.K.: Cambridge University Press.

Carmines, Edward G., and Richard A. Zeller. 1979. *Reliability and Validity Assessment*. Beverly Hills, Calif.: Sage.

Castles, Francis, and Peter Mair. 1984. "Left-Right Political Scales: Some Expert Judgements." *European Journal of Political Science* 12:83–88.

Centre de Recherche et d'Information Socio-Politiques. 1972. *Les elections provinciales du 7 Novembre 1971: Resultats et consequences*. Brussels: CRISP Courrier Hebdomadaire 547.

Centre de Recherche et d'Information Socio-Politiques. 1974. *Composition et organisation des gouvernements, 1972–1974*. Brussels: CRISP.

Cerny, Karl H. 1990. "Between Elections: The Political Parties, 1983–87." In Karl Cerny, ed., *Germany at the Polls: The Bundestag Elections of the 1980s*. Durham, N.C.: Duke University Press.

Cerny, Karl H., ed. 1990. *Germany at the Polls: The Bundestag Elections of the 1980s*. Durham, N.C.: Duke University Press.

Costard, Raymond. 1974. "Les élections des conseils provinciaux." *Res Publica* 16:547–72.

———. 1972. "Les élections des conseils provinciaux." *Res Publica* 14:667–724.

Culver, Lowell W. 1966. "Land Elections in West German Politics." *Western Political Quarterly* 19:304–36.

de Mayer, Jan. 1983. "Coalition Government in Belgium." In Vernon Bog-danor, ed., *Coalition Government in Western Europe*. London: Heinemann.

De Swaan, Abram. 1973. *Coalition Theories and Cabinet Formations: A Study of Formal Theories of Coalition Formation Applied to Nine European Parliaments after 1918*. Amsterdam: Elsevier.

Decoster, Jacques. 1987. "Le budget de la Province du Brabant." Brussels: CRISP Courrier Hebdomadaire 1165–66.

Delmartino, Frank. 1993. "Belgium: In Search of the Meso Level." In L. J. Sharpe, ed., *The Rise of Meso Government in Europe*. Newbury Park, Calif.: Sage.

Denters, Bas. 1993. "The Politics of Redistribution in Local Government." *European Journal of Political Research* 23:323–42.

———. 1985. "Towards a Conditional Model of Coalition Behaviour." *European Journal of Political Research* 13:295–309.

Deschouwer, Kris. 1992. "The Survival of the Fittest: Measuring and Explaining Adaption and Change of Political Parties." Paper delivered at the European Consortium for Political and Social Research, University of Limerick, Ireland.

———. 1989. "Belgium: The 'Ecologists' and 'Agalev.'" In Ferdinand Müller-Rommel, ed., *New Politics in Western Europe*. Boulder, Colo.: Westview Press.

Dewachter, Wilfred. 1987. "Changes in a Particratie: The Belgian Party System from 1944 to 1986." In Hans Daalder, ed., *Party Systems in Denmark, Austria, Switzerland, the Netherlands, and Belgium*. London: Frances Pinter.

Dewachter, W., and E. Clijsters. 1982. "Belgium: Political Stability Despite Coalition Crises." In Eric Browne and J. Dreijmanis, eds., *Government Coalitions in Western Democracies*. New York: Longman.

Dodd, Lawrence. 1976. *Coalitions in Parliamentary Government*. Princeton, N.J.: Princeton University Press.

Downs, Anthony. 1957. *An Economic Theory of Democracy*. New York: Harper & Row.

Downs, William M. forthcoming. "Belgium." In Vincent E. McHale, ed., *Political Parties of Europe: The 1980s and 1990s*. Westport, Conn.: Greenwood Press.

———. 1996. "Federalism Achieved: The Belgian Elections of May 1995." *West European Politics* 19:168–75.

———. 1995. "The Belgian General Election of 1995." *Electoral Studies* 14: 336–41.

Dunleavy, P. 1980. *Urban Political Analysis*. New York: Macmillan.

Duverger, Maurice. 1954. *Political Parties*. London: Methuen.

Eldersveld, Samuel J. 1964. *Political Parties: A Behavioral Analysis*. Chicago: Rand McNally.

Electoral Documents on Politics and Society in the Federal Republic of Germany. 1986. Bonn: Inter Nationes.

Esche, Falk, and Jürgen Hartmann, eds. 1990. *Handbuch der deutschen Bundes-länder.* Frankfurt: Campus Verlag.

Fitzmaurice, John. 1992. "The 1991 Belgian Election." *West European Politics* 15:4:178–82.

———. 1983. *The Politics of Belgium: Crisis and Compromise in a Plural Society.* London: Hurst.

Frankland, G. 1989. "The Green Party in West Germany." In Ferdinand Müller-Rommel, ed., *New Politics in Western Europe.* Boulder, Colo.: Westview Press.

Franklin, Mark N., and Thomas T. Mackie. 1983. "Familiarity and Inertia in the Formation of Governing Coalitions in Parliamentary Democracies." *British Journal of Political Science* 13:275–98.

Frendreis, John P., Dennis W. Gleiber, and Eric C. Browne. 1986. "The Study of Cabinet Dissolutions in Parliamentary Democracies." *Legislative Studies Quarterly* 11:619–28.

Gamson, W. 1961. "A Theory of Coalition Formation." *American Sociological Review* 26:373–82.

Gerstenlauer, Hans-Georg. 1995. "German *Länder* and the European Community." In Barry Jones and Michael Keating, eds., *The European Union and the Regions.* Oxford: Clarendon Press.

Groennings, Sven. 1970. "Notes towards Theories of Coalition Behavior in Multiparty Systems: Formation and Maintenance." In Sven Groennings, E. W. Kelly, and Michael Leiserson, eds., *The Study of Coalition Behavior: Theoretical Perspectives.* New York: Holt, Rinehart & Winston.

Groennings, Sven, E. W. Kelley, and Michael Leiserson, eds. 1970. *The Study of Coalition Behavior: Theoretical Perspectives from Four Continents.* New York: Holt, Rinehart & Winston.

Gunlicks, Arthur B. 1977. "Coalition Collapse in Lower Saxony: Political and Constitutional Implications." *Parliamentary Affairs* 30:437–49.

Hainsworth, Paul, and John Loughlin. 1989. "Coalitions in the New French Regions." In Colin Mellors and Bert Pijnenburg, eds., *Political Parties and Coalitions in European Local Government.* London: Routledge.

Harmel, Robert, and Kenneth Janda. 1992. "An Integrated Theory of Party Goals and Party Change." Paper delivered at the Annual Meeting of the American Political Science Association, Chicago.

Heidar, Knut. 1984. "Party Power: Approaches in a Field of Unfilled Classics." *Scandinavian Political Studies* 7:1–16.

Hinckley, Barbara. 1981. *Coalitions and Politics.* New York: Harcourt, Brace Jovanovich.

Hirschman, Albert O. 1970. *Exit, Voice and Loyalty: Responses to Decline in Firms, Organizations, and States.* Cambridge, Mass.: Harvard University Press.

Hoffmann-Lange, Ursula. 1986. "Changing Coalitional Preferences among

West German parties." In Geoffrey Pridham, ed., *Coalitional Behaviour in Theory and Practice*. Cambridge, U.K.: Cambridge University Press.

Hrbek, Rudolf. 1987. "The Political Dynamics of Regionalism: Germany, Austria, Switzerland." In Roger Morgan, ed., *Regionalism in European Politics*. London: Policy Studies Institute.

Hugé, Philippe. 1991. *La pérennité de l'institution provinciale*. Brussels: Bulletin du Crédit Communal.

———. 1989. *Province 2001: Pro Vincere*. Brussels: Association des Provinces Belges.

Inglehart, Ronald, and H-D. Klingemann. 1987. "Party Identification, Ideological Preference and the Left-Right Dimensions among Western Mass Publics." In Ian Budge, David Robertson, and Derek Hearl, eds., *Ideology, Strategy and Party Change*. Cambridge, U.K.: Cambridge University Press.

Johnson, Nevil. 1983. *State and Government in the Federal Republic of Germany*. Oxford: Pergamon Press.

Jones, Barry, and Michael Keating, eds. 1995. *The European Union and the Regions*. Oxford: Clarendon Press.

Kaase, Max, and Wolfgang Gibowski. 1988. "The Landtag Elections of 1987–1988 in West Germany: Crisis or Mid-Term Low for the Bonn Government?" *German Politics and Society* 15:8–21.

Kalton, Graham. 1983. *Introduction to Survey Sampling*. Beverly Hills, Calif: Sage.

Kelley, E. W. 1968. "Techniques of Studying Coalition Formation." *Midwest Journal of Political Science* 12:60–75.

Kesselman, Mark, and Donald Rosenthal. 1974. *Local Power and Comparative Politics*. Beverly Hills, Calif.: Sage.

King, Gary, James E. Alt, Michael J. Laver, and Nancy E. Burns. 1990. "A Unified Model of Cabinet Dissolution in Parliamentary Democracies." *American Journal of Political Science* 34:846–71.

Kitschelt, Herbert. 1989a. "The Internal Politics of Parties: The Law of Curvilinear Disparity Revisited." *Political Studies* 37:400–421.

———. 1989b. *The Logics of Party Formation: Ecological Politics in Belgium and West Germany*. Ithaca, N.Y.: Cornell University Press.

———. 1988. "Organization and Strategy of Belgian and West German Ecology Parties: A New Dynamic of Party Politics in Western Europe?" *Comparative Politics* 21:127–54.

Kitschelt, Herbert, and Staf Hellemans. 1990. *Beyond the European Left: Ideology and Political Action in the Belgian Ecology Parties*. Durham, N.C.: Duke University Press.

Klingemann, Hans-Dieter. 1985. "West Germany." In Ivor Crewe and David Denver, eds., *Electoral Change in Western Democracies: Patterns and Sources of Electoral Volatility*. London: Croom Helm.

Kloss, Günther. 1990. *West Germany: An Introduction,* second edition. New York: Macmillan.

Knapp, Andrew, and Patrick Le Galès. 1993. "Top-down to Bottom-up? Centre-Periphery Relations and Power Structures in France's Gaullist Party." *West European Politics* 16:271–94.

Kuiper, Wim, and Pieter Tops. 1989. "Local Coalition Formation in the Netherlands." In Colin Mellors and Bert Pijnenburg, eds., *Political Parties and Coalitions in European Local Government.* London: Routledge.

Laver, Michael. 1989. "Theories of Coalition Formation and Local Government Coalitions." In Colin Mellors and Bert Pijnenburg, eds., *Political Parties and Coalitions in European Local Government.* London: Routledge.

———. 1986. "Between Theoretical Elegance and Political Reality: Deductive Models and Cabinet Coalitions in Europe." In Geoffrey Pridham, ed., *Coalitional Behaviour in Theory and Practice: An Inductive Model for Western Europe.* Cambridge, U.K.: Cambridge University Press.

———. 1974. "Dynamic Factors in Government Coalition Formation." *European Journal of Political Research* 2:259–70.

Laver, Michael, Colin Rallings, and Michael Thrasher. 1995. "Policy Payoffs in Local Government." Unpublished manuscript.

———. 1987. "Coalition Theory and Local Government: Coalition Payoffs in Britain." *British Journal of Political Science* 16:501–9.

Laver, Michael, and Norman Schofield. 1990. *Multiparty Government: The Politics of Coalition in Europe.* New York: Oxford University Press.

Laver, Michael, and Kenneth A. Shepsle. 1990. "Government Coalitions and Intraparty Politics." *British Journal of Political Science* 20:489–507.

Lehmbruch, Gerard. 1978. "Party and Federation in Germany: A Developmental Dilemma." *Government and Opposition* 13:151–77.

Leiserson, Michael. 1970. "Game Theory and the Study of Coalition Behavior." In Sven Groennings, E. W. Kelly, and Michael Leiserson, eds., *The Study of Coalition Behavior.* New York: Holt, Rinehart & Winston.

———. 1968. "Factions and Coalitions in One-Party Japan." *American Political Science Review* 62:770–87.

Lemaître, Henri. 1982. *Gouvernements belges de 1968 à 1980: Processus de crise.* Brussels: Editions J. Chauveheid.

Lijphart, Arend. 1981. "Power Sharing versus Majority Rule: Patterns of Cabinet Formation in Twenty Democracies." *Government and Opposition* 16: 395–413.

Luebbert, Gregory M. 1986. *Comparative Democracy: Policymaking and Governing Coalitions in Europe and Israel.* New York: Columbia University Press.

Lupia, Arthur, and Kaare Strøm. 1995. "Coalition Termination and the Strategic Timing of Parliamentary Elections." *American Political Science Review* 89:648–65.

Mabille, Xavier. 1986. *L'élection des conseils provinciaux et des sénateurs indirects.* Brussels: CRISP Courrier Hebdomadaire 1110.

————. 1982. "Les élections des conseils provinciaux." *Res Publica* 24:195–205.

Mabille, Xavier, and Jacques Brassinne. 1992. *La formation du gouvernement et des exécutifs.* Brussels: CRISP Courrier Hebdomadaire 1356.

Mabille, Xavier, and Evelyn Lentzen. 1988. *Les élections législatives du 13 décembre 1987.* Brussels: CRISP Courrier Hebdomadaire 1179–1180.

Machin, Howard. 1989. "Stages and Dynamics in the Evolution of the French Party System." *West European Politics* 12:59–81.

Maor, Moshe. 1992. "The Institutional Determinant of Coalition Behavior." Paper delivered at the Annual Meeting of the American Political Science Association, Chicago.

Mazey, Sonia. 1993. "Developments at the French Meso Level: Modernizing the French State." In L. J. Sharpe, ed., *The Rise of Meso Government in Europe.* Newbury Park, Calif.: Sage.

————. 1989. "Centre-Periphery Relations in the Fifth Republic: The Legitimization of Local Politics." In Paul Godt, ed., *Policy-Making in France: From de Gaulle to Mitterrand.* London: Frances Pinter.

————. 1986. "The French Regional Elections of 16 March 1986." *Electoral Studies* 5:3:297–312.

Mellors, Colin. 1989. "Sub-National Government: A New Arena for the Study of Coalitions." In Colin Mellors and Bert Pijnenburg, eds., *Political Parties and Coalitions in European Local Government.* London: Routledge.

————. 1984. "Political Coalitions in Britain: The Local Context." In L. Robins, ed., *Updating British Politics.* London: Politics Association.

————. 1983. "Coalition Strategies: The Case of British Local Government." In Vernon Bogdanor, ed., *Coalition Government in Western Europe.* London: Heinemann.

Mellors, Colin, and Bert Pijnenburg. 1989. "Conclusion: Local Coalitions in Europe." In Colin Mellors and Bert Pijnenburg, eds., *Political Parties and Coalitions in European Local Government.* London: Routledge.

Mény, Yves. 1988. "Radical Reforms and Marginal Change: The French Socialist Experience." In Bruno Dente and Francesco Kjellberg, eds., *The Dynamics of Institutional Change: Local Government Reorganization in Western Democracies.* Beverly Hills, Calif.: Sage.

Michels, Robert. 1962. *Political Parties.* London: Collier-Macmillan.

Mughan, Anthony. 1985. "Belgium." In Ivor Crewe and David Denver, eds., *Electoral Change in Western Democracies: Patterns and Sources of Electoral Volatility.* London: Croom Helm.

Müller-Rommel, Ferdinand. 1989. "The German Greens in the 1980s: Short-Term Cyclical Protest or Indicator of Transformation?" *Political Studies* 37:114–22.

Nachmias, David, and Chava Nachmias. 1987. *Research Methods in the Social Sciences,* third edition. New York: St. Martin's Press.

Norpoth, Helmut. 1982. "The German Federal Republic: Coalition Government at the Brink of Majority Rule." In Eric C. Browne and John Dreijmanis, eds., *Government Coalitions in Western Democracies.* New York: Longman.

Orbell, J., and G. Fougere. 1973. "Intraparty Conflict and the Decay of Ideology." *Journal of Politics* 35:439–53.

Padgett, Stephen. 1991. "The New German Electorate: Dealignment or Non-Alignment?" Paper delivered at the Annual Meeting of the American Political Science Association, Washington, D.C.

———. 1989. "The Party System." In Gordon Smith, William E. Paterson, and Peter H. Merkl, eds., *Developments in West German Politics.* Durham, N.C.: Duke University Press.

Padgett, S., and T. Burkett. 1986. *Political Parties and Elections in West Germany.* London: Hurst.

Page, Benjamin I. 1994. "Democratic Responsiveness? Untangling the Links between Public Opinion and Policy." *PS: Political Science and Politics* 27:25–29.

Page, Edward C., and Michael J. Goldsmith. 1987. "Centre and Locality: Explaining Crossnational Variation." In Edward C. Page and Michael J. Goldsmith, eds., *Central and Local Government Relations: A Comparative Analysis of West European Unitary States.* Beverly Hills, Calif.: Sage.

Panebianco, A. 1988. *Political Parties: Organization and Power.* Cambridge, U.K.: Cambridge University Press.

———. 1982. *Modelli di partito: Organizzazione e potere nei partiti politici.* Bologna: Il Mulino.

Paterson, William E. 1989. "The Greens: From Yesterday to Tomorrow." In Peter H. Merkl, ed., *The Federal Republic of Germany at Forty.* New York: New York University Press.

Pedersen, Mogens N. 1983. "Changing Patterns of Electoral Volatility in European Party Systems, 1948–1977: Explorations in Explanation." In Hans Daalder and Peter Mair, eds., *Western European Party Systems.* Beverly Hills, Calif.: Sage.

Pedersen, Mogens N., and Jørgen Elklit, eds. 1995. *Kampen om Kommunen: Ni fortællinger om kommunalvalget i 1993.* Odense, Denmark: Odense University Press.

Perrineau, Pascal. 1986. "A l'ombre des législatives . . . les élections régionales." *Revue Politique et Parlementaire* 88:19–30.

Perrineau, Pascal, ed. 1987. *Régions: Le baptême des urnes.* Paris: Pédone.

Pierre, Jon. 1986. "Attitudes and Behaviour of Party Activists." *European Journal of Political Research* 14:465–79.

Pijnenburg, Bert. 1989. "The Multiple Dimensions of Local Coalition Formation in Belgium." In Colin Mellors and Bert Pijnenburg, eds., *Political Parties and Coalitions in European Local Government.* London: Routledge.

———. 1987. "Political Parties and Coalitional Behaviour in Belgium: The Perspective of Local Politics." *European Journal of Political Research* 15: 53–73.

Pijnenburg, Bert, ed. 1988. *Coalities in België, Tijdschrift voor Sociologie* 9.

Pridham, Geoffrey. 1989. "Local and Regional Coalitions in Italy: Party Strategies and Centre-Periphery Links." In Colin Mellors and Bert Pijnenburg, eds., *Political Parties and Coalitons in European Local Government.* London: Routledge.

———. 1988. *Political Parties and Coalitional Behaviour in Italy.* London: Routledge.

———. 1987. "Coalition Behaviour and Party Systems in Western Europe: A Comparative Approach." *Parliamentary Affairs* 40:374–87.

———. 1986. "An Inductive Theoretical Framework for Coalitional Behaviour: Political Parties in Multi-Dimensional Perspective in Western Europe." In Geoffrey Pridham, ed., *Coalitional Behaviour in Theory and Practice.* Cambridge, U.K.: Cambridge University Press.

———. 1985. *Political Parties and Coalitional Behaviour in Italy: An Interpretive Study.* London: Croom Helm.

———. 1984. "Parties and Coalitional Behaviour in Italian Local Politics: Conflict or Convergence?" *European Journal of Political Research* 12:223–41.

———. 1982. "The Government/Opposition Dimension and the Development of the Party System in the 1970s: The Reappearance of Conflictual Politics." In Herbert Döring and Gordon Smith, eds., *Party Government and Political Culture in Western Germany.* New York: Macmillan.

———. 1981. *The Nature of the Italian Party System: A Regional Case Study.* London: Croom Helm.

———. 1973. "A 'Nationalization' Process? Federal Politics and State Elections in West Germany." *Government and Opposition* 8:455–72.

Profession Politique. 1992. *Le guide: L'annuaire du monde de la politique et des pouvoirs.* Paris: Profession Politique.

Pulzer, Peter. 1982. "Responsible Party Government in the German Political System." In Herbert Döring and Gordon Smith, eds., *Party Government and Political Culture in Western Germany.* New York: St. Martin's Press.

Putnam, Robert. 1993. *Making Democracy Work: Civic Traditions in Modern Italy.* Princeton, N.J.: Princeton University Press.

Rallings, Colin, and Michael Thrasher. 1986. "Parties Divided on Hung Councils." In *Local Government Chronicle,* January 3, 1986: 12–13.

Reisinger, William M. 1986. "Situational and Motivational Assumptions in Theories of Coalition Formation." *Legislative Studies Quarterly* 11: 551–63.

Riker, William H. 1962. *The Theory of Political Coalitions.* New Haven, Conn.: Yale University Press.

Ritter, Von Gerhard A., and Merith Niehuss. 1987. *Wahlen in der Bundesrepublik Deutschland: Bundestags-und Landtagswahlen 1946–1987.* Munich: Verlag C. H. Beck.

Roberts, Geoffrey K. 1989. "Party System Change in Western Germany: Land-Federal Linkages." *West European Politics* 13:98–113.

Robertson, John D. 1983. "The Political Economy and the Durability of European Coalition Cabinets: New Variations on a Game-Theoretic Perspective." *Journal of Politics* 45:932–57.

Robinson, Robert. 1989. "Subnational Coalitions in Spain." In Colin Mellors and Bert Pijnenburg, eds., *Political Parties and Coalitions in European Local Government.* London: Routledge.

Rousseau, Jean-Jacques. 1978. *On the Social Contract.* Edited by Roger D. Masters. Translated by Judith R. Masters. New York: St. Martins.

Rudd, Chris. 1986. "Coalition Formation and Maintenance in Belgium: A Case-Study of Elite Behaviour and Changing Cleavage Structure, 1965–1981." In Geoffrey Pridham, ed., *Coalition Behaviour in Theory and Practice.* Cambridge, U.K.: Cambridge University Press.

Sani, G., and G. Sartori. 1983. "Polarization, Fragmentation and Competition in Western Democracies." In H. Daalder and P. Mair, eds., *Western European Party Systems.* Beverly Hills, Calif.: Sage.

Schain, Martin A. 1991. "Immigration and French Communism: The Changing Electoral Base and the Decline of French Communism." Paper delivered at the Annual Meeting of the American Political Science Association, Washington, D.C.

Schlesinger, Joseph A. 1984. "On the Theory of Party Organization." *Journal of Politics* 46:369–98.

Schmidt, Manfred G. 1983. "Two Logics of Coalition Policy: The West German Case." In Vernon Bogdanor, ed., *Coalition Government in Western Europe.* London: Heinemann.

Schmidt, Vivien A. 1990. *Democratizing France: The Political and Administrative History of Decentralization.* Cambridge, U.K.: Cambridge University Press.

Schofield, Norman. 1993. "Political Competition and Multiparty Coalition Governments." *European Journal of Political Research* 23:1–33.

Selle, Per, and Lars Svåsand. 1983. "The Local Party Organization and Its Members: Between Randomness and Rationality." *Scandinavian Political Studies* 6:211–30.

Sharpe, L. J. 1993. "The European Meso: An Appraisal." In L. J. Sharpe, ed., *The Rise of Meso Government in Europe.* Newbury Park, Calif.: Sage.

Sharpe, L. J., ed. 1993. *The Rise of Meso Government in Europe.* Newbury Park, Calif.: Sage.

Shubik, M. 1967. "The Uses of Game Theory." In James Charlesworth, ed., *Contemporary Political Analysis*. New York: Free Press.

Sjoblom, G. 1968. *Party Strategies in a Multiparty System*. Lund: Studentlitteratur.

Smith, Gordon. 1989. "Political Leadership." In Gordon Smith, William E. Paterson, and Peter H. Merkl, eds., *Developments in West German Politics*. Durham, N.C.: Duke University Press.

Steunenberg, Bernard. 1992. "Coalition Theories: Empirical Evidence for Dutch Municipalities." *European Journal of Political Research* 22:245–78.

Strom, Kaare. 1994. "The Presthus Debacle: Intraparty Politics and Bargaining Failure in Norway." *American Political Science Review* 88:112–27.

———. 1990a. "A Behavioral Theory of Competitive Political Parties." *American Journal of Political Science* 34:565–98.

———. 1990b. *Minority Government and Majority Rule*. Cambridge, U.K.: Cambridge University Press.

Strom, Kaare, Ian Budge, and Michael Laver. 1994. "Constraints on Cabinet Formation in Parliamentary Democracies." *American Journal of Political Science* 38:303–35.

Strom, Kaare, and Jorn Y. Leipart. 1993. "Policy, Institutions, and Coalition Avoidance: Norwegian Governments, 1945–1990." *American Political Science Review* 87:870–87.

Taylor, Michael. 1972. "On the Theory of Government Coalition Formation." *British Journal of Political Science* 2:361–86.

Taylor, Michael, and Michael Laver. 1973. "Government Coalitions in Western Europe." *European Journal of Political Research* 1:205–48.

Temple, Michael. 1991. "Power Distribution in Hung Councils." *Local Government Studies* 17:1–23.

Thomas, Alastair H. 1989. "Local Coalitions in Denmark: A Preliminary Approach." In Colin Mellors and Bert Pijnenburg, eds., *Political Parties and Coalitions in European Local Government*. London: Routledge.

Toelen, Danny. 1987. "De Provincieraadsverkiezingen van 13 December 1987." *Res Publica* 30:99–118.

———. 1986. "De Provincieraadsverkiezingen van 13 Oktober 1985." *Res Publica* 28:307–24.

Tsebelis, George. 1990. *Nested Games: Rational Choice in Comparative Politics*. Berkeley: University of California Press.

von Beyme, Klaus. 1983. "Governments, Parliaments and the Structure of Power in Political Parties." In Hans Daalder and Peter Mair, eds., *Western European Party Systems: Continuity and Change*. Beverly Hills, Calif.: Sage.

Weber, Henri. 1990. "Pluralisme interne: Il ne sert que lorsqu'on en use . . ." *Revue Politique et Parlementaire* 92:50–52.

Wilson, Frank L. 1989. "Evolution of the French Party System." In Paul Godt, ed., *Policy-Making in France: From de Gaulle to Mitterrand*. London: Frances Pinter.

Zariski, Raphael. 1984. "Coalition Formation in the Italian Regions: Some Preliminary Findings and Their Significance for Coalition Theory." *Comparative Politics* 17:403–20.

Zinnkann, Hans, ed. 1991. *The Landtag of North Rhine-Westphalia, 11th Legislative Period.* Bonn: Universitäts-Buchdruckerei.

INDEX

Rational choice theory, 6, 21–25, 31–
39, 43. *See also* Coalition theory
Refugee Party (GB/BHE), 112–13,
116
Representation, 5–8, 14, 275
Republikaner Party (Germany, REP),
69, 150, 196, 246, 248–49, 261–
62, 270

Social Democratic Party of Germany
(SPD), 142, 153, 233, 239–40,
246–49, 260–64; electoral constraints on, 178–83; government
participation, 8, 11, 112–20; internal party politics, 194, 196, 198,
200–201, 206, 212, 227, 229; in
"traffic light" coalitions, 60, 79
Socialist Party (Belgium/Flemish, SP),
26–28, 77–79, 90, 95, 142, 177,
227; government participation,
99–105, 107, 251–52
Socialist Party (Belgium/franco-
phone, PS), 26, 77–79, 90, 94;
coalition experimentation, 241,
246–49, 251–53; electoral volatility
and, 153, 176–78; government
participation, 98–105, 107, 189–
91; internal party politics, 194,
196, 198, 200–201, 206, 212
Socialist Party (France, PS), 80–82,
121, 124, 126–32, 181–83, 230,
241–42, 246, 248–49, 272; "big
bang" alliance strategy, 131–32,
230, 233, 247, 255–60; decision
making within, 193–94, 196, 198;
internal divisions, 59, 200–201,
212
Spain, 18, 275; decentralization in, 6;
regional coalitions in, 9

Statt Partei. *See* Instead Party
Strategic inertia, 173–74, 177, 186,
225
Subnational assemblies: as coalition
proving grounds, 7, 15, 59–60,
221–66; institutional universe in
Europe, 17–18
Subnational government, xiv; func-
tional relevance of, 9–10
Sweden, 18; decentralization in, 7;
minority governments, 23
Switzerland, 18

Union for France (UPF), 80, 255
Union for French Democracy
(France, UDF), 82, 121, 124, 126–
32, 182, 256; collaboration with
FN, 230, 243–44; electoral alliance
with RPR, 80–81, 255; internal
politics, 194, 196, 198, 200–201,
206, 209, 212; openness to coalition experimentation, 246–49
United States: coalition building in,
19; Democratic Party, 59; government formation in, 4

Vlaams Blok (Belgium, VlB), 26, 97,
107, 150, 178, 222, 244, 252
Volksunie (Belgium, VU), 78–79,
107, 178, 244, 252; coalition participation, 97, 99–100, 102–3; and
Limburg "coup," 26–28, 227

Wallonia, 68, 70, 90–92, 96–97, 103,
106; Walloon Parliament, 106,
189–90
Walloon Rally (Belgium, RW), 99,
101–3, 107, 226, 232